FLYING COLOURS

A HISTORY OF
COMMERCIAL AVIATION
IN CANADA

FLYING COLOURS

PETER PIGOTT

DOUGLAS & MCINTYRE
VANCOUVER/TORONTO

Douglas & McIntyre Ltd.
1615 Venables Street
Vancouver, British Columbia
V5L 2H1

CANADIAN CATALOGUING IN PUBLICATION DATA

Pigott, Peter.
 Flying colours

 ISBN 1-55054-593-0

 1. Aeronautics, Commercial—Canada—History. 2. Airlines—Canada—History. 3. Aircraft industry—Canada—History.
I. Title.
HE9815.A3P54 1997   387.7′0971   C97-910515-3

Editing by Barbara Pulling
Jacket design by Peter Cocking
Text design and typesetting by Val Speidel
Printed and bound in Canada by Friesens
Printed on acid-free paper ∞

The publisher gratefully acknowledges the support of the Canada Council for the Arts and of the British Columbia Ministry of Tourism, Small Business and Culture.

CONTENTS

INTRODUCTION

I can remember the first time I ever came close enough to touch an aircraft. I was five years old and it was the day that my mother met Errol Flynn. She had reminded us all that while her favourite actor was really Tyrone Power, Flynn was arriving at our local airport. Only a few years before, Flynn had starred in a movie (she thought) called *Burma Patrol*, where one scene had him shooting down Japanese fighters by cradling a heavy machine gun in the doorway of an aircraft. I imagine that my father, who had actually fought in Burma as part of the Chindits, was less than enthused. Now he worked for Trans World Airlines at the farthest end of its network—Bombay's Santa Cruz Airport, in India.

The airline sent Flynn out to publicize the inauguration of the latest in their series of Lockheed Constellations, the 1049G. We all stood on the airport's tarmac in the glare of the Indian sun and watched from behind a rope as the great man stumbled down the steps, making for the air-conditioned terminal. As he passed us, my mother did what any woman of her generation would have done. She pushed me under the rope towards Flynn. I was only vaguely aware of being propelled into the star, who crouched and asked me my name. That was my mother's signal to dart out and claim me. I couldn't understand why an otherwise sensible person like my mother would want to gush over the man with the moustache when there stood the silver beauty behind him. Flanked by two Indian Airlines DC-3s sitting on their haunches, the Connie's nose dipped down like a greyhound, its silver-metallic fuselage accentuated by the massive Wright engines, then curved gently away into a triple fan. It pleased my five-year-old eyes.

I knew that the Connie had flown all the way from Los Angeles and, now ignored by the grown-ups, I ran to touch the nose wheel as if it might pass on the magic. Years later, I read that Kelly Johnson, the Constellation's designer, used to say that he didn't build aircraft, he grew them. I was smitten with aviation and have remained so ever since.

This book is part of what began that day. It is, I hope, unlike others written of aviation in Canada. Neither a comprehensive history nor a technical manual, it is an exercise in a particular aspect of our country's recent memory, wading into that no-man's land of national identity. If as a people we see ourselves through our latest mode of transport, be it canoes, railroads or aircraft, this is an aerial exploration of who we are. It also explains our changing perceptions of the flying machine—the greatest invention of this century.

Canada and aviation began this century together, children of European and American parents, and, like all children, given to displays of independence while seeking reassurance. Aviation not only expanded our grandparents' views of the wilderness but imbued them with a sense of pride in the Dominion's sheer mass. The flight of the first bush pilot, Stuart Graham, showed them a country that bore no relation to the ordered European landscape that most Canadians knew. The collective image of tundra and polar ice only took form in the national consciousness when Bob Randall and Punch Dickins flew over it. We may have had no equatorial colonies to send flying boats or airships to, but the mouth of the Mackenzie River on the Arctic Ocean was equally distant. Other exploits, such as C. D. Howe's "dawn to dusk" marathon in 1937, the founding of Trans-Canada Air Lines, and the first flights across the Atlantic, have slipped into our image of ourselves.

Aviation, whether flying schools or airlines, aircraft manufacturers or clubs, has never been to Canadians a mere reflection of a technological revolution. Flying and politics in this country have always been wed, each supporting (or at times discrediting) the other. The first Canadian to fly, J. A. D. McCurdy, went directly to Ottawa with his *Silver Dart*, looking for financial support. In contrast, Wilbur and Orville Wright, the first Americans to fly, shied away from their government altogether, publicly demonstrating their machine first in France. In Europe, the earliest air companies were begun by wealthy entrepreneurs and railways, in the United States by aircraft manufacturers as outlets for their products. With a miniscule population, an economy impoverished by the First World War and a vast land mass to navigate, Canadian civilians

who sought to fly understood that only the federal government had the wherewithal to bankroll them. It is ironic that the greatest adventure of this century in this country—that of flying across it—was dependent on grubby, pedestrian dealings in Ottawa backrooms.

The shifting beliefs of the electorate, the economic swings of boom and recession, the political scandals within the House of Commons (from the Avro Arrow to the Airbus), and even the attitude of the various prime ministers towards the new form of transportation were all projected onto the skies above. As bush outfits and early airlines were changing the shape of the country, they were locked into the same political arguments and deals that had built the Canadian Pacific Railway fifty years earlier. It is ironic that while they could defy the Rockies and winter temperatures so extreme that the oil froze in their engines, aerial visionaries could not surmount obstacles like shortsightedness, pettiness and timidity. Erroll Boyd, the first Canadian to fly the Atlantic, did so, to our eternal shame, on hand-outs, and died three decades later more unknown than forgotten. The experiences of James Richardson and Grant McConachie proved that commercial aviation in a hostile environment was about risk-taking, about trusting one's intuition and, ultimately, about the unconquerable spirit of the soul. Future historians will wonder at the practices of the federal government in the immediate postwar years, as it behaved in the best tradition of a venture capitalist, funding aviation companies and then abandoning them to shift for themselves.

In the second half of this century, aviation soared into every aspect of our society—national security, commerce, communications, leisure, international relations and politics. Few realize that the democratization of air travel, with the introduction of cheaper fares and wide-body jets, had a more comprehensive effect on us than any other previous single facet of social engineering. By the 1980s, the spectre of mass destruction by Soviet bombers was replaced by soaring energy costs, faltering airlines and massive unemployment in the aerospace industry. Out of those ashes grew the privatization and deregulation of airlines in Canada and the foundations of what is today the sixth-largest commercial aerospace business in the world. In the end, Canadian aviation survived because, unlike in the United States and Europe, it had long since weaned itself off defence contracts. When the Berlin Wall came down in 1989, shrinking arsenals caused aviation manufacturers around the world, from Seattle to Khodinka, Saint-Cloud to Hatfield, to merge or disappear.

Within living memory, aviation reshaped our country and ourselves. For a people who gave the world bush flying, we have grown up mostly ignorant of the events and passions, knavery and heroics that contributed to our aeronautical present. The great aviators—McCurdy, J. A. Wilson, Richardson, Howe, McConachie and Gordon McGregor—possessed a scale and depth that contemporary pilots and airline presidents cannot match. Perhaps it is because today aviation is driven more by finance than passion—or perhaps, as Gloria Swanson put it in *Sunset Boulevard*, the old stars remained big but "the pictures just got smaller."

Without some memory and appreciation of its past, a society risks living in a permanent present. This book was written to give perspective to our aviation heritage, to link the many peaks and valleys since the first aircraft flew in Canada in 1909, and to celebrate our aerial achievements.

CHAPTER ONE

The Early Years: Bell, Curtiss and the AEA

On the wintry morning of February 23, 1909, some 150 people gathered by the frozen surface of Bras d'Or Lake at Baddeck Bay, Nova Scotia. In the previous four years, the local population had become familiar with Dr. Alexander Graham Bell's experiments using large kites. They counted themselves fortunate that a celebrity like Bell summered on Bras d'Or Lake, at his house Beinn Bhreagh, a

rambling cedar-shingled structure festooned with towers, gables, balconies and chimneys. Today it was rumoured that the scientist would actually launch a flying machine piloted by a local young man, John Alexander Douglas McCurdy.

The promise of a spectacle by Bell always drew a crowd. The day before, on February 22, his giant motorized kite *Cygnet II* had been carefully manoeuvred out of the Kite House, his workshop at Beinn

Bhreagh, and dragged onto the frozen lake. Fifty-two feet wide on top and tapering to forty feet on the bottom, the kite resembled a mammoth red honeycomb, with its 2,152 cells made of fabric. Many of the female spectators had helped sew the silk onto the frame, and there was considerable interest in the kite's debut. Its Curtiss engine was started up and two attempts were made to launch it into the air, but the kite's steel tube skids refused to leave the ice. On the third try, as the multicelled contraption slid along, the ten-foot propeller broke off and smashed, causing *Cygnet II* to grind firmly to a halt.

The kite's inability to defy gravity had only confirmed the belief of most of the audience that physical flight was an impossibility. A few had read of the success of the German glider pilot Otto Lilienthal; the September 1894 issue of that household regular, *McClure's Magazine*, had devoted nine pages to his flights. But they also knew that two years later, when one of his gliders stalled at fifty feet above the ground, Lilienthal had been killed, making the supreme sacrifice for his foolhardiness. Recently there had been vague stories that two American brothers, Orville and Wilbur Wright, bicycle makers from Dayton, Ohio, had actually flown. Even more fantastically, there were some Nova Scotians who half-believed these rumours.

Today, there would be an attempt by Douglas McCurdy to fly a gasoline-powered airplane. The Curtiss engine had been taken off the ill-fated *Cygnet II* and fitted onto a machine that the young man had designed himself, in the United States. The *Silver Dart*, so named because of the shimmering fabric that covered its wings, looked infinitely more capable of flight than the giant kite. In any case, in an era when most Canadians worked sixty-six hours a week, any distraction was welcome, and there was no lack of willing helpers to drag the machine out onto the lake. Some of the young men, conscious of the audience and of Bell's camera, even donned skates to help steady the *Silver Dart* when it took off. For not only was this the first airplane that had ever been seen in Canada: it was also being piloted by a native of Baddeck itself.

TAKING TO THE AIR

The new century had been eventful enough already. Queen Victoria had died in 1901. American president William McKinley had been assassinated the same year, and since then the world had seemed to move at a frenetic pace. Even in this far corner of the British Empire, the Boer War and the Boxer Uprising had shaken people's faith in a well-ordered, Western-dominated world. The streets of Toronto now had so many automobiles on them—8,000— that in 1907 the first parking tickets were distributed. Saskatchewan and Alberta had joined Confederation two years before the *Silver Dart* was built, and in Winnipeg Nellie McClung was agitating for women to have the same opportunities as men. While most people enjoyed *Harper's Weekly*, more adventurous Canadians were reading Sigmund Freud's *The Interpretation of Dreams*, in which the author had written "that the wish to be able to fly signifies in the dream nothing but the longing for the ability of sexual accomplishment."

Even though many were skeptical, travelling in the air, whether by balloon or by machine, had caught the public's fancy. The race to perfect whichever method promised sustained flight was on. As Bell's assistants were reassembling the *Silver Dart* in the workshop at Baddeck, the Halifax newspapers reported that a Frenchman named Louis Blériot had successfully flown 656 feet in his home-built monoplane, and had then foolishly promised the press that he would fly across the English Channel that summer.

Recorded history is full of dreamers and scientists who wanted to soar off the earth's surface. In 1783, the first aeronauts were carried into the air by air itself: air that had been heated and captured in a bag. By the turn of this century hot-air balloons had given way to safer hydrogen-filled ones, but both were unsatisfactory as methods of transportation, being at the mercy of the winds.

Even the military, that most hidebound of institutions, had operated gas-filled balloons early on. The United States Army had fielded a complete Balloon Corps since 1861, and the British since 1878.

In Europe, visionaries such as Alberto Santos Dumont and Count Ferdinand von Zeppelin took the concept further and made balloon flights in steerable, powered gas bags, called, quite literally, "dirigibles."

Like their European cousins, Canadians were quite familiar with balloons, the first having been exhibited in 1834 at the Champ des Mars, Montreal. Six years later, on August 10, 1840, Louis Anslem Lauriat ascended in a balloon from Barrack Square in Saint John, New Brunswick, and floated a distance of twenty-one miles to the Quaco Road, becoming the first aerial traveller in British North America. Perhaps the most imaginative use of balloons occurred in the unlikely location of the high Arctic, in what would become the Northwest Territories. In August 1850, the Royal Navy deployed its frigate HMS *Assistance* to search for the overdue expedition of Sir John Franklin. Hampered from proceeding any further than present-day Cornwallis Island because of the ice, the searchers released small hydrogen-filled balloons carrying messages in the hope that Franklin would see them.

In the two decades following Lauriat's ascent, balloons, some made in Canada, sailed over Montreal (1856), the nation's capital (1858), Lake Ontario (1859), Toronto and Hamilton (1862). The first aerial fatality in Canada took place at the Ottawa Exhibition on September 26, 1888, when Tom Wensley, one of the volunteer helpers at a balloon's ascent, held onto the rope for too long and was carried into the air, falling to his death. By 1900, no fair or agricultural exhibition was complete without at least one aeronautical display. No longer a curiosity, ballooning became an Edwardian institution, accepted if not as a practical means of transport then as a hobby for the young, idle rich.

EARLY EXPERIMENTS

When the Wright brothers began building gliders in August 1899, they had the results of centuries of experimentation to rely on. The brothers even studied German in the evenings at Kitty Hawk to better understand Lilienthal's work. Like George Cayley in Britain and the French-born Octave Chanute, the German experimenter designed gliders with vertical and horizontal stabilizers and angled wings. Even in Canada, there were attempts at serious aeronautical research. In 1895, C. H. Mitchell presented a paper called "Aerial Mechanical Flight" to the Engineering Society at the University of Toronto. Of more lasting value, in 1902 Wallace Rupert Turnbull, a New Brunswick engineer, built a wind tunnel in the barn behind his home. There he tested his theories about dihedral wing angles and airscrews. Two decades later, Turnbull's experiments would lead to the invention of the variable-pitch propeller.

Slowly, on both sides of the Atlantic Ocean, academics and backyard tinkerers accumulated the knowledge to understand the forces of lift and propulsion. One ardent inventor was the head of the Smithsonian Institution in Washington, Dr. Samuel Pierpont Langley, and it was his friendship with Alexander Graham Bell that brought aviation north of the border. Of the same generation as Bell, Chanute and Zeppelin, Langley was too old to actually fly his creations, but he hoped to become the first to make a powered glider that others could fly. In June 1891 Bell wrote to a friend from his home in Washington, D.C.: "They [models of Langley's flying machines] flew for me today. I shall have to make experiments upon my own account in Cape Breton. Can't keep out of it. It shall be up to us someday!"[1] Until his death in 1922, the old inventor's curiosity and his fortune, acquired after winning several lawsuits over telephone patents, allowed him to explore the development of objects as diverse as the photoelectric cell, the iron lung and the phonograph. As a regent of the Smithsonian Institution, he had access to the scientific journals in which articles on aviation appeared. Both he and Langley foresaw that it was powered kites, and not balloons, that held the key to the future of aviation.

While Langley worked away in Washington fashioning larger models of his steam-powered "aerodrome," Bell constructed giant box kites that were strong enough to carry a man.[2] In 1899, Bell published a paper in the magazine of the National

Academy of Science titled "Kites with Radial Wings," and he began to be obsessed with designing kites composed of layers of tetrahedral cells. (A tetrahedron is a pyramid with its base and sides composed of four triangles.) If two of the four sides of the cell were covered with fabric, Bell thought, the kite's wings would be strong and stable enough to make wire bracing unnecessary. Such a massive kite could be towed into the air, and, with a strong wind, would hover by itself. The kite's passenger could throw down a line to have the kite tethered to the ground, then climb down from the sky by means of a rope ladder. What practical purpose such a kite might serve, Bell had still to work out.

Because of his age, Bell employed Douglas McCurdy, the son of his secretary, to do most of the practical work. Born at Baddeck in 1886, McCurdy was studying at the University of Toronto to become an engineer. During their summer vacations, he and a college friend, Frederick W. "Casey" Baldwin, began helping Bell fly his kites.

THE RACE IS ON

The world of aviation was a competitive one, with Europe at its centre. An international aeronautical commission sponsored by the Aero-Club de France met in Paris to discuss aspects of powered gliding. Wealthy patrons put up large sums of money as prizes for longer flights, and "aeronauts" such as Gabriel Voisin and Ferdinand Ferber demonstrated their gliders at exhibitions. The first "airport" was proposed by the engineer Gustave Eiffel, who suggested that it be set up on the Champ de Mars, at the foot of his famous tower, so that aircraft to be launched could be hoisted up by cable to the tower's first stage. Across the channel at Aldershot, the British Army was testing Samuel Cody's "war kites." Begun as attractions for his popular Wild West show (in which Cody impersonated the more famous William F. Cody, Buffalo Bill), Cody's kites would eventually fly as high as 14,000 feet, impressing the Royal Meteorological Society enough to earn the flamboyant American cowboy a fellowship.

The United States attempted to catch up with Europe in all things, especially this new means of transportation. The U.S. War Department advanced Samuel Langley the enormous sum of $50,000 to build a flying machine that would have military applications. The idea of public funds appealed to the Wright brothers, but the scrutiny that came with them did not. Methodical loners, they improvised with used bicycle parts in a tiny shop while teams of carpenters completed Langley's elaborate aerodrome, its size and complexity growing by the day.

On December 8, 1903, before a huge audience and with his assistant as pilot, Langley prepared to have his gasoline-powered monoplane catapulted off the roof of a houseboat moored in the middle of the Potomac River. Onlookers watched in awe as his aerodrome, the first aircraft in North America, gathered speed. It rolled off the edge of the roof—and sank into the river.

The disaster did for North American aviation what the sinking of the *Titanic* would do for travel by ship nine years later. The newspapers of the day went into an orgy of smugness. If the secretary of the mighty Smithsonian Institution, with $50,000 and all his education, could not fly, then who could? Such was the ridicule and skepticism heaped on him by the press that Bell's old colleague never recovered, and he died soon after.

Nine days after the Potomac embarrassment, on December 17, 1903, at 10:35 A.M. on the sands of Kitty Hawk, North Carolina, Orville and Wilbur Wright made history with their *Flyer*. Mindful of Langley's experience, the brothers remained quiet about changing the course of history.[3] The Dayton mechanics never forgave the establishment of the day its patronage of Langley and later, Bell, both of whom, in their eyes, knew little about aerodynamics and even less about practical aeronautics.

THE CURTISS ENGINE

Bell pursued his aerial experiments at Baddeck. He had some success on December 28, 1905, when his box kite, *Siamese Twins*, composed of 1,829 tetrahedral cells each ten inches wide, lifted off carrying a passenger. The following January, the Aero Club of

America held its first convention in New York. Unlike the Wrights, Bell enjoyed the attentions of the media, and he brought a tetrahedral kite to display at the convention. The sign over his exhibit described it as "A Soaring Kite Adapted to Gliding Flight When Freed from Its Cord." His other purpose in attending was to search out a lightweight engine to power the kites, and it was at this exhibition that he met a second American who would have a profound effect on him and on Canadian aviation in general.

If ever a young man represented the new century, Glenn Hammond Curtiss did. When Curtiss was ten years old, in 1888, the British "safety" bicycle first appeared in America and changed his life forever. Using one as a Western Union messenger boy, he also took to cycling on weekends the seventy miles between his home in Rochester, New York, and Hammondsport, where his grandmother lived. Soon he moved to Hammondsport permanently, married and set up a bicycle repair shop.

Beinn Bhreagh, Alexander Graham Bell's estate on Cape Breton Island, Nova Scotia. COURTESY AND COPYRIGHT BELL FAMILY AND THE NATIONAL GEOGRAPHIC SOCIETY

Curtiss, like the Wrights, had a mechanical genius coupled with a familiarity with wood, metal and lathes. He was also fortunate to be born just as the German engineer Karl Daimler Benz was perfecting the internal combustion engine, an invention that freed designers from using clumsy, heavy steam engines as a means of propulsion. Curtiss's bicycles quickly evolved into motorcycles. At 125 pounds, his engines were light, double-cylinder and reliable—perfect for balloons and even gliders.

On July 12, 1906, crowds of Montrealers marvelled as one such engine powered Lincoln Beachey's airship as it rose from Dominion Park. But there were few witnesses a year later when the actual birth of aviation in Canada took place not far away. Lawrence Jerome Lesh, barely out of his teens, had

built a glider he christened *Montreal No. 1* in his back yard, and one day in mid-August he had it towed out over the St. Lawrence River. Then, strapped into the harness fastened under it in modern hang-gliding style, he flew from the docks down the river for a distance of six miles. Lesh was the first to fly a heavier-than-air machine in Canada, and would be the first in Canada to take an aerial photograph from something other than a balloon. More significantly, his next glider, *Montreal No. 2*, made use of ailerons—the first to do so in North America. But when this creation crashed, no more was heard of Lawrence Lesh, and other Canadians carried the torch into history.

In the United States, Glenn Curtiss had become a nationally known motorcycle racer. Fame had brought orders for his engines, and he was able to corner the North American market. In April 1906, Bell ordered a Curtiss No. 1 engine and asked that it be shipped to Baddeck, to be fitted onto one of his kites. As neither the old man nor his assistants McCurdy and Baldwin had any experience with internal combustion engines, Curtiss was invited to Nova Scotia to install it.

Members of the Aerial Experiment Association, formed October 1, 1907. From left to right: Glenn Curtiss, J.A.D. McCurdy, A.G. Bell, F.W. Baldwin, Lt. Thomas Selfridge. COURTESY AND COPYRIGHT BELL FAMILY AND THE NATIONAL GEOGRAPHIC SOCIETY

THE FOUNDING OF THE AEA

In September 1907, Mabel Bell suggested to her husband and his young colleagues McCurdy, Baldwin and Curtiss that they form an association to carry out flying experiments. She had recently come into some money and offered to finance the venture. A fifth member of the group was to be Lieutenant Thomas Selfridge. Impressed by the young U.S. Army officer who had volunteered his help, Bell used his friendship with President Roosevelt to have Selfridge assigned to temporary duty at Beinn Breagh.

The Aerial Experiment Association (AEA), founded in Bell's living room on October 1, 1907, would have a fundamental effect on aviation in North America. At the outset, Bell explained that this was a cooperative scientific effort, "not for gain, but for the love of the art and doing what we can to help one another."[4] Bell as chairman, and Curtiss as executive officer and director of experiments, would each receive a salary of $5,000 a year. Baldwin, the chief engineer, and McCurdy, the treasurer, would each be paid $1,000 annually. Selfridge, who took the role of secretary, declined any pay.

The object of the AEA, as minuted, was "to build a practical aeroplane which will carry a man through the air by its own power." But Curtiss, McCurdy, Baldwin and Selfridge all had the same unspoken motive: while they would allow their patriarch his impractical dream of monster tetrahedral kites, each had his own agenda for designing and flying a practical flying machine.

The members wasted no time in getting to work on *Cygnet I.* An unswanlike creation of 3,393 tetrahedral cells, it was fifty-two feet wide and ten feet high, made even more ungainly by being fitted with pontoons. On December 6, 1907, Mabel Bell christened it with a cup of water, and it was ready to be launched into the wind. To achieve lift-off, the kite was placed on a flat barge and towed behind a steam excursion ship out onto Bras d'Or Lake. Then, with Selfridge lying full length on board, swathed in oilskins and rugs, *Cygnet I* was pulled into the air. It reached a height of 168 feet and maintained that altitude for seven minutes. Then it floated gently back to the water like the bird it was named after. So overcome were they by such a sight that the steamer's crew did not release the tow rope in time, and the glider, with Selfridge still on it, ploughed into the chilly water. The kite was dragged behind the ship, disintegrating beyond repair.

The Association prepared to transfer to Curtiss's workshop at Hammondsport after the Christmas holidays. Curtiss wrote to the Wrights, inviting them to join the AEA there so that they might, in his words, "talk engine." Suspicious of Curtiss, and fearing that the AEA might use their aeronautical knowledge illegally, the brothers ignored the invitation. However, they did correspond with Selfridge, even answering his inquiries about aircraft design in some detail. They had hopes of the United States Army being a possible customer for the Wright *Flyer* and

besides, the AEA was not a serious threat to their monopoly . . . yet.

THE FIRST AEA AIRCRAFT

Through the winter of 1908, following endless nightly discussions, the AEA team constructed a series of aircraft, all powered by Curtiss's engines. Selfridge's design was the first to be built. Named the *Red Wing* because of the colour of the fabric used, the biplane had the elevator in front and the vertical rudder behind. Most of the flying machines Bell was associated with were coloured dark red, for good reason. He had fought long battles to protect his telephone patent, battles that could have been avoided if he had kept notes and photographs of his invention at every stage of its development. Determined to have everything well documented this time, Bell had all the evolutionary stages of the AEA's kites and airplanes photographed. Red stood out well on the black-and-white film of the day.

As all suitable fields were covered in snow, the slippery, frozen surface of nearby Lake Keuka was chosen to provide the necessary lift. But it was March 12, and the ice along the shore was starting to break up. The *Red Wing*, with its skids, was put on the deck of a small steamboat and taken out for its first flight. It was unloaded where the ice was thickest.

Unhappily, Selfridge had been ordered to report to Washington that day, so Casey Baldwin was chosen as pilot. The pilot's seat was a kitchen chair with the legs removed. The total weight of the aircraft, including pilot, was 570 pounds, and it needed all the power that Curtiss's eight-cylinder air-cooled engine could provide. Baldwin turned the motor to full throttle, and the *Red Wing* took to the air. It flew steadily for about 300 feet through a light breeze, although there were no lateral controls for stability. Then, suddenly, it dropped from a height of 20 feet and crashed onto the ice. Baldwin emerged unhurt from his chair.

Five days later, in a cold rain, a second flight was made. The *Red Wing*'s fabric became so sodden that this time it crashed after rising 120 feet in the air. The unlucky Selfridge returned from Washington to find his aircraft a soggy mess and the others working on Casey Baldwin's design.

The members of the AEA made sure their efforts were well covered by the local media, and thus many photographs and eyewitness accounts of their exploits exist. Those who saw the *Red Wing*'s flights realized that the Wrights' monopoly on powered flight in North America had been broken.

The Wrights had achieved lateral control in their *Flyer* by an ingenious invention called "wing-warping," which they patented. They entered into an exhaustive series of court battles to keep their competitors from using wing-warping or any related form of lateral control. In practice, wing-warping strained the airframe and bent already fragile wings out of shape. AEA members considered it dangerous, because it produced a drag on the wings and caused the aircraft to skid. Yet rather than experiment further, the Wrights continued for the remainder of their lives to perpetuate their invention in between serving legal writs on their competitors.

The AEA took a different approach, methodically adapting their successive machines to incorporate improvements. In their next model, Baldwin's *White Wing*, they added devices first used by the French aviator Robert Esnault-Pelterie in 1904. Called "ailerons," these movable surfaces at the edge of each wing improved lateral stability and were controlled by a yoke attached to the pilot's shoulders. The *White Wing* also became the first aircraft in North America to be fitted with wheels, arranged in a triangle configuration, instead of skids. Using the Hammondsport racetrack as a runway, Baldwin flew 279 feet on May 18, and on May 21, Curtiss, on his thirtieth birthday, took it 1,017 feet. The day after, McCurdy flew the *White Wing* 600 feet, crashing it and injuring himself.

The AEA's third aircraft had the unglamorous name of *June Bug*. Designed by Curtiss, and flown only by him, it embodied all the lessons learned and some innovations. It had a V8 40-hp air-cooled engine and, like its predecessor, stood on wheels. On the July 4 holiday, before a huge crowd at the Hammondsport racetrack, Curtiss took off in the

159. Leken 1909 Oct. 10 Jul.
Div. 1909 Oct. 13 Jm.

June Bug and flew more than half a mile, winning a trophy from the journal *Scientific American*.

When Orville Wright read of the flights, and heard that the AEA planned to sell copies of the aircraft, he calculated that the association had accomplished in six months what he and his brother had needed six years to do. This leap in technology could only be explained, he reasoned, by illegal use of the Wright's wing-warping invention. The Wrights sought legal advice. On July 20, Curtiss received a letter from Orville Wright reminding him that the Wrights' U.S. patent number 821,393 broadly covered all adjustable surfaces of flying machines. Wisely, Curtiss referred the issue to Bell. The old inventor, on the counsel of his lawyers, took out a patent on the AEA's ailerons, thus setting the stage for court

battles with the Wrights for many years to come.

On August 29, when McCurdy flew the *June Bug* for over two miles, association members knew they had perfected the balance between the wings, the engine and the ailerons. A sign of their growing confidence was the decision to extend the flying season into the fall. Planning to use water for a runway instead of ice, they renamed the *June Bug* the *Loon* and fitted it with pontoons.

At Fort Myer, Washington, Orville Wright demonstrated his *Flyer* on September 20, and as part of the requirement for its acceptance by the U.S. Army, took Selfridge up as a passenger. From a height of 100 feet, the *Flyer* suddenly plunged to the ground, injuring Wright but killing Selfridge, who became the first victim of powered flight in history.

Baddeck No. 2 at Bentinck Farm, Big Baddeck, with F. W. Baldwin in the aviator's seat. PHOTO BY J.A.D. McCURDY/ COURTESY AND COPYRIGHT BELL FAMILY AND THE NATIONAL GEOGRAPHIC SOCIETY

The four remaining members of the AEA voted to keep the association going for six more months, until March 31, 1909. Mrs. Bell once more agreed to finance them, no doubt in the hope that the younger members would now work exclusively on her husband's giant kites. But only Casey Baldwin accompanied Bell to Baddeck. McCurdy chose to return to Hammondsport with Curtiss, it being McCurdy's turn to design an airplane. While doing so, he gained some experience in flying by operating the tried and tested *Loon*, now fitted with a more

powerful Curtiss engine. In November, McCurdy failed to get the plane to lift off from the water, although he did reach a speed of 72 mph.

THE SILVER DART

By December, the AEA were confident enough to show off their latest and most famous creation. The result of a unique partnership between McCurdy and Curtiss, it would be the fourth aircraft to come out of the AEA workshop. So much silver fabric was used that the slender machine begged to be called the *Silver Dart*. Like the *June Bug*, it had a wheeled undercarriage, but it was powered by the latest Curtiss engine: a water-cooled 50-hp eight-cylinder engine that drove a twin-bladed propeller. The

aileron control surfaces tested on the *June Bug* were enlarged and, for the first time, there were seats for the pilot and a passenger in tandem.

On December 6, McCurdy flew the *Silver Dart* a distance of 600 feet, making ten more similar flights by Christmas. Becoming worried that the association was too attached to Hammondsport and Curtiss, Bell wired to have the *Silver Dart* sent to Baddeck for trials, and for Curtiss and McCurdy to accompany it. They arrived to find the old man and Baldwin with half the townsfolk of Baddeck dragging Bell's massive *Cygnet II* onto the ice. That it couldn't fly surprised no one but Bell.

The next morning, February 23, the engine was transferred from the kite to the *Silver Dart*, which

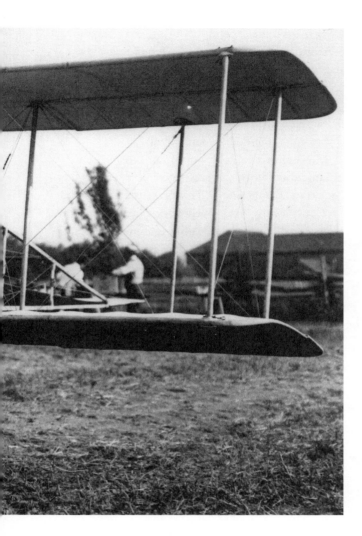

grated. Curtiss caught the train back to Hammondsport, relieved to be done with Bell's paternalism and his impractical kites. Curtiss had been approached about the possibility of forming his own aircraft manufacturing company in the United States by a shadowy, controversial figure in early aviation history, Augustus Heering. Heering was a seductive character, and under his spell Curtiss managed to overlook the fact that Heering had initially approached the Wrights and tried to interest them in financing a company to rival the AEA. Ultimately the two men quarrelled over the direction their company should take, and their argument ended up in court.

On the evening of March 31, Bell, McCurdy and Baldwin, the remaining members of the AEA, gathered in the living room at Beinn Bhreagh for their final meeting. Baldwin moved that the organization be dissolved, and McCurdy seconded the motion. Bell later wrote that "It had been a band of comrades on a great adventure . . . as if having four brilliant sons to share my life and work. Now it was over."

McCurdy flew for half a mile at a height of 60 feet and an estimated speed of 40 mph. It was another first: the first powered flight in the whole British Empire.

On February 24, before a crowd of excited onlookers, McCurdy flew the *Silver Dart* on a circuitous four-and-a-half-mile flight that lasted six minutes. On descending, the machine's right wing struck the ice and a wheel crumpled. But by early spring, McCurdy was back in the air, flying the *Silver Dart* for almost twenty miles in a closed circuit, making a total of two hundred flights without incident.

Just as they were on the brink of commercial success, the Aerial Experiment Association disinte-

THE CANADIAN AERODROME COMPANY

By the summer of 1909, Bell was becoming quite content to leave flying machines to his young assistants. He exchanged with Curtiss all of the AEA's assets at Hammondsport, including the *June Bug*, for the AEA's assets in Baddeck, which included the *Silver Dart*. In June, again with the financial backing of Mrs. Bell, Canada's first aircraft manufacturing firm was formed: the Canadian Aerodrome Company (CAC) of Baddeck, Nova Scotia. Its board of directors consisted of Bell, Baldwin, William Bedwin, who had joined the AEA after Selfridge's death, and McCurdy. That summer, the CAC built the *Baddeck No. 1*, a biplane that significantly had a 40-hp Kirkham engine instead of a Curtiss.

This was not the first attempt to put aviation on a commercial basis in Canada. Several months earlier, the Franco-American Automobile Company of Montreal had advertised for sale Voisin aircraft from France. Handmade, with custom-built engines, the airplanes were expensive, and owning them was the preserve of the government or the very wealthy.

Aircraft were still homemade affairs in Canada. In a Vancouver basement the Templeton brothers, William and Winston, along with their cousin William McMullin, hammered together a contraption they hoped would fly. For those without such skills, there were aviation societies and clubs forming in Winnipeg and Toronto, for the purpose of "promoting practical aeronautics and encouraging Canadian inventors." By far the most popular types of aircraft used in Canada were Blériots and Curtiss "pushers." Plans for both were commercially available; they were easy enough to build, and Curtiss did not seem to be worried about his design being copied. Between 1908 and the First World War, at Lindsay and Sarnia, Winnipeg, Calgary, Montreal and Red Deer, the first aircraft to take to the skies were copies of Blériots or Curtiss pushers.

Reading in the newspapers that European governments saw a future in military aviation, McCurdy and Baldwin turned to the Canadian Army in the hope that it might purchase the *Silver Dart*. Their old mentor, Dr. Bell, gave them a boost in a speech he made before the Canadian Club in Ottawa, with the governor general and most of the Cabinet present. The topic of aviation had reached the highest circles of power, and there must have been much nodding over brandy and cigars that Canada should adopt some sort of policy. Soon it was generally agreed that the young men should be given an opportunity to demonstrate their airplanes before members of the government.

McCurdy and Baldwin were fast running through Mrs. Bell's money; that summer, they dismantled both the *Baddeck No. 1* and the *Silver Dart* and took them by train to the Petawawa Army camp north of Ottawa. The military, in a rare moment of generos-

ity, approved the expenditure of $5 for lathes and rolls of tar paper to assist in the rebuilding of both aircraft. On July 26, 1909, as the machines were being assembled, news came that Louis Blériot had conquered the English Channel. The Canadian public, seized by patriotic fervour, called for a national feat to equal the Frenchman's flight.

On August 2, on a day of bright sunshine and unlimited visibility, the press and public gathered at Petawawa. Before the military brass and their wives, McCurdy swung the propeller and climbed into the *Silver Dart*. He flew a half mile at about 10 feet off the ground before making a flawless landing. Then he took Baldwin up as a passenger—the first time in Canada that an aircraft had carried more than one person. On his third flight, McCurdy took up the foreman from the army workshop. Now increasingly confident, he made a fourth and, unfortunately, final flight. Blinded by the sun, McCurdy hit a grassy knoll, and the *Silver Dart* crashed onto its starboard wing. The plane was damaged beyond immediate repair.

Even after witnessing three successful flights, observers were less than impressed. The problem was that no one could see any practical use for the flying machine on a battlefield. Balloons had the height for observation; in fact, the British Army had set up its own Balloon School at Farnborough, England. If *they* could not see any benefits to aviation, how could the Canadian militia be expected to?

Ten days later, on August 12, McCurdy demonstrated the CAC's other aircraft, *Baddeck No. 1*, to military officials and government representatives. This first flight of an aircraft completely designed and built in Canada was a historic one. But when, after flying at a height of 12 feet for about 100 yards, the *Baddeck No. 1* too stalled and crashed, the audience who had given the invention little hope took the train back to Ottawa.

Dejected and penniless, the two aviators returned to Nova Scotia. They pooled their last resources into one final biplane, *Baddeck No. 2*. Its first flight, on September 25, was a complete success, and after fifty successful flights, McCurdy begged the military to send an observer. It would be March 1910 before a Major G. S. Maunsell travelled to Baddeck. McCurdy took him up twice on March 9, impressing the major enough that he returned to Ottawa and wrote a favourable report on the Canadian Aerodrome Company. But they had missed their chance. The Cabinet had lost interest in the aircraft, and the whole project was buried in the time-honoured tradition of bureaucrats everywhere.

With the last of Mrs. Bell's money, the members of the company did manage to fulfil one order for an aircraft. Mrs. Bell's first cousin Gardiner Greene Hubbard II, of Boston, commissioned the Canadian Aerodrome Company to build him a monoplane. It took the company all winter to do so, and it was April before the Hubbard monoplane, powered by a 40-hp. Kirkham engine, took off from the ice at Baddeck. It made nine flights, each of about 15 seconds' duration, before crashing through the thin ice. But Hubbard seemed well satisfied, and he took his new acquisition to the Montreal Air Meet that summer and to Boston in September. It was the first aircraft to be sold in Canada, and the first to be exported. But for the Canadian Aerodrome Company, it was all too little too late.

Without names like Bell or Curtiss on the company's letterhead, it proved impossible for McCurdy to recapture the public's attention. Besides, there were too many other aircraft manufacturing competitors by now—Louis Blériot, the Wrights, and their former AEA colleague, Glenn Curtiss. The 1910 Montreal Air Meet held at Lakeside should have been the perfect opportunity for Canada's first aviation company to demonstrate its Baddeck-type aircraft. But when McCurdy crashed the rebuilt *Baddeck No. 1* the day before the meet opened, it seemed that his luck had run out. Although he repaired the airplane and tried to fly on subsequent days, the tattered old Hammondsport design had had its day. The Canadian Aerodrome Company was bankrupt, and McCurdy and Baldwin left to seek their fortunes in the United States. Not surprisingly, they both made their way to Curtiss, now the president of the Heering-Curtiss Company and recent winner of the Gordon-Bennett Trophy race at Rheims, France.

As for Bell, he continued to put his trust in tetrahedral behemoths. *Cygnet III* appeared in 1912. A smaller version of its predecessor, it consisted of only 360 tetrahedral cells. McCurdy even left his job with the Curtiss exhibition team and returned to Baddeck to help launch the new kite. But despite its 70-hp. motor, it barely managed to leap a foot in the air before crashing forever.

His passion for investigation undiminished, Bell finally turned from kites to "hydro dromes"—hydrofoil boats driven by giant propellers. In 1920, two years before his death, his 60-foot hydrofoil was demonstrated before some naval officers. Their verdict was that, while innovative, the hydrofoil was impractical; and like Bell's giant kites, it could charitably be described as an old man's fancy.

Like all of the early aviators, the members of the AEA believed that one day aircraft would span continents and oceans, shrinking the world and facilitating commerce. But less than a decade after the momentous events at Baddeck, their efforts were subverted into a perennial human occupation: using the latest invention to kill one's enemies efficiently and in greater numbers. In Toronto, however, far from the carnage of the First World War, the seeds of Canadian commercial aviation would be sown and then flourish.

The Canadian aerospace industry began in this workshop on Strachan Avenue, Toronto. To circumvent the legal issues concerning the Wright Brothers' patent on ailerons, Curtiss and McCurdy had the ailerons made here and fitted to JN-3s built across the border in Buffalo. CITY OF TORONTO ARCHIVES: JAMES COLLECTION

CHAPTER TWO

The Curtiss Aviation School

I n January 1915, the First World War was heading into its second year. It had become a global conflict, fought on fronts as far away as German East Africa and the Sinai peninsula. Most Canadians were hard pressed to locate Africa's Rufiji River or the Arab port of Aqaba on the map, let alone digest the fact that of the 6,000 Canadian soldiers sent to France the previous year, fully one-third had already been slaughtered.

AN AIR FORCE FOR CANADA?

On the home front, Canada afforded a rapidly expanding British war machine several advantages— wide-open spaces for training, unlimited foodstuffs, and a pool of volunteers for the trenches. While these attributes were to be expected from "bread-basket" colonies like Canada and Australia, Canada had a further asset: it bordered on the United States. Although their country was ostensibly neutral, American manufacturers eagerly cashed in on the

19

Allied appetite for armaments. The farseeing among them set up branch offices across the border so that their products could be stamped "Made in Canada" before they were shipped across the Atlantic.

One of those who saw the commercial potential in the war was Glenn Curtiss. By 1915, the Hammondsport motorcycle shop had grown into a conglomerate of companies that not only designed and manufactured aircraft and aero-engines but ran training schools for fliers as well. Now established in Buffalo, New York, the Curtiss organization, at an estimated net worth of $6 million, was the biggest, most aggressive aviation concern in North America. Canada did not have a native aircraft industry, and of all the foreign manufacturers, Glenn Curtiss was the most familiar with the Canadian aviation scene. He was also able to employ its nationally known aviator, his former colleague J. A. D. McCurdy.[1]

With the failure of the Canadian Aerodrome Company, McCurdy had taken up exhibition flying. On January 30, 1911, after becoming the first Canadian to receive a pilot's licence from the Aero Club of America, he made the first flight in history across an ocean. McCurdy flew a Curtiss aircraft between Key West, Florida, and Havana, Cuba— a distance of 96 miles—coming down a few miles short of the beach in shark-infested waters. Through the summer he took part in the great aviation meets held at Montreal and Toronto. On August 2 he made the first flight between two Canadian cities when he won an air race between Hamilton and Toronto. Yet despite McCurdy's impressive record of historic "firsts," exhibition flying was not financially rewarding, and he remained on the lookout for a more permanent position. In 1913, he returned to Hammondsport and learned to fly a Curtiss flying boat. He then accepted the position of "flying chauffeur" for the publishing millionaire George d'Utassy. When d'Utassy's machine was wrecked a year later, McCurdy became a consultant to the Curtiss Aeroplane Company. Lest it be thought that Curtiss hired his old AEA colleague only for McCurdy's connections with the military in Ottawa (he proved to have none), it should be

mentioned that the Hammondsport designer had fallen out with Augustus Heering, and the resulting court battles would continue for a decade afterwards.

With the start of the war, McCurdy, like many, speculated as to what the role of aircraft might be. Its potential as a weapon was no longer in doubt. In 1911, the Italians had used reconnaissance aircraft to conquer Abyssinia, and in 1913, Mexican rebel pilots had bombed government ships from a height of 2,500 feet. The major combatants, the British, the French and the Germans, had all entered the war with aircraft fleets that were rapidly evolving into fighter-bombers.

In December 1914, McCurdy set about lobbying Prime Minister Sir Robert Borden to form an exclusively Canadian air arm. While running for office, Borden had championed Canadian independence from both the British and the Americans. In both the Washington Treaty of 1871 and the Alaska dispute in 1903, Canadian ministers had been humiliated by having to negotiate with the White House as part of a British team. On the strength of Borden's election rhetoric, McCurdy guessed that a nationalistic idea such as a Canadian air force might find fertile ground. When he did gain an interview with the prime minister, he proposed that the aircraft for the air arm be built by Canadians employed at a factory which the Curtiss Aeroplane Company would set up in Toronto. As part of a package deal, the Curtiss company would also run training schools to teach Canadians to fly those aircraft. A further incentive was that for every aircraft the government bought, the Curtiss company offered to train a pilot without charge.

In 1914, the anteroom to every minister's office in Ottawa must have been crowded with salesmen, lobbyists and constituents, all clutching briefcases crammed with projects, all guaranteeing victory. Borden heard McCurdy out—he was after all a young man with influential connections—but the prime minister was not about to infect national defence with American-tainted private enterprise. McCurdy's offer was turned down. But Borden did pass McCurdy's proposal on to his Minister for Militia and Defence, Colonel Sam Hughes.

Hughes had already sanctioned and paid for a small Canadian air unit that had been sent over to England with the 1st Contingent of the Expeditionary Force. The unit consisted of three pilots and an American-made Burgess-Dunne biplane. As yet, neither the pilots nor the aircraft had done anything to justify his investment; in fact, when the Burgess-Dunne arrived in Britain, it was locked away in a shed and soon fell apart. The minister for militia had no wish or time to get involved with aviation once more. By April 1915, his pride and joy, the Ross rifle, was proving useless under combat conditions, and worse, the scandal of the Shell Committee (in which Hughes had given $170 million worth of contracts to his cronies to produce shells), had surfaced. The increasingly erratic minister performed the time-honoured Ottawa ritual and passed McCurdy's plan to—he hoped—oblivion.

But fortunately for Canada, and for its author, McCurdy's brief ended up in London at the British Admiralty, setting in motion a train of events that no one could have foreseen. Lord Kitchener, Secretary of State for War, had assigned responsibility for the overall defence of the British Isles against air attack to the admiralty and its recently formed Royal Naval Air Service (RNAS). The army, he said, would be too busy actually fighting the Hun. The RNAS protested that it did not have the men or machines to accept such an honour, as all suitable aircraft and pilots in Britain had already been slated for the Royal Flying Corps (RFC). What available aircraft there were had a very limited range and a poor operational ceiling, too low in fact to reach the Kaiser's airships. When the zeppelin raids over England began in early 1915, the inability of the RNAS aircraft to intercept the giant sausage-shaped dirigibles was particularly galling for the public to watch from below. Stung by criticism in Parliament and the newspapers, the admiralty was looking into recruiting pilots in Canada and purchasing training and maritime patrol aircraft from American companies.

In 1915, the governor general of Canada was Field-Marshal His Royal Highness the Duke of Connaught, the youngest son of Queen Victoria. Such was his status that his personal secretary was Lieutenant Colonel E. A. Stanton who, before he came to Canada, had been governor of the Sudan. Stanton, peculiarly for a man of his age (he was forty-eight) and class, had taken a personal interest in prewar Canadian aviation, and his reports on the subject remain invaluable to modern historians. On February 25, 1915, he wrote to the Canadian Chief of General Staff asking what arrangements had been made for enlisting aviators in Canada. It wasn't just an inquiry from an aviation enthusiast. Stanton had the authority of Rideau Hall and, consequently, of Buckingham Palace behind him, as Prime Minister Borden and his Cabinet were well aware.

As the war progressed, aviation's role had taken on a global significance. Land armies had become so large and unwieldy that, for the first time in history, commanders could no longer see with their own eyes what was going on. Remote from the advance or retreat of their troops, general staff were reluctantly forced to embrace the air squadrons as their main source of intelligence—whether photographic or by word of mouth. It was only a matter of time before the aerial scouts shot at one another, and they needed the protection of their own armed aircraft as they observed the enemy's movements. By 1915, aerial warfare had moved from the defensive to the offensive, and the cult of the dashing fighter pilot was born.

That April, advertisements for airmen appeared in newspapers across Canada, spurred no doubt by Stanton, who also arranged for recruiting to be handled by the governor general's office in Ottawa. Only British subjects "of pure European descent" and under thirty years of age were asked to apply. Preference would be given to those between nineteen and twenty-three years of age. On passing an interview and medical examination, the students were to be accepted into the RNAS—on condition they obtained a pilot's licence at their own expense. The overwhelming immediate response was tempered only by the inability of the few existing flying schools in Canada and the United States to take them.

CURTISS AEROPLANE AND MOTORS LTD.

During this time, the British Admiralty sent Captain William Elder to North America to purchase JN-3 training aircraft from Curtiss's company, now called the Curtiss Aeroplane and Motor Company. The JN-3s were undoubtedly the best such aircraft available on the market, their design hampered only by the continuing legal battle over the use of the aileron.

Orville Wright (Wilbur had died of typhoid in 1912) was still doggedly contesting the invention of the aileron with Curtiss (and everyone else), continuing to claim that the Wrights' patent for wing-warping covered all methods of lateral control. The Wrights held the patents for wing-warping and ailerons in France, Britain and the United States—wherever there was an aviation industry—and their lawyers served writs for illegal use of ailerons on aircraft manufacturers and exhibition pilots alike. Even with the war, no one was exempt, and they continued to enforce their legal right, imposing a 5 per cent royalty on each aircraft with ailerons manufactured in either the United States or Britain.

Without an aviation industry of its own, Canada had been excluded from the Wrights' claim, and Curtiss and McCurdy were quite aware of this legal loophole. If the ailerons could be made in Toronto and then fitted onto JN-3s built at the Curtiss works across the border in Buffalo, New York, the Wrights could not demand royalties. With 5 per cent saved from the total cost of the large Allied orders for aircraft, the profits for Curtiss would be considerable.

That McCurdy soon hoped to make more than just ailerons in Canada was obvious. As he had told the prime minister, he visualized the Toronto factory turning out complete aircraft. In February of 1915 McCurdy had been appointed secretary-treasurer and managing director of the Curtiss company in Canada. Curtiss Aeroplanes and Motors Ltd. (Toronto) started operations that April in a factory at 20 Strachan Avenue, near the Canadian National Exhibition grounds. Initially only ailerons were made, but, as a result of McCurdy's persistence, Elder's orders also stipulated that eighteen of the JN-3s be manufactured in Canada. With this official sanction, the factory expanded in May to accommodate the complete assembly of the aircraft, with the engines imported from the Buffalo plant. Six of the eighteen were earmarked for the Curtiss Aviation School in Toronto.

THE FIRST STUDENTS

Through the Curtiss Flying School program, students would receive their initial training on the Curtiss Model "F" flying boats, which were based at Hanlan's Point on Toronto Island, then move on to Curtiss-built landplanes. The instructors were initially American, and the course, providing four hundred minutes of flying time, was to be run on the standards of the Aero Club of America. It was a commercial arrangement from the outset. The fee was $400, and on graduation those students accepted by the RNAS were entitled to a gratuity of $365.

On May 6, the first thirteen students gathered at the aileron factory on Strachan Avenue to watch the two flying boats being assembled. Both had been built at the Curtiss workshop in Buffalo and sent to Toronto to be put together. The Model "F" was a "pusher," with the 90-hp Curtiss OX engine facing the tail. Student and instructor sat side by side in front of the biplane's wings and engine. In the patriotic fervour of the day, the first completed aircraft was named the *Maple Leaf.*

A corrugated-roofed hangar with a ramp that sloped from the door to the water was erected on one of Toronto Island's beaches. As part of its war effort, the city rented the beach to the flying school for a nominal sum of $1. McCurdy, the school's director, was assisted by Warner Perberdy, a British electrical engineer who had worked at the Hammondsport factory and was also learning to fly.

More than half the recruits accepted for training at the Curtiss school came from Ontario. Essentially middle-class, they were mostly in white-collar positions: clerks, teachers, chauffeurs, "students-in-law" and draughtsmen. Their education was comparable. While Warner Perberdy had been educated at Rugby Lower School and Oxford University, a majority of

the others were graduates of St. Andrew's College in Toronto (as was McCurdy), and Toronto "Tech" and Montreal High also featured in the school's files.

The actual issues of the war probably meant little to the flying school students: they were likely more familiar with singer Al Jolson and movie director D.W. Griffiths (who had just made a movie about Canada) than with the assassination of an Austrian archduke. But the Old Country was in danger, and as all the students were either British-born or of British ancestry, they saw it as their duty to repel the Hun. Besides, war was still seen as a dashing adventure, with aircraft taking the place of cavalry charges. The slaughter that was to take place at Vimy Ridge lay two Easters in the future.

Instructional flying at the school began two days after an official visit from the governor general and Lieutenant Colonel Stanton. By the height of sum-

Hanlan's Point, Toronto Island, in the summer of 1915 with all three flying boats of the Curtiss Flying School in action.
CITY OF TORONTO ARCHIVES: JAMES COLLECTION

mer, the flying boats were operating from 4:30 A.M. until dark. Some students camped near the hangar or were fortunate enough to rent a room among Toronto Island's residents.

The flights were an unexpected and free source of amusement for Torontonians that summer, taking place as they did within view of the city beaches with their fairgrounds and summer cottages. On weekends, when the crowds and curious crews of pleasure craft threatened to disrupt the circuits, a police boat had to be used to keep spectators away.

By mid-June, all thirteen students had completed the flying boat course and were ready to move into the second phase of training, which was held at the

Long Branch Rifle Ranges, eleven miles west of Toronto. Late that month, on a field at Long Branch that was prone to flooding during the summer rains, Canada's first airport came into being. As it had on the island, the school here consisted of a single three-bay hangar with a corrugated metal roof. Three Curtiss JN-3 trainers had been brought up from the Curtiss factory in Buffalo. Unlike the flying boats, the JN-3s were fitted with tandem controls in both cockpits, and the instructor would sit in the rear.

As flying began at 5:30 A.M. (even earlier in mid-summer), students either camped on the field or commuted from the city by the earliest possible train. Some of the more fortunate were able to stay at the nearby Toronto Golf Club, where they enjoyed playing privileges. Instruction stopped for lunch at noon, resumed at 2:00 and ended at 8:00 P.M., light permitting. To qualify for an Aero Club certificate, a student had to make three solo flights observed by club-appointed officials. Two of the flights, at least 3 miles in length, were to be in figure eights and around posts 546 yards apart. At the completion of each of these flights, the student had to land the aircraft, with the engine turned off, within 54 yards of a specified point. On the third and final flight, the engine was turned off once the plane reached a height of 328 feet, and the student had to glide to a landing.

Although a great improvement on the prewar pushers, the biplanes were still extremely frail and difficult to keep steady. There were no instruments except for a long rag that the pilot tied to the elevator. He judged his turns by the way it blew—if it wasn't straight back as he manoeuvered the aircraft, he knew he was slipping too much. Initially, aviators wore what they felt comfortable in, but as aircraft gained altitude and endurance, single-piece flying suits, goggles, helmets and gloves began to appear.

THE "CANADA"

The airfield at Long Branch was crowded. JN-2 biplanes bought by the Spanish government were being tested there, as well as the JN-3s being made at Strachan Avenue as part of the RNAS contract. The first Canadian JN-3 was ready on July 14, and by November the whole batch would be at the RNAS station at Hendon, England.

The Strachan Avenue factory, by now employing six hundred Torontonians, also built the twin-engined Canada. The large biplane was a copy of the flying boat America, which the Curtiss Aeroplane and Motor Company had designed before the war to fly the Atlantic. The admiralty liked the America but, rather perversely, wanted a landplane version of the flying boat. The Canada had two unusual features: a four-wheel undercarriage, and the first Sperry stabilizers to be fitted. In retrospect, it was an ambitious project for so unsophisticated a work force. At the Canadian National Exhibition that year, a Canada was flown by a crew who "bombed" a

J.A.D. McCurdy (*left*) in the cockpit of the twin-engined Canada bomber surrounded by the Curtiss Aeroplane and Motors Ltd. board of directors. Twelve of the aircraft were built, becoming Canada's first aircraft export order. CITY OF TORONTO ARCHIVES: JAMES COLLECTION

model of a German warship moored in the harbour with bags of flour. As a touch of reality, explosions were set off by remote control.

Of the twelve Canadas made, eleven went to the Royal Flying Corps and one to the admiralty. However, both customers complained that, given the speed at which aerial warfare had evolved, the design was now obsolete and of no use to them. That fact, combined with poor workmanship, doomed the Canadas to be scrapped by 1917 at Farnborough.

FINAL DAYS FOR THE FLYING SCHOOL

Winter flying was never contemplated, and with the fall, the Curtiss Flying School began to wind down. It was a hard winter for the students who, with no government support, hung around Toronto, frittering away what money they had until spring.

In early 1916, the Long Branch school expanded to four aircraft, four instructors and a total of forty-six pupils. Most of the instructors were now Canadian, some with RNAS experience overseas. The only crash to occur at Long Branch took place on August 4, when a JN-3 that was taking off turned and pitched into the field. The undercarriage and wings were damaged, but the instructor and student had only minor bruises. Gusting winds were blamed.

On September 7, the governor general arrived by special rail car for his first visit to the Long Branch field. His term of five years was almost complete, and he was soon to be replaced by the Duke of Devonshire. He was accompanied this time by the mayor of Toronto, two provincial cabinet ministers and the lieutenant governor of Ontario. After inspecting the students and their aircraft, the official party watched the instructors perform an aerobatic display of loops, rolls and even inverted flying.

Notably absent from the party was McCurdy's supporter, Stanton. The governor general's secretary was on his way to a desk job at home in the Army Pensions Department. Prime Minister Borden never forgot nor forgave what he considered the Englishman's interference in purely Canadian matters. In his memoirs, he would depict Stanton as vain and meddlesome, always running to the governor general on matters that did not concern him.

The skies over the Western Front now mirrored the brutality of the trenches below. With pilots on both sides using synchronized machine guns to deadly effect, the war was consuming trained airmen faster than either the British or the Canadian governments had imagined. It seemed inevitable that each government would develop a large-scale pilot training scheme under its own auspices. When this happened, McCurdy knew that the days of the privately run flying schools in Canada would be numbered.

As if to settle the issue decisively, Orville Wright formally gave up the litigation struggle in October 1916. There were now too many pilots and too many aircraft manufacturing companies to track down, let alone sue. Wright announced that as his contribution towards the Allied cause, he was donating the aileron patents to the British and French governments.

By December 12, the negotiations to establish twenty Royal Flying Corps training squadrons in Canada were completed. The Imperial Munitions Board would do all the purchasing and contracting, as well as the building of airfields, and it would use its own instructors. Ironically, in seeking to escape dependence on the British, Borden was forced in the end into allowing them to take over all aviation activities in Canada. The prime minister was by then immersed in political scandals within his Cabinet. The conscription crisis was looming, as was an election. McCurdy's school featured in his grand scheme of things as no more than a sideshow.

In its two short years, the Curtiss Flying School had trained 261 pilots; 106 were serving in the RNAS and 30 in the RFC. Its graduates would fly fifty different types of aircraft during the war, from Sopwith Triplanes to giant Handley Page 0/400s. Several pilots went on to be decorated for service at the Front. J. E. Greene shot down eleven enemy planes, sharing three more "kills" with others. Three pupils of the school, A. G. Knight, A. S. Todd and A. E. Cuzner, would fall victim to the guns of the infamous Red Baron, Manfred von Richthofen. Robert Leckie, destined to become an air vice-marshal of the RCAF by the next war, would shoot down a zeppelin.

THE CANUCK

Training ended at the Curtiss schools on December 15, even as Ottawa loaned London $1 million to buy the company's Toronto factory. Renamed Canadian Aeroplanes Ltd., and now run by the Imperial Munitions Board, the company took an order for two hundred copies of the Curtiss JN-4 aircraft then being made in the United States. Eventually, 1200 JN-4s would be built at the company's new nine-acre facility, with spares for 1700 more.

In the years to follow, barnstormers would prefer the Canadian member of the Curtiss "Jenny" family, called the "Canuck," because it had ailerons on the lower wings. Whatever they were called, the JNs would become the Model Ts of postwar aviation. Although the plane's Curtiss engine was imported from the United States, almost everything else was made in Canada. The Canucks, the Canadas and later the 50 Felixstowe F5s, large twin-engined maritime patrol aircraft built for the United States Navy, were the beginnings of the aviation industry in Canada.

THE WAR COMES TO A CLOSE

Prime Minister Borden's patience with his minister of militia finally wore thin in late 1916, and Hughes was forced out of office. The colonel had dispensed enough favours to be reelected in Victoria-Haliburton the next year. But this time, the prime minister did not allow him near the Cabinet, and Hughes disappeared into political anonymity. In London, Stanton was rescued from his desk in the pensions department and made military governor of Palestine.

Unhappily, Douglas McCurdy did not fare as well. In his enthusiasm for a Canadian air force, he had misrepresented Ottawa's intentions to the British government, and vice versa. Borden, or more precisely Loring Christie, his new external affairs advisor, treated McCurdy with suspicion bordering on contempt and kept him at an arm's length for the remainder of the war. McCurdy was viewed as being tarred by the commercial brush—and an American one at that.

At one point he tried to interest Canadian Vickers Ltd., a shipbuilding company, in manufacturing aircraft engines. The company's British parent was already doing so, and the Canadian factory at the edge of Viau Street on the Montreal waterfront indicated some interest—if only Ottawa could provide it with firm orders. But with the war drawing to a close and the increasing availability of surplus aircraft, nothing came of McCurdy's initiative. Decades went by before the Father of Canadian Aviation was officially recognized. It would take another war (and another generation of politicians) for the federal government to appoint McCurdy assistant director general of aircraft production in the Department of

Munitions and Supply, a post he held from 1939 to 1947. But perhaps vindication took place for him on February 23, 1959, when he stood on frozen Bras d'Or Lake at Baddeck and watched a reproduction of his *Silver Dart* take off. It was the fiftieth anniversary of his country's entry into the Air Age. Bell and Curtiss were long gone, and Casey Baldwin had died on August 7, 1948. The AEA and the Curtiss Flying School lived only in dusty archives. But John Alexander Douglas McCurdy had come full circle.

By the autumn of 1917, egged on by a campaign in the newspapers, the Canadian public had begun agitating for the creation of a wholly Canadian air force. All Canadians flying overseas were part of the Royal Flying Corps or the Royal Naval Air Service, and national pride in reading about Captain W. A. Bishop singlehandedly attacking a German airfield or N. A. Magor sinking a German submarine made itself felt across the country. In Ottawa, several members of Parliament—including the ubiquitous Sam Hughes—began hounding the prime minister to organize a Canadian air service.

Borden and his Cabinet were lukewarm to the idea, and the British government was very much opposed. But all were astute enough to realize that it was an idea whose time had come. On May 29, 1918, with Ottawa's approval, the British agreed to allow for the formation of two Canadian Air Force (CAF) squadrons, staffed and commanded by Canadians, to be based at Upper Heyford in England.

On September 5, Prime Minister Borden ordered that the Royal Canadian Naval Air Service (RCNAS) be created. With its divisions being shipped overseas through Halifax, the United States Navy was mounting ever-increasing patrols of the Atlantic approaches to the St. Lawrence River and Nova Scotia. In August, the U.S. Navy had commissioned a naval air station at Baker Point, Dartmouth, to patrol the Halifax harbour entrance for German submarines. Equipped with Curtiss HS-2L flying boats, it was commanded by Lt. Richard E. Byrd, famous in later years as a polar navigator. It was understood that the American base would remain in operation until the RCNAS could take it over. The Royal Canadian Navy, already overstretched, had nothing to spare to counter this "friendly invasion," and Borden, worried about Canadian sovereignty in the future, saw RCNAS air patrols as a cheap method of maintaining some sort of token Canadian presence. Apart from the recruits themselves, there was nothing Canadian about the RCNAS; the men were sent off to the Massachusetts Institute of Technology for training on the Curtiss flying boats.

Predictably, with the Armistice, the initiative (and funds) to maintain both the CAF and the RCNAS petered out, and the latter was disbanded in December 1918. The United States Navy returned home, leaving their HS-2Ls at Dartmouth as a gift to Canada. The CAF survived a little longer. The two squadrons were brought home, but with the creation of the Air Board in 1920, they also ceased to exist.[2]

By the end of the Great War, the Royal Flying Corps (now the Royal Air Force) had 22,500 aircraft and 300,000 men—a far cry from the motley collection it had fielded four years before. A full 40 per cent of its pilots were Canadian. Of the twelve acknowledged British air aces, eight were Canadian —the first being Lieutenant Colonel W. A. Bishop from Owen Sound, Ontario, who shot down sixty of the enemy's planes. When it came to effective use of air power, the Canadians had proven they had no equals. Yet Borden, for all his nationalism, did not seize on the opportunity to create a wholly Canadian flying corps, a decision that would have given him the leverage he needed at London and later Versailles.

The large-scale training program of the RFC in Canada left the accomplishments of private flying schools far behind. But while Canadians also learned to fly at schools in Dayton, Ohio; San Antonio, Texas; Vancouver and Montreal, the Curtiss Flying School was unique. For two summers, McCurdy and his instructors had run an efficient, successful operation with no encouragement from Ottawa. That it was accomplished without a single fatality is to their credit. And that the Curtiss company made a sound profit from the school cannot be denied. After all, that is what commercial operations are all about.

A JN-4 Canuck flies over a bucolic scene. Because the planes were utilitarian and cheap, the lure of barnstorming in a Canuck attracted many unemployed, ex-military pilots in the 1920s. CITY OF TORONTO ARCHIVES: JAMES COLLECTION

CHAPTER THREE

Coming of Age: Barnstormers and Bureaucrats

" I used to do this crazy flying . . . they'd dress me up like an old woman, you know and put me in an ambulance. Then they'd drive out on the field in front of the crowd and I'd get out. They'd announce that I was going for a ride to cure my deafness. (Flying was supposed to be good for your hearing troubles back then!) I'd climb into the back cockpit of the plane. Then there'd be this pilot—helmet, goggles, breeches and boots . . . busy doing his stuff

with the switches, going round turning the prop and all that, and then—by gosh!—the propeller would catch! He'd stand back surprised, I'd open the throttle a bit and the aeroplane would start to move. He'd step back out of the way, waving his arms. I'd open the throttle a little more and he'd start to run, trying to catch up and rescue . . . the poor old lady. Then I'd bounce her around . . . and finally pull her up into the air . . . while everyone in the crowd screamed in horror for that little old lady all alone

up in that plane. I'd manoeuvre around, flopping all
over the sky then come back in, heading right for
the crowd. Everybody'd scatter! I'd finally come in,
make a terrible landing, and bounce up and down
awhile before I stopped. The pilot would run
over . . . then they'd lift me out and drop me flat on
the ground. I'd get up, squawking like mad, and
chase him right off the field. That was the end of the
act. It always went over very well." —Ernie Boffa[1]

THE BEGINNINGS OF BARNSTORMING

The Roaring Twenties—flappers, "flivvers" (Model T
Fords) and Buster Keaton movies. From below the
border came rumrunners, skyscrapers, flag-pole sit-
ters, the Charleston and "barnstorming." The last
had actually come to Canada just before the First
World War. Then called exhibition flying, it was
brought by itinerant American aviators like Charles
F. Willard, who had been taught by Glenn Curtiss
himself.

In late August 1909, Willard arrived at
Scarborough Beach amusement park east of Toronto
with his Curtiss *Golden Flyer*. Though he tried several times before the Labour Day crowds for a
record-breaking flight, they were all of a disappointing five minutes' duration and barely a few miles
over the lake. In any case, the Toronto newspapers
were full of Peary's discovery of the North Pole and
found only enough space to comment drily, "Airship
went up, airship came down."[2]

Another American, Charles K. Hamilton, flew
before a crowd of 3,500 spectators on March 25,
1910, at Minoru Park racetrack near Vancouver, the
cradle of aviation in British Columbia. From June 25
to July 5 of that year, the first aviation meet in
Canada was held at Lakeside on the west island of
Montreal. Promoted by John Bassett, a reporter from
the local newspaper the *Daily Witness*, and sponsored
by the Royal Automobile Club and Montreal
Tramways, the event attracted 20,000 spectators and
more than a hundred aircraft and airship owners.
Montreal became the first Canadian city to be flown
over when one of the exhibitors, French aviator
Count Ferdinand de Lesseps, the son of the Suez

Canal builder, circled it in his Blériot XI monoplane
Le Scarabee. Some of the aviators moved on to
Toronto the following week and took part in a "fly-
in" at the farm of J. W. Trethewey at Weston, with
de Lesseps making the first flight over Toronto on
July 13.

There were only two Canadians licensed to fly
before the First World War: J.A.D. McCurdy and
William M. Stark. Stark had achieved notoriety in
Vancouver in 1901 for driving the first gasoline automobile on the city's streets. He bought a Curtiss
biplane, and on April 12, 1912, flew from the Minoru
Park racetrack out to the mouth of the Fraser River
and back. The Vancouver press did cover his flight,
but news of the sinking of the *Titanic* relegated the
achievement to the back pages. Stark became succes-
sively more daring, and would later take his wife,
Olive, aloft, making her the first female passenger in
Canada.

The attraction of seeing the first Canadian
woman to pilot an aircraft at a time when none of
her sex could vote brought hundreds of British
Columbians to Minoru Park on July 31, 1913. The
Daily News-Advertiser reported that Alys McKay
Bryant flew her husband's Curtiss biplane "quite
competently." Her husband, John Milton Bryant,
was less fortunate. On August 6, while flying the
same aircraft, he crashed and became the first
Canadian to be killed by the new invention.

SHOW BUSINESS

Not for the first time, the interests of show business
merged with science. As greed for gold had fuelled
exploration of the New World, so too did the gate
receipts of the curious finance early aviation. The
posters and handbills that preceded an exhibition
trumpeted the pilots as "Birdmen!" and "Death
Mockers!" As they had in Europe and the United
States, airshow promoters toured Canadian cities and
communities, promising, for a mere twenty-five
cents, admission to "aerial feats, formation flying,
acrobats and crazy flying."

For early aviators, barely able to sustain level
flights, being made to attempt the exotic was noth-

ing short of suicidal. To satisfy the crowds of thrill-seekers, they flew in figures of eight and under bridges, dropped parachutists and messages to pretty women in the bleachers, and looped the loop. Both the Wrights and Glenn Curtiss encouraged exhibition flying because of the free publicity for their products, Curtiss even fielding teams of "aeronauts" that toured the continent.

Without government support, or even private funding, aerial showmen were dependent upon sometimes unscrupulous fairground promoters, who made it clear that neither high winds nor technical difficulties should prevent them from taking off. It was a brave aviator who refused, for whatever reason, to fly. On September 22, 1912, when G. A. Gray could not take off in his biplane from Lafontaine Park, Montreal, the 100,000 people who had paid to see him perform became an angry mob. Police protection saved the poor pilot, though not his aircraft.

The first night flight in Canada took place at the Dominion Livestock Show and Fair at Brandon, Manitoba, on July 23, 1913, when H. W. Blakeley landed on the bonfire-lit grounds. The first interprovincial flight occurred October 8, when William Curtis Robinson flew from Montreal to the Ottawa "Ex" fairground at Lansdowne Park. Unfortunately, because of the size of the crowds waiting for him, Robinson was forced to land at nearby Slattery's cow pasture, where today a plaque commemorates the event. The earliest commercial flight was surely on December 6, when a Baldwin biplane came down at Fletcher's Field, Montreal, bearing no less a personage than Santa Claus himself. The flight had been sponsored by Goodwin's department store, and Cecil Peoli—under the disguise—had taken off with a sack of toys from the Bois Franc polo grounds a few miles away.

The Great War, which began the following year, was the first such conflict to be captured in detail on celluloid, and movies of aerial battles over the Western Front increased the public's hunger for demonstrations of spiral dives and "Immelmann" turns. And with the Armistice in 1918, thousands of demobilized airmen were forced to invent their own livings. Exhibition flying came into its own. If air aces such as Billy Bishop and William George Barker had to put their Victoria Crosses in mothballs and earn a living flying wealthy sportsmen between Toronto and Muskoka, what other chance did lesser-known pilots have?

What there were in abundance in 1919 were JN-4s. Over 8,000 of these training aircraft had been manufactured in Toronto and other locations in North America between 1916 and 1918, costing taxpayers about $5,000 each. Released from government stocks, they now sold for anything from $50 to $500. With its 90-hp engine and cruising speed of 60 mph, the JN-4 was not a highly strung fighter or a lumbering, long-range bomber. It was utilitarian, slow and simple enough to operate with a minimum of investment. For many an ex-military pilot, the lure of travelling around the continent with only his bedroll, seeking his fortune in a "Canuck," was irresistible.

FARMSTORMING

Canadian aviation pioneer and historian Frank Ellis coined the term "farmstorming" to describe what he and other aerial gypsies did on the prairies. Accompanied more often than not by a mechanic, pilots would work their way across rural Canada, landing in farmers' fields. If the landing ground was suitable, that is, without gopher holes, the pilot would get the farmer's permission to use it as a temporary base from which to stage joyrides. This usually involved, as twenty-two-year-old Grant McConachie found out, first taking the whole family up for a ride, and then sitting on the porch with the farmer and discussing the next harvest and the wonders of the age they lived in. McConachie was able to charge $2.50 a ride in 1930, since his high-winged Fokker offered an unobstructed view of the country-side. Having established his base, and more than likely cadged a meal, the barnstormer then took off and flew over the main street of the nearest community, dropping pre-printed handbills with the time and place for the rides inserted. To get the show started, the first person to bring the handbill back to

the pilot was promised a free ride. Another barn-stormer discovered that if he gave the local priest a free ride, several of the flock were then sufficiently encouraged to pay for the privilege. Sometimes, if the flights took place on a Sunday, the pilot might return to a reception with the local police, having contravened the provincial laws of the Sabbath.

Every barnstormer soon came to know that his most profitable time was as harvest season ended. Before the use of combines to harvest grain, the farmer depended on the arrival of steam-driven threshing machines and gangs of men called harvesters who came by train from the east. By early fall, the harvesters had pockets full of money. For $10 and a signed release of liability in case of accident, a harvester was taken up for a ten-minute ride and the thrill of waving to his friends below.

One feature that always seemed to work if business was slow was weighing the passengers. Maurice McGregor, who went on to become one of Trans-Canada Air Line's original pilots, recalled that barnstormers would borrow a weighing scale from one of the feedstores and take it out to the fairground. Then they would fly customers at a penny a pound—150 pounds meant $1.50 a ride.

If money was really scarce, the barnstormer flew into "the bush" to look for trade. On a Saturday morning, he would follow a railroad track or power

Throughout the 1920s, aerial gypsies such as these toured rural Canada, thrilling crowds at fairgrounds with their aero-batics and selling rides. Shown here are barnstormer H. S. McClelland (*second from left*) and E.G. Hamilton (*far right*).
MARTHA HAMILTON HILL/SASKATCHEWAN ARCHIVES SB 7008/S82-195

line until it came to a likely town. One Vancouver pilot remembered arriving at Merritt, British Columbia, circling the town a few times, and then flying low up and down the streets. Children and adults began looking up, pointing and running down the streets. That was the signal to choose a place to land.

> [We] no sooner got down when here came everyone. One old gentleman came along; he had an umbrella, and he walked up and he poked it through the wing and he says "Oh my God, that isn't solid!" Put a hole right through it! . . . By now the dogs were fighting under the machine, and the kids were leaning their bikes against it. We finally got everybody away . . . We'd make maybe three or four or five hundred dollars sometimes. That was a lot of money . . . Then we'd be invited into town for dinner with the local officials. Oh, we used to have a lot of fun. We wore breeches, and these big boots, leather jackets and scarves around our necks, helmets and goggles—really dressed up.[3]

Dominion Day, bank holidays, sports events and agricultural fairs found the pilot and his Canuck much in demand. The luxury of operating from a smooth sports field, of having the crowd controlled by the local RCMP constable, of sampling the unlimited municipal hospitality after weeks on a bachelor's diet and, best of all, of being the most popular dance partner at the compulsory social: these were what every barnstormer dreamed of. The open cockpit aircraft were too cold to use after Thanksgiving, and the pilot often hibernated in a rude hangar. If he was far-sighted, he took advantage of the "refresher" course in flying that the Royal Canadian Air Force held annually at Camp Borden.

A CRAZY WAY TO EARN A LIVING

It was a crazy way to earn a living, and one that became more dangerous as the twenties spiralled out of control. In July 1918, Ruth Law, flying a Curtiss biplane, raced Gaston Chevrolet in Chevrolet's specially designed sportscar at Lansdowne Park, Ottawa. Chevrolet won. Two years later, over Calgary, Ormer L. Locklear performed, for the first time in Canada, the death-defying stunt of changing aircraft in mid-air.[4] It was soon taking more than races and steep turns to keep the spectators coming. The public could see better aerial action in movie theatres. Hollywood movies like *Hell's Angels* and *Wings* were so realistic because the extras who flew the Spads and Sopwiths were unemployed veterans. Dwindling gate receipts were forcing promoters to look for alternative attractions, and the romance of flying took a ghoulish turn as it was no longer the pilot the public came to see but his "wingwalker."

Once the plane was airborne, the mechanic, or more sensationally, a nervous-looking young woman, would clamber out of the biplane's cockpit. With the JN-4's air speed at 50 mph, the wind would keep her pressed against the crosswires—as long as she didn't "freeze" and tip forward. When the crowd tired of this, the wingwalker could ease down the fuselage to the rear of the plane and sit astride the body, waving with both hands! The more foolhardy (or desperate) could claw their way under the aircraft and hang from the undercarriage as in a trapeze act, using only one hand in the finale.

At grander airshows, a standard aerobatic routine soon developed that called for two aircraft and their pilots to work together. In this manoeuvre, the wingwalker made his way out onto the bottom wing of the first aircraft, climbed up the struts to the top wing and then crouched between the bracing wires until the other aircraft came up beside him. Then he would step up to the second aircraft's bottom wing and walk along it to the cockpit. The pilots needed all their skill to make this stunt successful. As the wingwalker moved across the top wing, the first pilot had to compensate for his weight by tilting the Canuck gradually to one side. Once the stunt performer got to the middle of the wing, the pilot would begin to tilt in the other direction. But the worst moment for both pilots was when the wingwalker got ready to step onto the other plane. At precisely the right moment, the first pilot had to "turn into" the second aircraft, since the loss of weight on his own wing would cause it to rise up sharply, potentially bumping the wingwalker into mid-air.

As strong as Canadian Aeroplanes Ltd. had made their Canucks to be, the years and indignities took their toll, and the war-surplus machines gradually came apart. Reliable records are scanty, but by 1925, the number of crashes at shows had risen with regularity. When the ultimate spectacle became watching a barnstormer actually crash into a barn, the tired old Canuck had performed its swan song.

Their livelihood and their lives increasingly dependent on disintegrating spars, avaricious agents and fear-crazed wingwalkers, barnstormer pilots changed from a carefree, picturesque band to a superstitious, fatalistic, usually hard-drinking one. A rhyme that had made the rounds of exhibitions since the prewar days perhaps best summed up their situation:

There was an old woman who lived in a hangar
She had many children who raised such a clangour
That some she gave poison, and some aeroplanes
And all of them died with terrible pains.[5]

Even so, barnstorming in Canada wasn't killed off until the Depression. Ernie Boffa was part of a group called "The Flying Frolics" who put on demonstrations at fairs. In 1930, in Medicine Hat, Alberta, they were so broke that they couldn't afford to have handbills printed, so they drummed up business by advertising with chalk on the sidewalks.

Barnstormers gave thousands of Canadians their first sight of, and sometimes their first ride in, an aircraft. Their gypsy existence glamourized aviation in isolated communities, and their antics probably gave a lot of people a lifelong aversion to flying. But they encouraged farmers to think of the possibility of crop dusting, and sportsmen and foresters of reaching inaccessible areas by air. The fields municipalities had set aside for airshows often became the town's first airport. Waning popularity and mounting fatalities caused pilots to diversify into fixed-base operations that the federal government was reluctantly forced to take notice of.

EMPTY SKIES OVER CANADA

Even as early as 1919, a few pilots attempted to turn their skills to commercial purposes other than exhibition flying. On May 5 of that year, Ervin E. Ballough transported 150 pounds of furs in a JN-4 Canuck between Toronto and Elizabeth, New Jersey. It was the first cross-border commercial flight in Canada. A year later, on September 2, W. R. Maxwell flew 100 pounds of airmail from Remi Lake to Moose Factory, Ontario, in a Curtiss HS-2L flying boat. In northern Ontario, Ballough flew a patient to hospital in the first ambulance flight in Canadian history. These incidents were worthy of record because they were so isolated. Because the aircraft were still two- or three-seaters, passenger travel in them lay far ahead—as did all the infrastructure necessary to maintain such services over a country as vast as Canada.

By contrast, in the United States, a system of electric beacons had joined together a series of airports (all floodlit) across the country by 1923, courtesy of the U.S. Post Office. Washington bureaucrats required that the airmail pilots fly on schedule on regular routes—and at night. There were so many crashes that the pilots called themselves "the Suicide Club," and their de Havilland 4s were dubbed "Flaming Coffins" because they caught fire at the slightest mishap.[6] Liquor was carried to ward off the bone-chilling cold and numb the fear. By the time the U.S. government gave over the mail service to private operators in 1925, only six of the forty pilots hired in 1923 were still alive. Yet because of the operational procedures that evolved, American aviators took the lead worldwide in long-distance flying.

There were no airports or beacons in Canada, and airmail was still a stunt. Away from the railway and the agricultural belt, two-thirds of the country had not even been properly mapped yet. The federal government was at a loss as to what the role of aviation, whether civil or military, should be. By 1919, the Royal Air Force airfields, with the exception of Camp Borden, Ontario, were derelict. What aircraft and equipment the RAF and the United States Navy had left behind were put into storage or sold off. The science of aviation was a mystery to most politicians, and aviation's commercial possibilities were still unknown.

Besides, the government was not convinced that Canadians really needed another form of transport. They already had the best, most extensive railway system in the world, one that not only transported travellers between every major city centre and town but did so in complete luxury. The few airports that existed were muddy cow pastures in the suburbs, buried under snow in the winter, operable only during daylight hours and good weather. Between 1914 and 1918, the War Measures Act had prevented all civil flying. When the Canadian Pacific Railway decided in February 1919 to apply for the extension of its charter to include the operation of aircraft, no one was even sure who the application should be addressed to.

The problem was that responsibility in Ottawa for the new mode of transport fell to no one. There was no budget, no staff and no regulation. Aero clubs imposed their own rules on members, but the

Dominion lacked a legal foundation to control or encourage flying. The British and the French had promulgated air navigation acts as far back as 1911, and in 1919, the victorious Allies drew up the International Convention on Air Navigation (ICAN) to divide up the air space over Europe. It was these legal precedents on which Ottawa would frame its own laws.

THE AIR BOARD

Prompted by the CPR's application, Parliament created the Air Board, an autonomous seven-member body responsible for regulating all aerial operations in Canada, on December 31, 1919. At best a stopgap until more settled times, the board was at worst a half-hearted, low-cost compromise to appease both the military and the pacifists. The board employed former air force pilots and mechanics, still in uniform, to conduct duties like forest fire patrol, anti-smuggling surveillance and delivering treaty money to First Nations groups. Little capital investment was necessary, since the aircraft used were surplus bombers, fighters and trainers from Britain and flying boats left behind by the United States Navy in Halifax. As in Europe, the government, through the Air Board, was to prescribe all air routes, license all airports and pilots, and inspect aircraft. The city of Regina was issued Airharbour Licence No. 1, and its pilot, Reginald Groome, became the first to be licensed in Canada. The first civil aircraft to be registered was "G-CAAA,"[7] a JN-4 Canuck belonging to Groome's Aerial Service Company of Regina.[8]

The first woman licensed to fly in Canada was a textile analyst from Hamilton, Ontario. As a teenager, Eileen Vollick had watched with envy the men who flew Canucks at Jack Elliot's Flying School. After overcoming her fear of approaching the instructors for lessons in what she called "this man's game," she obtained her Private Pilot's Licence in March 1928 at the age of twenty. Her flying school presented her to the press on every occasion; her fur-lined flying suit was copied by other aviatrixes, and American aircraft manufacturers wanted her to endorse their aircraft. (She declined.) Vollick went

John Armistead Wilson, Canada's first controller of civil aviation, was primarily responsible for the construction of the chain of airports across the country known as the Trans-Canada Airway. DEPARTMENT OF NATIONAL DEFENCE PL 117438

on to take up aerobatic training and became the first Canadian woman to parachute.

Flying may have caught the imagination of ordinary men and women across Canada, but unlike in France and Britain, here no public subsidies were given to the aviation industry. The European railway system and merchant marine had been destroyed by the war, and airlines offered an alternative. Many countries also understood from the start that aviation was bound up with politics. As early as 1919, the Germans had consolidated their influence in South America by founding an airline in Colombia. Holland, France, Belgium and Britain poured money into their "flag carriers" to protect overseas investments and link them with their capital cities. But in Canada, fledgling air companies were placated with a

few airmail contracts and told to look to the free market. It was a short-sighted philosophy that would dam civil aviation in Canada for the next two decades.

Canada's first Controller of Aviation, appointed as secretary of the Air Board on June 6, 1920, was a visionary Scottish immigrant, John Armistead Wilson. Until the Department of National Defence was created in 1923, Wilson's Air Board was responsible for all aviation activities, both civil and military. Wilson had been assistant deputy minister of the Royal Canadian Navy in 1918, and he was profoundly influenced by the navy's complementary relationship with the merchant fleet. Consequently, he held that the successful development of civil aviation was the foundation of a country's air force. In 1922, he was credited with organizing a Canadian Air Force expedition to Ellesmere Island in the Arctic to search for potential landing strips. Wilson would later say that there was precious little civil aviation to actually *control* in Canada—as late as 1925 there were only fourteen aircraft companies in the whole country.

THE FLYING CLUB SCHEME

After the Canadian Air Force was reformed as a provisional military arm under the Air Board in 1920, it spent the first few years building up its squadron personnel. Former members of the RAF were invited to join, and refresher courses and cadet training schemes begun at Camp Borden, Ontario. King

George V approved the designation "Royal" for the Canadian Air Force in 1923.

By 1925, the majority of commercial pilots in Canada were still drawn from the ranks of Royal Flying Corps veterans. What few flying schools there were were beyond the reach of most Canadians. The RCAF was becoming alarmed at this, since in the event of an emergency, there would soon not be a ready reserve of pilots to call upon. As secretary of the Air Board, Wilson had suggested that the government organize a flying club scheme, as the British and the Australians had. The air force was supportive. (The Air Board had ceased to exist on January 1, 1923, when the National Defence Act created the Department of National Defence [DND]. Wilson was made civil aviation secretary to the Canadian Air Force, and when the DND was reorganized in 1927, with the air force taking over civil operations, Wilson was named controller of civil aviation.) In September 1927, the government offered every community flying club with a qualified flying instructor, a mechanic and at least thirty members two aircraft, one parachute and a grant of $100 for each pilot undertaking training. The clubs were also encouraged to look for other revenue. Less than a year later, there were fifteen clubs in existence: Halifax,

Montreal, Granby, Toronto, Hamilton, Ottawa, London, Windsor, Winnipeg, Regina, Saskatoon, Moose Jaw, Edmonton, Calgary and Victoria. In all, twenty-six clubs were established through the flying club scheme, and twenty-two survived the Depression. As Wilson had hoped, the airfields that the clubs maintained became the first airports for many cities, and when the Second World War began, the investment in pilots and instructors paid dividends.

One important component in the training of this second generation of pilots was the availability of a new light biplane, the de Havilland D.H.60 Moth. It was British aviation pioneer Geoffrey de Havilland's sixtieth model, and in Britain, private owners (including the Prince of Wales), flying schools and university air squadrons were snapping them up, making the D.H.60s popular successors to the battered World War 1 Avro 504s. The federal government in Ottawa ordered a single D.H.60 for the Hudson Straits Expedition, and the Ontario Provincial Air Service bought four to replace their aged Curtiss flying boats. Scenting expansion, de Havilland sent his sales director, Francis St. Barbe, to Ottawa in December 1927 to meet with J. A. Wilson. To succeed, Wilson's flying club scheme needed well-tested, cheaply built aircraft that could provide enthusiasts with basic instruction. Following some enthusiastic lobbying by Wilson, the federal government contracted with de Havilland to buy their Moths for the scheme. In the winter of 1928, the company set up in a disused canning factory at Weston, Ontario, to assemble the aircraft sent out from Britain. The neighbouring de Lesseps airfield was used to test the finished product. So optimistic were the company's directors about sales that a year later de Havilland moved to larger quarters at Downsview, three miles away.

The flying club scheme proved very successful. It was the determination of men like Murton A. Seymour, a lawyer who drafted the Canadian Flying Clubs Association's constitution and served on the association's executive and later as president, that kept the flying clubs going through meagre times to train some 3,000 pilots before the Second World War. Every pilot who graduated from a local club has anecdotes of tyrannical instructors, boisterous social "events" and muddy airfields.

Bob Randall, later famous as the Canadian pilot who flew with Bradford Washburn, the American explorer, signed up in the spring of 1928 at the Saskatoon Aero Club, the first club in the country to fulfil all the scheme's requirements and receive its pair of de Havilland Moths. That summer was the wettest on record, and the runways would take two days to dry. Seven decades and many types of aircraft later, Randall still recalled the advice his instructor gave him before his first solo: If your aircraft is in trouble, you haven't got all day and all night to figure out where to land—just put her in the trees.[9] The Saskatoon *Star-Phoenix* reported that the club celebrated the end of a successful first summer by flying in formation and stunting over the Saskatoon Industrial Exhibition.

Herb W. Seagrim was told by an over-eager salesman from the Winnipeg Flying Club that he would be flying solo in four hours at a total cost of $60. When it took Seagrim six hours, he was in some debt and not a little perturbed. Then he realized that without accumulating a lot more airtime he couldn't qualify for a job as a pilot. In exchange for flying time, he arranged with the club to work as a mechanic's assistant, and he and a friend also hauled cinders to surface the club's car park. It took him two years, but when he left the Winnipeg club in 1933, Seagrim had the required flying time—and an air engineer's licence.

Grant McConachie, who learned to fly with the Edmonton Flying Club, discovered a source of income while working on his hours flying solo. One day the club's manager, Jimmy Bell, received a phone call congratulating Bell on hiring "such a nice young man who had been taking people up for five dollar rides in the Club's aircraft."[10] As McConachie didn't yet have a commercial licence—and as the rides were not entered in the logbook—he was lectured and grounded temporarily.

Most of the great pilots of the early airline era

were flying club alumni: Frank Young (Brant-Norfolk Aero Club), Dennis Yorath (Calgary Flying Club), Jack Showler (Regina Flying Club), J. L. "Lindy" Rood (Cape Breton Flying Club), George Lothian (Aero Club of British Columbia), Wilbert "Mel" Knox (Moose Jaw Flying Club). For his instructional talent—and patience—Maurice Burbridge, the instructor at the Edmonton Flying Club, was awarded the McKee Trophy for 1932. That he was also Grant McConachie's instructor probably had nothing to do with the judges' decision.

AN INTERESTED PRIME MINISTER

The year 1927 saw several initiatives by Ottawa towards the aviation industry, and if a single event can be credited for this, it was Prime Minister William Lyon Mackenzie King's meeting with Charles Lindbergh. King, first elected prime minister in 1921, held public office in Canada longer than any other politician. He is remembered as a paradoxical man: devious and deeply religious, genial and obnoxious. He somehow managed to guide the country he genuinely loved through Depression and war, sharing his thoughts only with his late mother (through seances) and with a succession of terriers all called Pat. Unlike his predecessor, Borden, King had no antipathy towards aviation, and a 1918 photograph taken at Ottawa's Rockcliffe Airfield to commemorate the first airmail flight to Toronto captures King, wearing a straw boater, prominent among the onlookers. To celebrate the country's sixtieth year of Confederation, the prime minister invited Lindbergh to lead a flypast of aircraft over the Parliament Buildings' new Peace Tower. King planned to write a book on the whole event and, as every author knows, a few glittering personalities thrown in doesn't hurt sales.

Having flown the Atlantic solo less than two months before, the "Lone Eagle" had been lionized in Paris (an American diplomat wrote that so enamoured were the French with Lindbergh that they agreed to sign the Kellogg-Briand Pact symbolizing American-French friendship without their usual suspicion).[11] Canadian newspapers reported that President Coolidge had sent a battleship to bring

Lindbergh home, and afterwards, to Mackenzie King's delight, the shy aviator had taken his mother to meet the president. Lindbergh was, at that hour, the most famous man on the planet—and to everyone's surprise, he agreed to come to the backwoods of Ottawa. On July 2 at 1:13 EDT, escorted by twelve United States Army Air Corps Curtiss Hawks, Lindbergh's Ryan monoplane, the *Spirit of St. Louis*, landed at Uplands Airfield. It required five hundred soldiers from the Governor General's Foot Guards and the Cameron Highlanders to keep at bay the crowds who came out to the airport. "Lucky Lindy" was mobbed wherever he went. Ottawa's muddy airport was renamed Lindbergh Field in his honour (the name lasted a single year before it reverted), and on July 4, when he circled Ottawa for a full thirty-five minutes before flying home, one witness remembers that it seemed every car horn and every bell in the city saluted him in utter frenzy.[12]

But Lindbergh's effect on Mackenzie King was even more startling. In his diary on July 2, King wrote: "A more beautiful character I have never seen! He was like a young god who had appeared from the skies in human form . . . as noble a type of the highest manhood as I have ever seen." The prime minister was a deeply sentimental man, brought up on the novels of Sir Walter Scott, and the young, clean-living flier appealed to his romantic nature. The flypast was the climax of the Jubilee celebration, which King had personally organized as an opportunity to foster national unity. For the first time in history, his speech and the sounds of the Peace Tower carillon could be relayed by radio from coast to coast. As did aviation, the broadcast symbolized for King prosperity and national pride.

Even before the Lindbergh cross-Atlantic flight, King had considered divorcing civil aviation from the military and placing it under its very own Department of Transport. Dazzled by the pomp and circumstance of his visits to the annual Imperial Conferences, and in gratitude to King George V for bestowing the title "Royal" on the Canadian Air Force, King rashly promised to strengthen imperial bonds with a strong Canadian air defence. More

importantly for civil aviation, he committed the Canadian government to taking part in the British globe-girdling airship route by building the first government airport at St. Hubert near Montreal.

But the country King returned to after each conference was closer in mood (and budget) to the Weimar Republic of Germany than to ancient Sparta. In the 1920s, Canada was impecunious and decidedly pacifist. It had fought an expensive and bloody "War to End All Wars" with little to show for it. Members of Parliament were loath to spend money on even a minimal aerial defence. As they pointed out, with an ocean on either side, no enemy had the capability to invade the country. King was also aware that most of his Liberal support in Parliament came from Quebec, a province that had not forgotten the conscription crisis. There could be no funding to inject into civil aviation when there was barely enough to keep the tiny RCAF alive. Ever the political chameleon, King recognized that the timing wasn't right for commercial aviation, and he proceeded to dismantle what little there was.

King's biographer, J. W. Pickersgill, would later write that King believed (and frequently said) that the real secret of political leadership was more in what was prevented than what was accomplished. In the summer of 1927, he sacrificed whatever ideas he had for an autonomous Department of Transport in order to keep the RCAF on a life-support system. The Air Board was disbanded, its civilian duties given to the air force; Wilson and all aspects of commercial aviation were put under the jurisdiction of the

The unlikely looking Curtiss HS-2L was Canada's (and the world's) first bush plane. Extensively used by the Air Board, the RCAF and Laurentide Air Service, it was the work horse of early bush aviation. DEPARTMENT OF NATIONAL DEFENCE PL 114176

Department of National Defence. The RCAF was instructed to spend its time and energies conspicuously on purely civil tasks such as aerial surveying, crop dusting, forest-fire spotting and mounting the Hudson Straits Expedition to the Arctic for the Department of Fisheries. As King had shrewdly guessed, none of his political opponents would argue with funding a military that performed such community-minded tasks as this.

To keep it functioning, the air force was given all the government contracts that would otherwise have gone to small aircraft companies. Its personnel trained in armament, wore uniforms and had squadron crests, but they described themselves as "bush pilots in uniform" or, more facetiously, "the Royal Comical Air Force." Yet the service survived a decade of cost-cutting and preserved a nucleus of experienced officers to fight another war.

BUILDING CANADIAN AIRCRAFT

The work of suppressing forest fires, catching smugglers, spraying crops and taking treaty money to the aboriginal peoples caused premature wear and tear on the RCAF's war-surplus HS-2Ls. Never designed for prolonged use—especially in the Canadian environment—or to be flown so deep into the hinterland,

the workhorse Curtiss flying boats soon fell apart. Air force officers complained that deteriorating wood and cracked main spars made their aircraft not only unreliable but dangerous to operate in isolated areas. Soon the situation was so critical that even a miserly Parliament authorized the immediate purchase of six flying boats. Wilson wanted the replacement aircraft to be built in Canada, and Canadian, British and American companies bid for the contract. Canadian Vickers Ltd. of Montreal, the company J.A.D. McCurdy had initially approached, was the winner. Its British parent had built amphibian flying boats for the RAF.

The six Vikings built at Vickers in Montreal were delivered to the RCAF in 1923. They were beautiful to look at, with mahogany planking and polished rivets, but hopelessly underpowered for the photographic surveys and forestry patrols they were put to. However, Vickers had made a profit from manufacturing them, and the company now looked to develop other aircraft for the Canadian market.

Chief Engineer Willfrid Thomas Reid, who had come from Vickers in England to work at the Canadian plant, had brought with him plans for a

Redolent with the smell of wood and dope, the Vickers factory on the Montreal waterfront turns out Vedettes in 1924 for the Royal Canadian Air Force. This first postwar government order revitalized the aviation industry in Canada.
CANADAIR ARCHIVES CL 28550

small flying boat. In 1924, he adapted them to design the first aircraft ever built in Canada for local conditions, the delightful Vedette. It was lighter and smaller than the Viking, more reliable than the HS-2L and easier to manoeuvre than the clumsy Felixstowe. It carried three passengers, was ideal for photographic operations and served the RCAF until 1941. Len Birchall, the RCAF Catalina pilot who in 1942 discovered the Japanese fleet off Ceylon, flew Vedettes and remembered them with affection. Reid designed other flying boats for Vickers, but none were as successful as the Vedette, and he left Vickers in 1928 to form his own aircraft manufacturing company. Vickers struggled on through the Depression until 1936, when Ottawa contracted it to build forty Supermarine Stranraer flying boats under licence for RCAF coastal patrol squadrons.

With little capital, Reid built two hangars at

A Vedette is prepared for launching. Designed by W. T. Reid, the aircraft was a commercial success, lasting through the inter-war years until 1941 and even exported overseas. CANADAIR ARCHIVES F 4055

Cartierville. His creation was a handsome sportsplane he called the Rambler. It attracted the attention of the American conglomerate Curtiss Aviation and Motor Company. Curtiss Aviation bought Reid's company, seeing it as a foothold into the Canadian market, and hiring J.A.D. McCurdy as a director.

As Glenn Curtiss had done two decades before, Curtiss-Reid began a flying school to demonstrate their product. The Depression and the government's decision to purchase de Havilland Moths effectively killed any hope the company had of sustaining itself, although the Cartierville flying school remained in operation until 1959, when it was destroyed by fire.

In their expanded role, and now equipped with the Vedettes, the RCAF was viewed by commercial pilots as unfair competition. Seasonal markets and unsympathetic creditors made commercial flying risky enough without the government becoming involved. Donald Roderick MacLaren, a World War I air ace and now chief pilot of Pacific Airways in Vancouver, protested as much—first with the minister for public works and then the minister for national defence—but to no avail. MacLaren's memorandum reached J. A. Wilson, who had always been sympathetic to the problems of civil aviation. But although the chief of defence staff, General A.G.L. McNaughton, was Wilson's ally, King's minister of defence, J. L. Ralston, saw the RCAF's participation in civil air operations as essential to the force's very survival.

By 1927, a real border had been crossed in Canada. The establishment of the Air Board, and later the Department of National Defence, meant that the day of the pioneer had ended.

Flying machines were now too complex and expensive for a solitary amateur to design in his workshop and test-fly from the field out front. Aviation was now a business and, like pilots and airfields, aircraft had to be certified by a government inspector. The day of the individual pilot was over. The science of flight had become a career.

CHAPTER FOUR

Bush Pilots: Putting Aircraft to Work

Bush flying was invented by
Canadians. The aviation lore of
both the United States and France
is full of larger-than-life pilots who
landed aircraft in hitherto inaccessible locations: the
Koufra Desert, the Alaskan tundra, Central African
jungles, Salt Lake City flats. But in 1919, when
Stuart Graham piloted a flying boat from Halifax,
Nova Scotia, to Lac-à-la-Tortue, Quebec, covering
645 miles in four days, he not only set a record for

the longest flight in Canada to date—he became the
world's first bush pilot.

THE CURTISS HS-2L FLYING BOATS
Even after the First World War, much of the world
remained unexplored. Unless there were strategic or
commercial considerations, governments and mining
or pulp and paper companies had little interest in
what was known as "the bush." Describing any terrain that wasn't farmland, the term "bush" was

The Ontario Provincial Air Service was the greatest user of Curtiss HS-2Ls, basing the aircraft at strategically chosen lakes around northern Ontario for forestry patrols. NATIONAL DEFENCE CANADIAN FORCES PHOTOGRAPHIC UNIT RE 19262

brought to Canada by troops that had served in South Africa. By 1920, it had come to include all wilderness areas—from tundra to equatorial jungle—over which aviators flew.

The major communication lines in Canada have traditionally been the St. Lawrence River and the Great Lakes and, in the last century, the railroads that run east to west, usually hugging the shores of rivers and lakes. What north to south routes there were in the early 1900s had been carved by canoe and dogsled, paddlewheel steamer and barge. Motor transport was in its infancy and, outside the thinly populated southern belt, there were no alternative means of transport. Once a traveller left the railway station or port, he or she faced a long walk, ride or paddle.

Vast expanses of Canada were liberally coloured red on maps as part of the Empire and left at that. Even the maps of the most populous province, Ontario, could not be trusted, especially away from the southern belt. They had been drawn up by surveyors who had used river transport, and so did not show any of the province's 250,000 lakes. As the pioneer bush pilots were to find out, maps of the Arctic coastline had been drawn up by whalers and missionaries for their own purposes, but it was only when the Armistice made so many aircraft and pilots

available that the bush could be economically explored. No one really knew much of the land mass that comprised the Dominion.

It was adapted technology developed by the military during the First World War, especially in the areas of aircraft design, engine technology and aerial reconnaissance cameras, that made cross-country flying economically viable and possible. Until then, all flying had been done in large cities or at country fairs, where aviators depended on attracting audiences for their livelihood. Now aircraft that had been designed to bomb Berlin or fly long-range patrols over convoys were available.

In 1918, Ellwood Wilson, chief forester of Quebec's Laurentide Pulp and Paper Company, saw that the forests his company owned would be easier to patrol against forest fires if done from the air. A group of pulp and paper companies in the St. Maurice River region of Quebec had set up the St. Maurice Forest Protective Association to look after their vast assets, and they were interested in Wilson's idea of aerial surveillance. He first thought of using dirigibles, but when these were unavailable, looked to the war-surplus flying boats stored in neighbouring Nova Scotia.

In August 1918, the United States had set up a naval air station at Baker Point, Dartmouth, Nova Scotia, to patrol Halifax harbour for German submarines. Three months after the station opened, the war ended, and its Curtiss HS-2L flying boats were generously left to the host country. But by then, the Royal Canadian Naval Air Service had also been demobilized, and all aircraft were put into storage at Dartmouth. Two of the flying boats could thus be loaned to the St. Maurice Forest Protective Association to form Canada's first bush "outfit." The awkward-looking HS-2L (nicknamed "Pregnant Pelican" by its pilots) was ideal for forestry patrols as it was slow (its cruising speed was about 65 mph) and it could land on any large lake. The observer's position in the bow was perfect to watch from for forest fires. Stuart Graham, who had flown similar craft with the Royal Naval Air Service, was hired to ferry them to Lac-à-la-Tortue, three miles east of Grand-Mère on the St. Maurice River.

Graham, his wife, Madge, and Air Engineer William Kahre lifted off from Halifax Harbour in the first HS-2L at 2:55 P.M. on June 5, 1919. The Curtiss, later registered as "G-CAAC" with the Air Board, had been christened *La Vigilance* and, as the original bush plane, has premier place in the aviation lore of Canada. Less is known of its navigator, Madge Graham. Divorced when she met Graham, Madge married him when he was convalescing after injuries received during the battle of Ypres. In 1919 the couple came to Canada with their two daughters. Although never having flown before, when her husband was hired to deliver the two aircraft, she volunteered to become his navigator.

The absence of any maps and the freezing temperatures in the observer's cockpit would have daunted many. But Madge, a landscape artist, was able to discern the contours of the countryside they flew over to keep the Curtiss on track. Communicating her instructions to her husband was a problem. The pilot and the engineer sat behind her and almost below the 400-hp Liberty engine, so shouting down a speaking tube was impossible. Ingeniously, Madge had a mini-clothesline rigged up between her and Stuart. Writing her directions on a note and attaching it to a clothespin, she was able to pass her observations down.

Their first stop was Saint John, New Brunswick, where a tumultuous welcome was staged for the three aviators. The mayor even arranged to take the very tired trio to the opera *La Traviata* that night. But as Stuart and Bill had been sitting below the flying boat's engine, both were temporarily deaf, and only Madge could appreciate the performance. The next day they took off for Lake Temiscouata, Quebec, but because of severe thunderstorms went off course and landed across the U.S. border at Eagle Lake, Maine. No one in the little lumber community there had ever seen an airplane, let alone a woman in one, and there was a mad rush of lumberjacks to gawk at both. Two days later the three taxied up to the beach at Lac-à-la-Tortue, the flying time from Halifax nine hours and forty-five minutes. On June 21, the trio took off from Halifax with the second HS-2L, and despite an unplanned landing at Long Lake, Maine, arrived at their destination in twelve hours and twenty-three minutes.

After delivering the "boats," Graham and Kahre began flying patrols from Lac-à-la-Tortue. After the aircraft had been in use for a month, on July 7 the first forest fire was spotted and put out.

As Graham soon discovered, however, one could not fly out of gliding distance of lakes or rivers in an HS-2L. A flying boat had to fly above or near water, so that if the engine cut out, it could glide safely down. The flying boat's other drawback was that it had to be hauled out of the water periodically to ensure that the wooden hull didn't get waterlogged—a problem at a rural location. But then, the aircraft was never meant to be a bush plane. The Curtiss HS-2L (Model "H," "S" for single-engined, "2" for second version and "L" for Liberty engine) was the only American-designed aircraft to fly operationally during the First World War. An ungainly creature at best, it had a wingspan of 74 feet, making it too unwieldy for all but the wider lakes and rivers. To steer while taxiing, the engineer was required to climb out on the lower wing and weigh down the float underneath so that the plane could pivot. It resembled nothing more than a bathtub that had sprouted layers of wings, and its Liberty engine, sandwiched between the wings, was difficult for the engineer to access, especially in the bush when persecuted by mosquitos and black flies. As it required an engineer to service and dock it, the HS-2L could only carry one or two additional passengers, and it had little cargo space. The plane's water-cooled engine and its inability to land on ice meant that its use was confined to the short summer months. But it was cheap and readily available, and before airports existed, the HS-2L was the workhorse of bush companies and of the RCAF. It was flown in Canada until 1932, a record for the series that Glenn Curtiss had launched in 1912.

The success of Laurentide encouraged Price Brothers of Quebec City to buy a Martinsyde floatplane. The plan to base it at Chicoutimi and fly forest patrols in the area was shortlived, however; the pilot, H. S. Quigley, soon left to form his own outfit, the Dominion Aerial Exploration Company, using HS-2Ls from Lac Ste. Jean. In 1926, his company was reorganized as Canadian Airways and moved to Montreal to fly airmail. Postal authorities were experimenting with an imaginative mail service to meet trans-Atlantic ocean liners entering the St. Lawrence off Farther Point, near Rimouski. Mail bags would be unloaded into a seaplane and flown to Montreal, saving forty-eight hours in the process. Using an HS-2L on the first trip, Quigley took thirty-seven bags off the *Empress of Australia*. The "pony express" scheme was dramatic but impractical, and out of character for the Post Office. With the opening of the government airport at St. Hubert in 1927, the mail was brought by a pilot boat to Rimouski airfield, and landplanes were used from there.

LAURENTIDE AIR SERVICES LTD.
In 1920, the St. Maurice Forest Protective Association disassociated itself from air operations, and the Laurentide Company confined the flying boats to its own area. Stuart Graham worked for them, staking the first mining claim in history from the air. In late 1921, the Laurentide Company's directors sold out to William Roy Maxwell. A former Royal Air Force instructor, Maxwell saw the economic potential in aerial surveying and convinced Thomas Hall, a wealthy Montreal shipbuilder, to put $10,000 into the company, which he then renamed Laurentide Air Services Ltd. Maxwell obtained contracts for forest protection and aerial photography from the Ontario government and, through government subcontracting, Fairchild Aerial Surveys Company, supplementing this by beginning the first scheduled air service in Canada.

Laurentide Air Service's planes took scheduled passenger flights into the Quebec gold mining area, between the railway station at Angiers and the twin cities of Rouyn/Noranda. The company bought nine more HS-2Ls and transferred its base to Haileybury, charging clients $40 between Angiers and Rouyn or $60 from Haileybury. Laurentide issued the first airline timetable in Canadian history, and all flights conveniently took place in the morning, for maximum sunlight. In 1924, Laurentide carried 1,004 passengers, and in September of that year the company established the first regular airmail service, even issuing its own stamps. But with rail and road systems entering the area, air service could not hope to achieve a profit. In 1925, Laurentide went bankrupt and sold off its aircraft.

THE ADVENTURES OF BOUNCING BRONCO
One of the flying boats they sold was a Vickers Viking "G-CAEB," which would embark on an odyssey straight out of a Jack London novel. The city of Calgary was still a frontier town in the 1920s, and its bankers were used to being accosted by grizzled old prospectors begging for financial backing to develop some fabulous gold motherlode they had discovered. In 1926, one such individual made the rounds of the city's bankers and businessmen, this time with samples of gold that he said were from a strike in the Northwest Territories. He didn't know

The first cross-border commercial flights in 1919 were more sensational than profitable. The aircraft used were adapted World War I trainers with little room for cargo. Note the improvement in flying suits, an outcome of the Great War. CITY OF TORONTO ARCHIVES: JAMES COLLECTION

exactly where his claim was on a map, but assured everyone it would not be difficult to locate from an aircraft, as he had marked the location on the edge of a lake with a rough cross cut into the bush.

The skepticism that normally greeted such claims was absent this time, no doubt because of the high-grade gold samples the prospector passed around. Investors quickly formed themselves into the Northern Syndicate Ltd. They bought the Vickers Viking from Laurentide and hired two of its former employees, Jack Caldwell as pilot and Irenee Vachon as engineer. Caldwell had operated the Viking, which he named *Bouncing Bronco*, throughout northern British Columbia and the Yukon, and Vachon was a master at aircraft engine maintenance. The plan was that the flying boat would take the prospector to find the lake while the main party would hack their way up to meet them.

Like all good stories, this one had a twist to it: before anyone could set out, the prospector got involved in a barroom brawl and was hit on the head with a bottle. He recovered from a skull fracture, to the relief of the syndicate. However, his memory was affected, and he could not recollect the exact loca-tion of the gold. All the businessmen could get out

of him was that the claim was east of Great Slave Lake in the Barren-lands. A vast, treeless slab of Pre-cambrian rock, the Barrenlands are the size of France and studded with lakes. The area had a sinister reputation and was reknowned for its eskers, herds of caribou and packs of wolves.

The investors decided to set off for the Territories anyway. The flying boat was dis-mantled and transported by rail to Lac La Biche. By June 22, *Bouncing Bronco* was in the air. Caldwell and Vachon flew to Fort Fitzgerald, where the rest of the party was waiting for them, and established a base camp at a lake they modestly named Lake Caldwell.

Throughout the summer, Caldwell and Vachon flew in ever-widening circles, looking for the lake the prospector had described. They ventured as far as the Yukon without maps or navigational aids. Like all bush pilots then, Caldwell flew by visual reference. Compasses were unreliable in northern Canada because of the magnetic pole, and there were few distinguishing landmarks to steer by. The pair were very careful about where they landed, realizing that no one knew their location—they barely knew themselves. A single crack in the hull, a blocked pipe or a broken propeller would mean certain death.

By August, ice was forming on Lake Caldwell, and the search was called off. The flying boat was sold, and six years later, after numerous owners, caught fire over the Strait of Georgia in British Columbia. Its Napier engine was rescued and donated to the National Aviation Museum. Seventy years later, one of the world's greatest diamond deposits would be discovered in the Barrens, a single deposit on Lac de Gras that would come to account for 3 per cent of total world production.

THE ONTARIO PROVINCIAL AIR SERVICE

Laurentide's demise had been hastened by the fact that its main customer had set up its own air service. In 1924, the government of Ontario had purchased a fleet of thirteen Curtiss HS-2Ls to begin the Ontario Provincial Air Service (OPAS), headquartered at Sault Ste. Marie. Each summer, the aircraft were based at lakes strategically sited around northern Ontario for forest-fire spotting, returning to the Soo before the freeze-up. In their first summer, OPAS pilots flew 2,600 hours in forest patrols. In a single day, one pilot, C. J. Clayton, was airborne for ten hours and forty minutes. If anything proved the value of aircraft, it was a forest fire in 1926—flying boats would ferry twenty-seven men and 6,420 pounds of equipment to fight it.

The OPAS provided an apprenticeship for several future pioneers in bush flying, such as Romeo Vachon, C. A. Schiller, H. A. Oaks, F. J. Stevenson and G. A. Thompson. During the winter, the idle pilots became well-known at various bars in the Soo, and on occasion were in court for drunk and disorderly charges. This might be where the bush pilot's reputation for hard drinking and carousing first began.

If the career of any one OPAS pilot mirrored the evolution of bush flying, it was that of Harold Oaks. Called "Doc" because he was a doctor's son and better educated than the other bush pilots, he had served in the Royal Flying Corps with distinction. Oaks graduated from the University of Toronto in 1922 as a mining engineer. In 1924, he began flying for the OPAS in the Soo. There he teamed up with pilot Roy Maxwell, and the two left the OPAS in 1926 to begin Patricia Airways & Exploration Ltd. They purchased a two-seater Curtiss Lark, which was too small for economical use but, unlike the OPAS flying boats, could be fitted with skis as well as floats, making it suitable for year-round use. The plane man-aged to carry airmail, 260 passengers and 140,000 pounds of freight that year. The Lark demonstrated that, to become viable, aircraft had to be able to land on water, in snow and on runways. This meant interchangeable undercarriages—pontoons to wheels to skis.

NEW DESIGNS TAKE TO THE AIR

By 1926, World War I surplus planes were being overtaken by the second generation of aircraft—high-winged monoplanes with radial engines and steel-tubed fuselages. These were the type of aircraft used in the great long-distance flights of the day—Richard Byrd to the North Pole in 1926 and Charles Lindbergh across the Atlantic in 1927. The design of these aircraft owed much to European manufac-turers. Byrd used a Fokker, and although Lindbergh's aircraft was made by the Ryan Company in California, it incorporated much of what Dutch, German and British designers had developed.

Forbidden by treaty after the war to make mili-tary aircraft, European companies concentrated on manufacturing sturdy civil aircraft. Dutch aircraft manufacturer Anthony Fokker, maker of highly suc-cessful World War I fighters, now put his energies into building commercial monoplanes with steel-tubed frames and plywood-covered cantilever wings. And in Germany, Dr. Hugo Junkers advanced aero-nautical science with the F-13. Resembling a car with wings, the F-13 was a low-wing monoplane made of corrugated duralumin. The most appreciated feature of the North American version of the F-13 was an enclosed cockpit, and it could carry five men, or their equivalent weight, in comfort—a vast improve-ment on the HS-2L. As good as the F-13 and the later Junkers W-34 were, customs duties put them out of reach of all except large companies because they were made in Germany.

In 1921, Charlie Taylor, Imperial Oil's manager at Edmonton, decided to use aircraft to service his company's wells in the Northwest Territories. He purchased two F-13s and had them flown up from New York by W. R. "Wop" May and W. Gorman. The Junkers, christened *Rene* and *Vic*, were initially put to work carrying fuel to build up caches between Peace River and Great Slave Lake. Once, while landing in deep snowdrifts at Fort Simpson, the propellers of both aircraft were smashed, and it looked as though the two Junkers would be stranded until summer. But exhibiting the typical resourcefulness of those who live in the North, a cabinetmaker at the nearby Roman Catholic mission fashioned propellers out of oak sleigh-boards and used babiche, made from the hide and hooves of moose, to bind the laminations together. The homemade propellers enabled the aircraft to return to Peace River and have factory-made ones fitted. Both Junkers continued to haul freight in the North, passing through several owners, with *Vic* finally falling apart in British Columbia in 1929.

If the best airframe designs for bush aircraft were Fokker and Junkers, the United States led the world in aero engines. The U.S. Navy had been searching for a light aircraft engine to power its carrier-launched fighters far over the vast Pacific. The engine could not be water-cooled, as this would add to its weight and mean less fuel for the aircraft. In 1924, the Wright Aeronautical Corporation developed the Whirlwind. Air-cooled because it was radial—the engine cylinders were exposed to the air to maximize cooling—the Whirlwind later evolved into the Pratt & Whitney Wasp, an engine favoured by aircraft manufacturers such as Bill Boeing, in his line of new aircraft, and the bush-pilot fraternity. The Wasp remained in production until after the Second World War, and the history of aviation owes much to its design.

Using the new radial engines, Fokker brought out his Universal monoplane in 1926. Although the pilot was still seated in the open and the wings had struts, the plane could carry four passengers within its cabin, and it had interchangeable pontoons, skis and wheels.

Fokker's competitor in the United States was the aerial photographer Sherman Fairchild. During the war, Fairchild had designed aerial cameras for use at the Front, and he later adapted them for his own mapping company, Fairchild Aerial Surveys. When he could not find aircraft steady enough to carry his cameras, he began building his own in Farmington, Long Island. By 1927, he had produced the FC-1 and the FC-2 as small, high-wing monoplanes with radial engines, excellent visibility and enclosed cabins. The significance of the heated cockpit was evident in their designations: "F" for Fairchild and "C" for Closed Cabin. Because of their ability to provide pilot and passenger comfort, Fairchild's aircraft began outselling Fokker's open-cockpit models in Canada as soon as they were launched. In 1928, Canadian Vickers built twelve FC-2s under licence for the bush pilot market. They sold so quickly that the next year Fairchild built his own plant at Longueuil, near Montreal, to make more. With the arrival of the Depression, the company struggled for a decade. Yet it managed to turn out a distinctive series of bush aircraft: the Fairchild 71C, the Super 71, and its most successful, the Fairchild 82. Until the arrival of low-wing, retractable undercarriage aircraft such as the Douglas DC-3 and the Boeing 247, Fairchild and Fokker were the mainstay of the aviation industry in Canada.

WESTERN CANADA AIRWAYS

The Father of Commercial Aviation in Canada was an unlikely candidate for the title. No aviator, he was more familiar with the floor of the Winnipeg Grain Exchange than with an aircraft cockpit. James Armstrong Richardson was born at Kingston, Ontario, on August 21, 1885. On graduating from Queen's University, he joined the family grain business in Winnipeg. He started up the first commercial radio stations in Western Canada and served on several boards, including those of banks, railways, and power, insurance and trust companies. Commercial aviation caught Richardson's eye when he was on his summer holidays in 1926 at Minaki, Ontario. While at the resort, he watched a Curtiss HS-2L take off from and land on the lake, carrying freight and passengers to prospectors' camps. He was sufficiently intrigued to arrange to meet Jack Clarke, its pilot, and they discussed the use of aircraft in isolated mining areas. Aircraft were the perfect instruments with which to exploit Canada's mineral resources, and by the end of the summer, Richardson had started his own aviation company, Central Canada Air Lines Ltd., to serve the mining districts of northern Ontario.

Investing the enormous sum of $100,000, Richardson sent Clarke to New York to buy Fokker Universals. But seduced by other opportunities for flying while there, Clarke resigned from the company, leaving his own HS-2L and a newly purchased Fokker Universal in New York. J. A. Wilson, as Canada's controller of civil aviation, was keenly interested in fostering bush outfits, and when he heard about Richardson's predicament he saw it as an opportunity to introduce Richardson to a few other bush pilots. Doc Oaks was then struggling to keep his own Patricia Airways & Exploration solvent, an impossible task with only the tiny Lark. On Wilson's suggestion, Oaks travelled to Winnipeg to talk to the industrialist. Richardson convinced him to become general manager of a new company they named Western Canada Airways (WCA), based at Hudson, Ontario. Oaks's first job was to go down to New York and fly up the open-cockpit Fokker, which he accomplished in a blinding snowstorm. The new company's first commercial flight took place on December 27 from Hudson to Lac Seul to Narrow Lake, some 217 miles, with a cargo of dynamite. In January, WCA was awarded the contract to fly mail from Hudson to Red Lake, and it was in business.

The timing was propitious for WCA. Its performance in two important airlifts would allow it (and bush flying) to break away forever from the summer-only flying boat era. In 1926, the federal Department for Railways and Canals wanted to link the port of Churchill, Manitoba, and Winnipeg with a railway line, so that grain could be shipped through Hudson Bay to Europe. Ice-bound for most of the winter and surrounded by miles of frozen wasteland, the port was isolated from an inland approach. With such terrain, the railway had become bogged down 280 miles away at Cache Lake. If construction was to continue in the spring, all surveying would have to be done that winter, and by air. The survey team consisted of twelve geologists with a box of dynamite, a churn drill, a gasoline engine and 17,894 pounds of supplies. The government asked WCA if it were possible to organize an airlift on such a large scale. Oaks accepted the challenge, and Richardson sent him back to New York to buy two more Universals. Between March 22 and April 17, WCA pilots Steve Stevenson and Bert Balchen flew twenty-seven round trips between Cache Lake and Churchill, carrying eight tons of machinery and fourteen engineers. As a result of their efforts, Churchill was established as the terminus of the grain railway.

The following summer, when Sherritt Gordon Mines began drilling for diamonds at Cold Lake, north of The Pas, WCA was again contracted to transport all food, oil, building supplies, gasoline and dynamite to the site. Through August and September, Stevenson shuttled back and forth in the Universal, carrying a total of 45,708 pounds and fifty-eight passengers. Now every mine owner was convinced of the value of aircraft in speeding up his operations. Oaks, sensing that he could do better, left WCA in 1928 and formed an air mining concern with Jack Hammell, the Northern Aerial Minerals Exploration Company. Richardson became a director and major shareholder in the company.

By early 1929, Richardson's airline had justified his investment. In 1927, it had carried 420,730 pounds and 1,747 passengers over 145,834 miles. The next year this increased to 1,192,646 pounds, 9,648 passengers and 545,193 miles—an increase of 360 per cent. More importantly, as the first all-year airline in Canadian history, WCA had demonstrated that tedious, expensive travel over hostile country could be eliminated by using aircraft. The company attracted men who would become aviation legends: the station manager Con Farrell (who, like Wop May, had flown in the Royal Flying Corps), Art Rankin, Rudy Heuss, North Sawle, Jack Moar, Don Lawson, Jack Hames, Jack Wright, Casey Vanderlinden and Dick Leigh. Soon, WCA extended its operations to the Pacific coast and installed radio

communications at some of its bases. It was now large enough to have its own maintenance base at the foot of Brandon Avenue, Winnipeg, with twenty-six aircraft and a pool of experienced pilots.

Cashing in on the publicity from both the record-breaking flights in its planes and the Churchill airlift, Fokker now brought out the Super Universal. The aircraft had an enclosed cockpit and a more powerful Wasp engine, and was able to carry six, instead of four, passengers. Canadian Vickers Ltd. built fifteen Super Universals under licence, and WCA bought fourteen of them.

If the company's balance books satisfied Richardson, for Oaks and all former OPAS and Laurentide alumni the best news was that one of their colleagues, F. J. "Steve" Stevenson, had been awarded the prestigious Harmon Trophy for 1927 as the most outstanding pilot in Canada. (Charles Lindbergh was the winner in the international category.) Sadly, Stevenson would not live long to enjoy it.

On January 5, 1928, at the WCA airfield at The Pas, Stevenson took one of the Fokkers up on a test flight. He was suffering a heavy cold, and this may have impaired his judgement as he later attempted to land. The plane overshot the runway, tried to turn, stalled and crashed. Stevenson was killed instantly. That May, the City of Winnipeg named its first airport Stevenson Aerodrome in his memory. The name would not be changed to Winnipeg International Airport until 1959, by the Department of Transport, in accordance with International Civil Aviation regulations.

THE GATEWAY OF THE NORTH

No Canadian city embraced bush aviation as passionately as Edmonton, which billed itself as "The Gateway of the North." Edmontonians knew that they owed their city's frontier flavour to the very circumstances that had created it: it was at the end of the railroad. To get to the fabulous North, with its wealth of gold, uranium, furs and oil, adventurers and geologists who had traditionally used canoes, steamboats, horses or dog teams now went there to hire bush planes, and the Magee Building in downtown Edmonton became the headquarters for bush airlines. Aircraft taking off from Edmonton, whether at the airfield or at Cooking Lake, remade the North within a decade. They did it with an abruptness that no one really understood at the time, least of all the aboriginal people who had barely had time to come to terms with the steam engine.

Edmonton was also on the direct route to Alaska for American aviators, and in 1920, Imperial Oil laid out a permanent airfield at Hagmann Farm as a home for its two Junkers. One of the Junkers pilots, Wilfrid Reid May (called "Wop" because that was the closest his young cousin could get to saying Wilfrid), persuaded Mayor Ken Blatchford to designate the farm as the city's official airport, and then had it named Blatchford Field in the mayor's honour. The airport was officially opened on January 8, 1927, by RCAF Flying Officer Punch Dickins in his ski-equipped Siskin fighter. When the federally financed flying club scheme began that year, May was hired as the instructor for the Edmonton flying club. It was an opportunity to begin his own company, Commercial Airways, for which he brought an Avro Avian two-seater biplane from England.

In December 1928, events far to the north of Edmonton suddenly thrust Wop May into the headlines. Dr. Hamman, the doctor at Fort Vermilion, received an urgent message brought by Louis Bourassa, a dog sled driver from the Little Red River settlement, some two hundred miles down the Peace River. There had been an outbreak of diphtheria in the village, and there was not enough antitoxin to prevent it from spreading across the whole territory. It had taken Bourassa two weeks to make the journey, and the fear was that it might be too late for many in the settlement. Hamman telegraphed Edmonton. To be effective, the antitoxin had to be delivered immediately. The RCAF air base at High River, Alberta, had closed down for the winter, and all Western Canada Airways' aircraft were at Winnipeg. Alberta's deputy minister of health, Dr. Bow, phoned Wop May, whose reply was short: "Get your antitoxin ready. Vic and I'll take off in the morning."

On January 3, 1929, May's little Avian staggered off Blatchford Field carrying the pilot, engineer Vic Horner, a tracheotomy set and 600,000 units of antitoxin wrapped in rugs around a charcoal burner. The ground temperature was 33° below zero. In Philip H. Godsell's 1936 account *Pilots of the Purple Twilight*, photos taken of the historic occasion show May fashionably dressed in what look like plus fours, a knitted sweater and a tweed cap, better outfitted for the golf club than the bitter weather. (The photos may have been taken at a recreation of the event for the media.) The Avian looks like the large toy it was, completely unsuited to the Canadian winter. Designed as a flying club aircraft, it had an open cockpit and, because it had just been delivered, it was still on wheels.

May followed the railroad line north, and then the Peace River. Through blizzards and snow squalls, the pair raced to cover as much distance as possible before the northern darkness closed in. Edmonton radio station CJCA began broadcasting messages to anyone along the route to look out for the aircraft. Blowing snow made it necessary for May to fly at treetop level, and soon both the Avian and the men were covered in frost. At noon, they landed and refuelled from a gasoline drum on board, and stamped about to get some feeling back in their arms and legs. Three hours later, they landed on a frozen lake at McLennan Junction in almost total blackness.

Alerted by the radio, the whole town turned out to help. The antitoxin was rushed indoors, while May and Horner drained the oil and put the hood over the engine. The next morning, despite suffering from severe frostbite, they took off at dawn for the last lap to Fort Vermilion. They flew all day, keeping the widening Peace River below them, their faces bleeding from the raw wind that whipped by the aircraft. It was 4:30 P.M., and just minutes before darkness fell, when the Avian bounced down on a clearing at the Fort. The antitoxin was rushed by a fast dog team to Little Red River, and the settlement was saved.

The dramatic flight—the stuff of boys' adventure comics—had been carried by newswire around the world, and when May and Horner returned to Blatchford Field on January 6, an estimated 5,000 spectators were there to cheer them. More than any other event until then, the Little Red River rescue publicized the value of bush flying. For these exploits and for inaugurating the airmail route into northern Canada, Wop May would be awarded the Trans Canada Trophy in 1930 and the Order of the British Empire by His Majesty King George V in 1935.

MERCY FLIGHTS AND CLOSE CALLS

Then, as now, bush flying also meant continual mercy flights that never made the headlines. The following excerpt, taken from the 1929 log of W. Leigh Brintnell, the operations manager of Western Canada Airways, gives some idea:

Field Ambulance Notes

Sept. 2nd—Cranberry Portage. Wire from Cold Lake asking for machine to take in seriously wounded man, otherwise weather unfit to fly in. Tried to get through to The Pas but unable, could not see ground from 200 ft. for fog, smoke and rain.Cranberry to Cold Lake to Cranberry 90 miles—Farrell.

Sept. 10th—Stewart to Burns Lake 260 miles—Gilbert. Extremely hot—transportation of Consolidated Engineer to Vancouver Hospital. (Take-off Burns Lake 9.45 arrive Vancouver 16.25—520 miles.) Total 780 miles—Gilbert.

(These trips were for the purpose of conveying Mr. H. C. Hughes, Superintendent of Emerald Mine, Ootsa Lake from Burns Lake to Vancouver. Mr. Hughes, when engaged in prospecting at Ootsa Lake, had encountered a grizzly bear which had mauled him and finally left him minus a finger, with his face badly chewed and badly bruised about the body and legs. When attacked, Mr. Hughes, who was unarmed, feigned death and to this he attributes the fact that the bear left him without doing greater damage. Later, when in hospital at Burns Lake, infection set in and it was considered imperative that he be removed to Vancouver).

Sept. 13th—To North Washagamis Lake to pick up man seriously ill. 120 miles—Westergaard.

Sept. 14th—Camp cook (appendicitis) from Pickle Lake to Allanwater. 90 miles—Garten.

December 4th—Gold Pines to Sioux Lookout—Dr. O'Gorman and sick man. 72 miles—Stull.

December 5th—Red Lake to Sioux Lookout—Man badly burned, needed hospital treatment urgently. 116 miles—Stull.

December 19th—Man killed at mine brought to Sioux Lookout. 116 miles—Stull.

December 22nd—Man with frozen feet had no money, brought to Gold Pines. Ticket 284, Mr. H. A. brought to Sioux for medical attention. He was walking to Red Lake to look for job and his feet were frozen—no money—no friends—no job. Red Lake to Sioux Lookout 116 miles—Stull.

Jan. 1st 1930—Corporal Cummings, RCMP. Sick, partially paralyzed. Brought from Good Hope on the Arctic Circle to McMurray. Transferred at McMurray to "Punch" Dickins for Edmonton hospital in six days with adverse weather. Good Hope to Edmonton 1440 miles.[1]

Punch Dickins, the pilot who flew the RCMP corporal to Edmonton, was destined to become the greatest bush pilot of them all. Born on January 12, 1899, at Port la Prairie, Manitoba, Clennell Haggerston Dickins flew for 211 Squadron in the Royal Flying Corps and, in 1918, shot down seven enemy aircraft.

He remained in the Royal Canadian Air Force after the war and was posted to Edmonton. It was there that he gained experience flying in winter conditions, helping test the RCAF's British-made Siskin fighter aircraft. In January of 1928 Dickins left the air force to join Western Canada Airways, and a year later, he achieved fame with its Fokker "G-CASK." Dominion Explorers of Toronto had contracted WCA to fly mineral exploratory flights over the Barrenlands. Carrying Lieutenant Colonel C. D. H. MacAlpine, the company's president, and Richard Pearce, editor of the *Northern Miner*, Dickins set off from Winnipeg. He flew along the Nelson River to Jackfish Island, then across to Churchill on Hudson Bay, to Chesterfield Inlet and then west to Baker Lake. MacAlpine was well pleased with having covered more than 4,000 miles in twelve days—it would have taken him two years to do as much on foot. For this, and because he was the first commercial pilot to fly across the Arctic Circle, Dickins was awarded the Trans Canada Trophy in 1929.

It must be emphasized that for the early bush pilots there were no navigation beacons, no weather reports, no aeronautical charts at all. All flights were conducted according to what would later be described as Visual Flight Rules (VFR): the pilot flew within sight of the ground or water at all times. In the populated south, this meant orientating yourself with the "iron compass," the railroad, or with a major highway and, as rural electrification spread, the web of power lines. Once in the bush, there was little to guide the pilot. The terrain, especially in the tundra, could be featureless, the patchwork of lakes confusing. Because of the closeness of the magnetic pole, the aircraft's compass could not be relied upon. Even today, the bush pilot flying VFR relies on his memory of physical landmarks.

Crossing mountain ranges, the VFR pilot resorted to what he called "valley crawling." River valleys served as highways and as refuges in case of emergencies. Bush pilots took sextant readings; they chose landing sites and assessed local weather and terrain very carefully. If successful, they stored all the details up for the next time. Float pilots especially needed excellent memories. Before the Second World War made aeronautical charts commonplace, the pecularities of every shoreline, the location of every sunken log and every shoal had to be filed away and hoarded for future use.

Once a pilot was away from base, there could be no communication with him until he returned. Radios were just coming into use and had a very limited range. But the pilots who flew HS-2Ls from the Air Board's seaplane base at Jericho Beach, Vancouver, were equipped with a small wicker basket that contained pigeons. In case of a forced landing, they could write a message on very thin paper, put it into a tube clipped to the pigeon's leg and then release the bird to fly home. This was not a very reliable method, however; pigeons were sometimes attacked by hawks in mid-flight.

Without radio communications, there could be no organized search and rescue operations if a pilot was overdue. There were no emergency beacons, and the area he flew over might be too vast for accurate searching. If a missing pilot was employed by WCA, the company sent available aircraft out along his intended route. The RCMP would be contacted, and anyone else who knew the area asked for advice. The native peoples who really knew the bush were invaluable. Unless a pilot worked for an airline or a mining company, his family paid for all the fuel used in the search. Every pilot took extensive emergency equipment when he flew into the Barrens and the

Northwest Territories, including an eiderdown, a rifle, an axe, a shovel, a jack and two pairs of snowshoes, as well as spare airplane parts and repair equipment. All told, emergency provisions could weigh up to 400 pounds.

The floats used in summer flying were another hazard. They were vulnerable to damage by rocks and submerged logs, and bush pilots recall that the early ones built by Hamilton lost their rivets every time an aircraft landed. And in winter, servicing a bush plane in the North was an exercise in madness. The inadequacies of the aircraft for the uses they were put to were the subject of continous complaints. Punch Dickins reported that at 50° below zero, the rubber shock absorbers on his aircraft's undercarriage would freeze solid.

When a pilot set down for the night, he closed the fuel line and allowed the carburetor to run dry before switching the engine off. This avoided the danger of fire the next morning. The engineer would drain the oil from the engine while it was still warm. The plane's skis would then be jacked up on poles to prevent them from freezing to the snow.

Called the "black gang," engineers were indispensable, the unsung heroes of bush flying. One of their main tasks was to get the aircraft started on winter mornings, a routine performed long before the sun rose so that maximum use could be made of the short daylight hours. The unfortunate engineer would crawl out of his sleeping bag, which contained his flashlight (he slept with it so that the batteries wouldn't freeze), then put on three pairs of long underwear, calf-length buckskin moccasins and fur-lined mitts. He heated up the frozen lump of oil on the wood stove, stirring it until it was a hot liquid. This was done on what was called "a Hudson Bay breakfast"—a stomach full of wind and a drink of water.

To get the engine warmed up, the engineer used his "plumber's pot," which looked like a big blowtorch with a small metal shield over the top. The flaming torch was put into the engine, which was covered with an asbestos blanket. The poor engineer then sat with the pot, breathing in its poisonous carbon monoxide fumes, waiting for the block of useless metal to heat up. Once this happened, he ran over to the stove, quickly took the oil off and poured it into the engine. He then wound the engine over a couple of times to make sure the hot oil flowed satisfactorily through it. Depending on the aircraft, he might climb a ladder, insert the crank into the inertia starter and rotate it a few times to get it going.

If everything had gone just right, the engine would fire when the pilot, sitting in the cockpit, engaged the starter. If the engine missed, the process was started over again. Depending on temperature and wind, the whole operation took between an hour and an hour and a half. It was, as one sufferer recalled, an unavoidable routine every morning until Tommy Siers, the WCA chief engineer, perfected his oil dilution system in 1940.

The cold that made aircraft inoperative also killed humans. Bush pilots knew temperatures so low that their lungs would hurt unless they took shallow breaths. At 60° below zero, their spit froze solid in mid-air. Yet they serviced and operated their aircraft as a matter of routine, motivated by what could only be described as love, for it brought them little financial reward. They transported humans, dogs, oxen, pigs, blasting caps, fuel drums, phonograph records, newspapers and heavy mining equipment. They died in sudden snowstorms, and crashed and disappeared in the dense British Columbia forest. Their beloved aircraft rotted from carrying fish, or caught fire and burned. On March 31, 1933, in a freak accident, the most famous Fokker Super Universal of them all, "G-CASK," was engulfed in flames as it was being refuelled. The subsequent investigation showed that a hose had broken, and static electricity had ignited the leaking gasoline. The plane's pilot, Walter Gilbert, would later write that "the unfortunate accident . . . divorced me from my best friend—flesh and blood and human—that I have ever known."[2]

On July 29, 1929, the Manitoba *Free Press* ran the following headline: "New flying record for coast to Winnipeg is set by Brintnell Saturday." The 13,000 air miles between Winnipeg and Vancouver had been covered in ten hours and thirty minutes, with one stop for refuelling at High River, Alberta. The story reported that Manitoba Premier John Bracken, with a party of Winnipeg businessmen and aviators, had breakfasted in Vancouver and dined in Winnipeg the same day. The flight was made in a ten-passenger Fokker tri-motor owned by Western Canada Airways and flown by W. Leigh Brintnell.

The WCA flight had taken place ten years and one month to the day that Stuart Graham lifted *La Vigilance* off at the other end of Canada. Graham retired from aviation in 1963. His last job was as air advisor for the International Civil Aviation Organisation. In that capacity, he served in Latin America, Haiti, Rwanda and Ethiopia. As he was presented at the court of Emperor Haile Selassie and decorated with the Star of Menelik, Graham must have been secure in the knowledge that no other bush pilot could claim such an award.

G-CAFU

Fokker Universal.
A typical aircraft of W.C.A.

Facing page: During the Depression, the public's fascination with aeronautical achievements like the flight of this American autogyro at Barker Field, Toronto, popularized commercial aviation in Canada. CITY OF TORONTO ARCHIVES: JAMES COLLECTION

Western Canada
Airways Insignia

G-CASK

Fokker Super Universal.
The standardized colors of W.C.A.

CHAPTER FIVE

CF-ATZ

Fairchild 71C.
The standardized colors of C.A.
Aircraft of the early thirties.

Flight in a Cold Climate

Canadian Airways
Insignia

CANADIAN AIRWAYS LTD.   CF-AQV

Junkers W-34.
A typical Junkers coloring and insignia was also frequently displayed.

Canadian Airways
Insignia Eastern Lines

CF-AAN

ith the signing of the Treaty of Versailles, the British, the French, the Dutch and the Belgians had all moved to consolidate links with their overseas colonies through airlines such as Imperial Airways, Air France, KLM and SABENA, all government controlled and subsidized. In the United States, it took the passing of the Airmail Act (the Kelly Bill) in February 1925 to spark Washington's interest in commercial aviation. The act took the air-

mail contracts away from the Post Office, whose pilots had suffered such frightening casualties, and gave them to private companies.

The Air Commerce Act created the U.S. Aeronautics Branch in 1926, putting the branch firmly within the Department of Commerce. The distribution of airmail contracts under the aegis of President Herbert Hoover's Postmaster General, Walter Brown, forced American air companies to consolidate, but more importantly it accelerated the introduction of

Fairchild FC2-W2.
In the late thirties an all aluminum finish was used with orange wing tips.

59

The Basic Color Schemes of the Aircraft of Western Canada Airways Limited and Canadian Airways Limited
ILLUSTRATED BY R. W. BRADFORD

improvements such as radial engines, variable-pitch propellers (patented by Canadian Wallace Rupert Turnbull in 1922 but developed by the American company Hamilton Standard), and enclosed, all-metal airliners such as the Ford trimotor.

AVIATION BELOW THE BORDER

The 1929 stock market crash devastated many industries in the eastern United States, but it hardly slowed research in aeronautical engineering or business opportunities in aviation. Throughout the Depression, Donald Douglas, Allen Lockheed and

John K. Northrop turned out airliners that surpassed those of the Europeans, introducing such advanced concepts as retractable undercarriages, cowled engines—and a big attraction for passengers—sound-proofed fuselages.[1] The advent of the first modern airliner, the Boeing 247, which could carry ten passengers from coast to coast in less than a day, encouraged young entrepreneurs like Juan Trippe and Howard Hughes to begin their own airlines, Pan American Airways and Trans World Airlines respectively.[2] Imagination, cutthroat competition and Madison Avenue publicity all combined in the 1930s

The Canadian Airways Junkers 52 freighter was an initial disappointment because of its BMW engine, but until the Second World War it was the largest aircraft in Canada.
CANADIAN AIRLINES ARCHIVES

to give the United States the lead in world aviation.

U.S. railway magnates such as W. A. Harriman and Robert Lehman poured money into developing air companies that connected with their trains—in Harriman's case, American Airlines. Aircraft manufacturers began their own airlines to market their products. Boeing, part of the United Aircraft & Transport conglomerate, built the Boeing 247 exclusively for United Airlines, the conglomerate's "in-house" air company. C. M. Keys, chairman of the Curtiss company, began North American Aviation, which would evolve into Eastern Airlines, to sell his

Condor aircraft. In what must have been a supreme irony, Keys merged Curtiss with the Wright Aeronautical Company in 1929 to form Curtiss-Wright, bringing together the nation's greatest early aviation pioneers—and its greatest rivals.

Transcontinental and Western Air (later Trans World Airlines), which did not have a parent aircraft supplier, was forced to buy Fokkers. When football star Knute Rockne was killed in one, the airline went to Donald Douglas, who had begun building aircraft in 1922 in an abandoned movie studio on Wilshire Boulevard in Santa Monica, and asked him to design an aircraft that would compete with the Boeing 247. Legend has it that Douglas drew up the initial proposal for the DC-1, grandfather of the immortal DC-3, on a train from Los Angeles to TWA's office in New York, finetuning it as he came into Penn Central.[3]

FLYING THE MAIL

In Canada, civil aviation was still controlled by the Department of National Defence. And in contrast to the American situation, financing for Canadian air companies was usually scrounged by the pilots themselves, who substituted boyish derring-do for sound business principles. J. A. Wilson, Canada's controller of civil aviation, identified it correctly when he wrote in a November 1929 memo to the government, "The weakness of the operating firms is that they are run almost entirely by men whose experience is limited to flying. They have no experience in transportation as a business and its many ramifications." [4] The only Canadian businessman so far to underwrite an aviation company was James Richardson, and by the end of 1929 his Western Canadian Airways was prospering. Its pilots carried Mounties and missionaries, prospectors and civil servants from Quebec's North shore to Vancouver and as far north as Aklavik on the Arctic Ocean. In September 1930, its Fokker "G-CASK" was the first aircraft to fly over the magnetic pole. Impressed, the federal government awarded WCA a four-year contract to deliver airmail on the Prairies and, on the basis of this, Richardson bought six large Fokker F.14s and three Boeing 40B aircraft. Commencing March 3, 1930, WCA transported the mail between Winnipeg, Regina, Moose Jaw, Medicine Hat, Lethbridge, Calgary, Saskatoon and Edmonton.

Passengers were another matter. Why they put their lives at risk—hunched on cane seats, deafened in freezing, drafty cabins, clutching "erp" cups accurately named for their use in turbulence, and finally deposited on muddy fields far outside of town—when they could have taken a warm, comfortable train with dining car service was beyond the comprehension of most pilots. The only advantage flying could offer was speed.

The Post Office did its level best to discourage WCA from transporting any passengers at all, fearing that the pilots might put the passengers' welfare—and schedules—above that of the mail bags. To them it was "Letters First, People Perhaps." At least Ottawa didn't go to the extreme of making Canadian pilots carry a handgun. In the United States, every pilot entrusted with the mail packed a revolver, a throwback to the Pony Express days.

In Eastern Canada, the competition from an established network of railways left the struggling air companies heavily dependent on government airmail contracts to survive. Canadian Transcontinental Airways Ltd. (CTAL) operated out of Quebec City, serving Rimouski and Montreal, while International Airways of Canada (IAC) flew the Hamilton-Montreal-Toronto route. Halifax, Moncton and Charlottetown were irregularly serviced by Canadian Transcontinental Airways, which began flying an airmail service between Moncton and the Magdalen Islands in 1927. A sympathetic federal government gave CTAL and IAC higher rates to carry mail in the east, but that wasn't nearly enough to sustain them.

One Montreal-based company that was not faltering was Canadian Colonial Airways. Its aircraft carried the mail between St. Hubert, the government airport near Montreal, and Albany, New York. Despite its name, Canadian Colonial was wholly owned by American interests, in this case, the Aviation Corporation of Delaware conglomerate. Its president, Major-General J. F. O'Ryan, planned to snap up both IAC and CTAL, and he began making overtures to their shareholders. In this way, he hoped to get a foothold in eastern Canada, not only to service the mining industries but to be well placed on the eastern seaboard when trans-Atlantic flying became a reality.

The transparency of O'Ryan's scheme alarmed

such air-minded Canadians as J. A. Wilson, James Richardson and Ellwood Wilson of Laurentide. To thwart it, they formed a syndicate in 1929-30 with Drury Brothers, an investment firm, and the Canadian Pacific Railway and bought controlling shares in the two airlines. The holding company, Aviation Corporation of Canada, would, they hoped, withstand American encroachment. The scheme might have worked except for the Wall Street crash, which put the future of the Aviation Corporation in jeopardy. In April 1930, its directors asked Richardson to shore it up by selling them his financially sound WCA. Instead, he negotiated a deal whereby the corporation and Western Canada Airways would be merged into one giant company.

On June 27, 1930, Canadian Airways Ltd. (CAL) came into being as a virtual monopoly that operated from coast to coast. Richardson was made its president and, significantly, both the Canadian Pacific and the Canadian National Railways now opted to become its main shareholders. The two railways invested $250,000 each in return for 10,000 shares, and Sir Henry Thornton (the CNR's president) and Sir Edward Beatty (the CPR's president) became vice-presidents of the airline. Within three years, the Winnipeg grain merchant had built a bulwark against American expansion—for patriotism and for profit.

But the ripples of the stock market crash and the taking on of the bankrupt corporation weakened WCA more than Richardson expected. There was little venture capital now for aerial surveying or transport, and in 1931, when the Conservatives came to power, even airmail contracts were taken from the commercial sector. As the new prime minister, R. B. Bennett, told the House of Commons, "Because of the crop failure in western Canada, and with 300,000 of a population receiving some form of relief, there was very little gratification in seeing an aeroplane passing day by day, when the unfortunate owner of the soil could hardly see the aeroplane because his crop had gone up in dust." Bennett informed J. A. Wilson that Canada couldn't afford an airmail service at a time when the federal

government was trying to raise $500 million. Furthermore, he continued, it was no use for Richardson to remind the prime minister that his company's airmail contracts still had three years to run, when both knew that the RCAF would be grateful for any service it could perform. In 1931, the air force was fighting for its life, with its staff cut by 70 per cent and air operations curtailed.[5] When the minister of national defence asked the RCAF to take over the mail service from the air companies, it was pleased to do so.

First the Maritime service, then the lucrative Montreal-Toronto route, and finally the prairie network was removed from WCA's operations. This last was a severe blow to Richardson, who was still paying for the new Fokkers, and for his most extravagant purchase, the Junkers 52 freighter "CF-ARM." (The largest aircraft in Canada for many years, the "CF-ARM" was an initial disappointment; its BMW engine gave pilots so much trouble that in its first year of service the aircraft was unused for 297 days.)

The plight of Canadian commercial aviation during the Depression elicited little sympathy from either the government or the public when compared with the widespread devastation caused by bankruptcies and the plight of destitute families all around. But the losses substained by Canadian Airways were alarming. In 1931, although CAL airlifted a large number of lumberjacks across the St. Lawrence in an emergency, it ended the year with a deficit of $76,928. The next year, when W. Leigh Brintnell, the airline's assistant general manager, struck out on his own and formed Mackenzie Air Services in the Northwest Territories, this competition in CAL's busiest sector lost the company $227,973.

WOLF BOUNTIES AND PROSPECTORS

The problem was that the busiest Canadian Airways sector, the far North, specifically the Mackenzie River district, wasn't very profitable, at least in currency. (The unwise licencing practice of the federal government had allowed more than one operator to provide service on many routes, resulting in too many companies chasing too little business.) Punch

Dickins, who was in charge of air operations, indicated why in an annual report:

> The balance of our business is done with numerous other persons, independent traders, trappers, restaurant keepers, woodcutters, police, doctors, government employees, Indians and half breeds.
>
> In collecting accounts from these people is where our great difference from normal routine lies. There are no banks in the country and no cash to speak of, as it is the policy of the two large trading companies to keep as little cash as possible as it is adverse to them in dealing with Indians and trappers when buying furs. When there is no cash then sellers of fur are obliged to accept an order for credit at the company concerned and take it out in trade on which the company makes a profit.
>
> It is therefore, in many cases, impossible to get cash settlements of accounts. Settlement is made . . . by turning in "Wolf Bounties" or in fur. An example of the collections received is given when on my last trip . . . I arrived back at McMurray with $15 in cash, $240 in wolf bounties, $320 in beaver and destitute ration orders, 400 muskrats, 2 red foxes, 2 cross foxes, 7 marten, 5 mink, 1 lynx, and 50 extra muskrat to come and go on. It is difficult to see any change in the monetary system . . . as the main trade in the future will still be controlled by the two fur trading companies.[6]

More negotiable than the "wolf bounties" was business from a rich mineral strike made by Gilbert Labine. The prospector came to Richardson in 1929 with his theory of large mineral deposits in the Great Bear Lake region of the Northwest Territories. At the time, Brintnell was flying "G-CASK" to the Yukon, and Richardson allowed Labine to go with him. Brintnell left his passenger off at Great Bear Lake on August 5, and Dickins picked him up from there three weeks later. Dickins would later remember that Labine was very excited over the mineral discoloration in some rocks they were flying over. Labine returned in March 1930 and discovered the richest deposit of pitchblende in history. Other prospectors

No one typified the bush pilot spirit better than the ubiquitous Grant McConachie, shown here at Takla Lake in the summer of 1934.
CANADIAN AIRLINES ARCHIVES

had seen it, but only Labine recognized it for what it was. He staked several claims immediately, and through the years his Great Bear Lake mine yielded not only silver but large quantities of radium and uranium oxide.

The mine proved a minor boon to Canadian Airways, as it was 800 miles from the nearest railhead and, except in the short summer, all supplies had to be flown in and the radium itself to be flown out. Soon there were 4,000 prospectors staking claims, and their requirements for food, fuel and machinery at Great Bear Lake kept CAL pilots busy throughout the 1930s. It still wasn't enough for a healthy operating margin, but with the end of the mail contracts, it was all there was.

Relying on prospectors for a living had its own hazards. The worst nightmare of these eccentric loners was that the location of their claim would leak out to competitors. They trusted no one with the information, not even the airline who was flying them in. Often the prospector submitted a false route to the air company manager, then had the pilot make for the real destination once they were actually in the air. As there was no radio on board, no one on the ground would know of the change. It was a dangerous practice that had the potential for disaster.

A CLOSE CALL

One prospector's need for secrecy eventually led to competition for Canadian Airways from an unlikely source, the owner of a shoestring air company in Alberta. At twenty-four, Grant McConachie was the owner of Independent Airways, a grandiose title for the two Fokkers and a DH Puss Moth biplane that he kept at Edmonton's Blatchford Field.

Like all other bush outfits, Independent barely made ends meet, and McConachie survived by hauling fish from Peter Pond Lake to the railhead at Cheecham, Alberta. Fresh fish commanded premium prices in Chicago, especially among the Jewish community, but flying it to the train was an indicator of a bush pilot's penury. The stench from the fish not only permeated the pilot and his aircraft, making both unwelcome at airports (and worse still for the pilots, at bars), but in time caused the fabric on the fuselage to rot. And when McConachie smashed up one of his Fokkers (realizing later that his propeller blade had iced up), breaking his leg, ribs and fingers and fracturing his hips, his Independent Airways was in imminent danger of going under.

One cold February night in 1933, as McConachie sat worrying about finding the money to repair his Fokker, a scenario familiar to most bush pilots occurred: a prospector walked in and offered him a contract to fly to a secret gold strike. All Barney Phillips would say was that his claim was located somewhere in the Stikine country of British Columbia. Crushed between the Skeena and the Omineca mountain ranges, even today the Stikine is little known or inhabited. There are no roads, power lines or settlements in its narrow mountain valleys, and the steep river valleys of the Hogem range make low-level flying dangerous.

McConachie, whose total flying experience had up until then been barnstorming or transporting fish over the flat prairies, had only the tiny Puss Moth and his desperation to go on. Caught up in the moment, he agreed to take Phillips into the labyrinth of mountains then covered in deep snow. Phillips wanted first to go to Takla Landing, northwest of Prince George, British Columbia, where three other men would be waiting to be ferried to the mystery location.

The flight through the Rockies in the little aircraft must have been frightening enough. After a refuelling at Takla Landing, Phillips guided McConachie over Bear Lake, up Sustut Pass, then along the frozen Injenica River to Tobogan Creek. Just as McConachie thought they were lost, the prospector pointed to a small lake below. They landed in the deep snow. McConachie, fearing that

the engine wouldn't start again, didn't turn it off; Phillips helped him unload the supplies, and they both put on snowshoes to trample out a makeshift runway. McConachie then headed back to Takla Landing to pick up the others. In all, he made seven trips to the lake, taking the other three prospectors and enough supplies to last until the middle of June, when he was scheduled to return.

McConachie returned to Edmonton's Blatchford Field exhausted, but sure that Phillips's gold mine would pay off all Independent Airways' debts. As he taxied the little Moth to his hangar, he saw Jimmy Bell, the airport manager, and the local sheriff waiting for him. Even before McConachie could climb out of the cockpit, the officer plastered a "Repossessed" sticker on the Moth, and McConachie noticed that there was already one on the Fokker. The assets of Independent Airways now belonged to McConachie's creditors.

Summer came, and by mid-June McConachie began having nightmares about his abandoned clients. He became crazy with desperation, knowing that the fate of four men depended on him. But the banks and the police remained deaf to his pleas. And when he finally convinced a friend to fly him to the site, they crashed north of Takla Lake because of mechanical problems.

Frantic, McConachie trekked back through the bush to the nearest town, where Ken Dewar, a pilot for a mining company, offered to fly him to the gold camp. There was no sign of life when they landed on the lake, and McConachie was certain Phillips and his men were dead. But then four emaciated figures staggered out of a tent. The survivors were flown out and, after hospital care, began cursing McConachie for deserting them. Only Phillips did not. He had struck it rich, and out of gratitude for the young man's efforts, proposed to invest in McConachie's

Western Canada
Airways Insignia

Canadian Airways
Insignia

Canadian Airways
Insignia Eastern Lines

G-CAFU

Fokker Universal.
The colors of the early aircraft of W.C.A.

G-CASK

Fokker Super Universal.
The standardized colors of W.C.A.

CF-ATZ

Fairchild 71C.
The standardized colors of C.A.L.
Aircraft of the early thirties.

CF-AQV

CANADIAN AIRWAYS LTD.

Junkers W-34.
A typical Junkers coloring and le
The C.A.L. insignia was
also frequently displayed.

CF-AAN

Fairchild FC2-W2.
In the late thirties an all aluminum
finish was used with orange wing tips.

The Basic Color Schemes of the Aircraft of Western Canada Airways Limited and Canadian Airways Limited
ILLUSTRATED BY R. W. BRADFORD

company. Phillips had indeed discovered gold, and he would need heavy equipment, men and supplies flown in.

McConachie could not get his old aircraft back, so he formed a new bush flying outfit, United Air Transport. Three new Fokkers were purchased, and this time he registered them in the names of his pilots' mothers.

CAL STRUGGLES TO SURVIVE

Competition from yet another bush company was all Canadian Airways needed just then. Not for the first time in national aviation history, there were too many airlines chasing too small a market. In eastern Canada, the directors of the Clark Steamship Company started up Quebec Airways. In Montreal, the millionaire Molson brewing family was backing Dominion Skyways and bought the company three Fairchilds, a Bellanca and the latest Noorduyn Norseman. The competition from both raised CAL's annual deficit in 1933 to $431,000. There seemed little hope of getting the airmail contracts back. Post Office officials unpatriotically and publicly hoped for Britain's Imperial Airways to submit a proposal to take Canadian mail internally. As hard-headed businessmen, James Richardson and the presidents of the two railways knew that this could not go on indefinitely and began to discuss shutting the air company down completely.

There was one faint hope on the horizon. In February 1929, the Department of National Defence had been authorized to begin work on the Trans-Canada Airway. The airway was envisaged as a chain of airports, emergency airstrips and lighting beacons spaced 100 miles apart that would allow an aircraft to fly safely, on schedule and at night from coast to coast. The airports along the prairie section were completed by March 1930. As the Depression settled in, Ottawa incorporated the construction of the airway into a relief scheme. Destitute men were transported from the cities by the DND to labour camps along the length of the proposed airway. At the project's height in 1933, over 10,000 men were housed at forty-six camps, building ninety-three airports and

emergency airstrips. As the acknowledged godfather of the airway, J. A. Wilson, using rail, road and biplane, shuttled back and forth between the sites, closely monitoring their progress.

A popular Depression song in 1934 was "Let's Face the Music and Dance!" and this sentiment described the atmosphere at the CAL annual general meeting on April 26. Richardson explained the company's situation to the shareholders, pointing out that it would cost $48,000 in storage and insurance fees to close the company down. The directors agreed that their only salvation was to hang on grimly in the hope that Ottawa would make CAL the national airline. There was a faint glimmer of optimism that with a general election in the offing, either party might encourage an aviation policy for political reasons. Until then, certain economies were implemented. The company's head office was moved to Winnipeg, staff were laid off, and the airline concentrated on freighting in the mining areas. The reorganization did work. That year in October alone, CAL carried 997,908 pounds of freight, more than it had for all of 1931. In fact, in 1934 the air freight total for CAL was 5,766,691 pounds, higher than the totals for either Britain's Imperial Airways or any airline in the United States.

On October 14, 1935, Mackenzie King's Liberals swept into office with 173 seats, the largest majority (until 1993) for any party since Confederation. Richardson immediately sent a memo to all CAL staff: "As the possibility of the inauguration of the trans-Canada Air Mail looks more favourable at the present time, would you please advise whether you wish to be transferred from bush operations to mail operations in the event of Canadian Airways being awarded this contract." Then Richardson called on the new prime minister—not as the owner of a struggling airline, he said, but in his capacity as chancellor of Queen's University, a position he was appointed to in 1929. King was not fooled and noted as much in his diary.

Although the Winnipeg grain merchant could not know, it was already too late for his airline. King had appointed to the portfolio of Railways, Canals and Marine a man who would shape the destiny of air transport in Canada for the next three decades. Clarence Decatur Howe, born in Waltham, Massachusetts, was the son of a house-builder and a schoolteacher. His high school motto had been "Deeds, Not Words," and after graduating as an engineer from the Massachusetts Institute of Technology, his yardstick for the remainder of his life was "Will it work?" Howe was an underpaid professor at Dalhousie University when Robert Borden, his local member of Parliament, was elected prime minister in 1911. Because of his support of Borden, Howe was given the government contract to build grain elevators at Fort William, Ontario. He formed his own elevator construction company, and within five years had made his fortune. When he sold out and entered politics in 1934, he was the wealthiest man in the House of Commons.

No sooner had Howe settled into his new office than the trio of Richardson, Beatty and S. J. Hungerford (Thornton's successor at the CNR) bombarded him with inquiries concerning the future of Canadian Airways Ltd. Richardson was becoming more nervous with each day. He was aware that other well-connected entrepreneurs were starting to see the value of investing in aviation—and, as Liberal supporters, were closer to Howe. They included the young E. P. Taylor, J. H. Gundy, one of the founders of the investment firm Wood Gundy, and George McCullagh, soon to merge his *Mail and Empire* newspaper with the Toronto *Globe*.

Worried that he might be in disfavour with the Post Office, Richardson demonstrated his commitment to fast mail delivery by squandering what little money CAL had left on a pair of the latest Lockheed Model 10 Electras. Then the ultimate in aircraft, this Lockheed model had been made famous by Amelia Earhart, who had flown one across the Pacific Ocean alone earlier that year.[7] At $60,000 each, the sleek, stressed-skin, fast monoplanes were equipped with flaps and retractable undercarriages and could carry ten passengers at 200 mph—hardly bush equipment.

It is unclear when and why Howe turned against Richardson. As late as the summer of 1936, Howe assured the businessman that CAL would be the national airline. He had told Richardson's general manager, G. A. Thompson, quite specifically that he intended to "form one large company with Canadian Airways as the backbone." And in August Howe wrote to Richardson that he was about to present to Cabinet a very definite program for flying the mail and carrying passengers in which Canadian Airways would figure.[8] But perhaps Howe had promised his Liberal friends Gundy and McCullagh too much, and they were now exerting subtle pressure on him to accept their own airline company (which existed only on paper) as the official carrier. Or was it that the heat from Dominion Skyways (which now had Billy Bishop, V. C., the most famous Canadian air ace of all time, on its letterhead) was too strong? Prime Minister King was content to watch the drama from the wings.

TRANS-CANADA AIR LINES

By September 1936, Howe had stopped returning Richardson's calls, and he refused to hear a compromise plan put forth by Sir Edward Beatty. On November 2, Canada's first minister of transport gave an inkling of what was to come when he spoke before the Canadian Club in Montreal:

> The Department of Transport, which today takes over the work of the former Department of Railways and Canals, the former Department of Marine, and the Civil Aviation Branch of the Department of National Defence, results from the plan of the Prime Minister . . . In the field of civil aviation, steps are now being taken to set up a transcontinental service for passengers and mail. While Canada has an enviable record for transportation of mail, passengers and freight by air, in districts not served by any other forms of transport, it is behind most countries in providing air service along the main arteries of travel . . . without a bold transportation policy on a national scale, Confederation could not have been accomplished and efficient operation is required to prevent it from being a drain on the public purse.[9]

Even before the Christmas recess, the minister had worked it all out—and CAL was not part of his plan. Howe's airline would be called Trans-Canada Air Lines Company, and it would operate all air services between Halifax, Montreal and Vancouver, with the exclusive right to airmail contracts on trunk routes, where it was an essential service. Howe proposed that the new airline be owned half by the CPR and any aviation interests it wanted, and half by the CNR and any aviation interests it wanted. Each railway would put in $2.5 million. The airline's board would ultimately have seven members—four appointed by the CNR and three by the government, of which J. A. Wilson was one and C. P. Edwards, the director of radio in the Marine Department, another. The men chosen by the railway all came from the boards of banks, breweries and the mining industry, except for H.J. Symington, an unassuming Winnipeg corporate lawyer. Despite his mild appearance, Symington was an indefatigable worker, handpicked by Howe and destined to become the airline's president one day. The federal government would provide the new airline with airports, weather reports and radio services, and it agreed to pay all the company's operating costs for the first two years.

As a consolation prize, Howe offered Richardson a seat on the TCA board and shares in the government airline, finally holding out the possibility of feeder lines to the transcontinental route as well. But the proud Father of Commercial Aviation wanted no part of it. For the remainder of his life, Richardson held certain members of the Post Office responsible for poisoning his relations with Howe. He complained of this to King, but no evidence was found to support his claim.

Beatty was also dismayed. He knew that, as the CNR was a government-owned company, the cards would always be stacked against his own railway, although it was expected to contribute half the capital. On March 17, 1937, to the surprise of no one, the Canadian Pacific Railway formally withdrew from participating in Trans-Canada Air Lines.

The bill to create Trans-Canada Air Lines (TCA) was introduced in the House of Commons on March 22, 1937, and received royal assent on April 10. Howe, somewhat surprised at the speed of its passing, told the House, "I think that most of us are aware of the necessity for such a service. Canada is one of the few countries in the world without a national scheduled air service." He did not need to point out that one of the benefits of a national airline was that the RCAF could be taken off civil duties to assume a more belligerent stance, even as the newsreels showed German bombers laying waste to the Spanish city of Guernica.

The Canadian National's S. J. Hungerford was appointed TCA's first president. For the rest of the senior staff, Howe went to the United States. When criticized, the minister defended himself by saying that there were no Canadians qualified to run an airline. The minister's own role on the airline's board was left unexplained; if the term "puppet master" was bandied about, it was done out of earshot.

Richardson, bitterly disappointed, gave up his Vancouver-Seattle service to TCA, selling it the two Lockheed Electras as well. With the RCAF out of the way, airmail contracts became more plentiful, but even here CAL fared no better. Brintnell's Mackenzie Air Services underbid it for the Mackenzie River and Lake Athabasca region, as did Starrat Airways at Red Lake, Ontario. Richardson would later write in disgust that Starrat's bid for the contract was only a half a cent less per pound than his own.

Nevertheless, at the end of a disastrous decade, CAL was still the largest airline in Canada. Of the sixty commercial aircraft then registered in the country, twenty-six wore its "Flying Goose" insignia. Apart from the tried and tested Universals and Fairchilds, there were now four Junkers W-34s in its fleet. The disappointing Junkers 52 "CF-ARM" had been refitted with a Rolls-Royce Buzzard engine and began to make a name for itself carrying the bulkiest loads—albeit very slowly.

On June 26, 1939, at fifty-three years of age, James Richardson suffered a fatal heart attack. Even before his death, Canadian Airways Ltd., in deep financial trouble, withdrew from several routes to concentrate on what it did best: bush flying. The Winnipeg grain dealer–turned–aviation entrepreneur had stitched the country together before other less patriotic interests could, laying the foundations of commercial aviation in Canada. But in one of those extraordinary reversals that characterized the industry, by doing so he had somehow alienated the new minister of transport who, in his own way, was as committed to Canada and the industry. Later, during the war, it was reputed that those C.D. Howe took a dislike to suffered his wrath, which was delivered with the zeal of a biblical avenging angel. It might be said that this was entirely consistent with his genetic make-up—after all, one of his ancestors, Julia Ward Howe, had composed "The Battle Hymn of the Republic." Whatever the reason, James Richardson had earned Howe's displeasure and was made to pay the price.

Ironically, the Winnipeg financier would have the last laugh. Thirty-one years later, when Gordon McGregor, the president of Air Canada (as TCA had been renamed) retired, Ottawa looked around for a politically acceptable successor. By 1968, the days of Howe and Hungerford's friendship were long gone, and there was no love lost between the current minister of transport, Paul Hellyer, and McGregor.[10] In a twist of fate, the Liberal member of Parliament for Winnipeg and deputy minister of transport was Richardson's son, James Richardson Jr., and Hellyer gave him the job of shortlisting candidates for the Air Canada presidency.

CHAPTER SIX

Created by an Act of God: Trans-Canada Air Lines

Jim Spilsbury, the colourful founder of B.C.'s Queen Charlotte Airlines, once wrote that all airlines in Canada were begun by bush pilots, with the exception of Trans-Canada Air Lines, which was created by an act of God.[1] Perhaps because of its divine birth, the "official instrument of the government" was a quantum leap ahead of all others. By the last years of the 1930s, barnstorming and home-made aircraft had gone out of fashion. Commercial aviation emphasized a high degree of scientific knowledge, professionalism, rigid standards—and making a profit.

FIRST ON BOARD

On April 15, 1937, five days after the Trans-Canada Air Lines Act was proclaimed, its first employee was hired. Donald MacLaren was a Royal Flying Corps air ace, his forty-eight victories putting him in the exalted ranks of Billy Bishop, W. G. Barker and Ray

The first 71 employees hired by TCA were expected to do everything—besides working on the engines, engineers loaded mail and baggage and rolled the passenger steps up to the door of the aircraft. AIR CANADA ARCHIVES

Collishaw. Like many pilots of his generation, he returned to Canada after the war and in 1921 formed his own air company. Operating around English Bay, Vancouver, Pacific Airways Ltd. owned a single HS-2L used for fisheries patrol and sightseeing and, when that crashed, a Curtiss Jenny. Through the 1920s, emboldened by his prestige as a war hero, MacLaren protested the government's use of the air force for business that should have gone to commercial operators. He flew for Western Canada Airways and later served with Canadian Air Lines as superintendent of the western division, during which time he pleaded Richardson's case in Ottawa. Howe was impressed enough to hire MacLaren and later make him as assistant to the new vice-president of Trans-Canada Air Lines, Phil G. Johnson.

President of Boeing at the age of thirty-one and of United Airlines seven years later: it was little wonder that the newspapers called Phil Johnson "King of the Air." Then, in 1934, the Roosevelt administration conducted an investigation into airmail contracts and Johnson was blacklisted by the industry. Although later exonerated, he retired from the airline business and from public life. As a major shareholder in Boeing and United, he was so wealthy (and restless) that he bought the entire Kenworth truck company to run as a hobby. When Howe flew across the

United States on a fact-finding tour in 1936, he met Juan Trippe and C. M. Keys. Both recommended Johnson to him as a man who would enjoy the challenge of starting up an airline in another country. Howe hired him on June 24, 1937, as vice-president of operations and set him up in an office at the CNR building on McGill Street in Montreal. To the minister's delight, Johnson brought with him three talented executives from United Airlines—Don B. Colyer, O. T. Larson and H. T. "Slim" Lewis—and later hired Steve Stevens from Eastern Airlines. Lewis, in charge of training the pilots on the airline's new Lockheeds, was one of the few survivors of the original Suicide Club of U.S. airmail pilots. The Americans would play an essential part in TCA until there were enough Canadians with the skills and the confidence to take over.

The seventy-one employees hired in 1937 were a close-knit, enthusiastic group, aware not only of their good fortune at having steady government jobs during the Depression but also of being part of a great adventure. "The drill back then," said Al Took, the airline's first dispatcher, "was to work a long day, literally from sun up until your work was done—and seven days a week, if necessary. It was hard alright, but somehow we didn't mind.[2] Bill Harvey, an accounts clerk then, remembered that "Unfortunately for their families, TCA took over employees' lives. We didn't want to do anything but work." Russ Bulger joined as radio technician. "Because the Western Electric equipment used was so utterly reliable," he said, he had little to do. So he sold tickets, performed airport passenger check-ins, made out manifests, tested the radio, helped with the engine run-ups, and flew on the inaugural run to Seattle on September 1, 1937. Proof of Bulger's enthusiasm was that he wasn't even put on the company payroll until September 6. He remembered, "I was so happy to be working for TCA, I worked for love for the first six days."

Several experienced Canadian Airlines employees, such as E. P. Wells, Z. Lewis Leigh, Maurice McGregor, Duncan McLaren, George Lothian and Stan Knight, left to join TCA. Some, like W. L. English, F. T. Wood and Jack Smith, were drafted

American Phil G. Johnson had been president of Boeing and United Airlines when C. D. Howe hired him in 1937 as vice-president of operations at the newly established Trans-Canada Air Lines. AIR CANADA ARCHIVES

from the CNR infrastructure, chosen for their skills in accounting, sales or administration. The status of new employees ranged from McKee Trophy winners Romeo Vachon and John Henry "Tuddy" Tudhope to unknown youngsters such as Herb Seagrim and J. L. "Lindy" Rood, both of whom joined on the same day.

The staff were well paid for the Depression years. A vice-president earned $17,500 annually, and a captain received $400 monthly, more if he instructed. Considering that sirloin steak cost twenty-three cents a pound, a chocolate bar five cents, a movie twenty cents and a new Chevrolet sedan $700, Canadian salaries were comparable with those at airlines in the United States.

Flying was entering a glamorous period. Aircraft were no longer antiquated wood and canvas biplanes with more wires than a bird cage, their pilots bundled up in heavy clothing, goggles and leather helmets. The new generation of all-metal, stressed-skin monoplanes like the Boeing 247, the DC-3 and the Lockheeds were enclosed, smooth, shiny and sound-

proofed—sexy, in a word. The public was dazzled
by the latest version of the aviator as well. Enclosed,
heated cabins meant pilots could now wear
uniforms. By midsummer 1938, even Grant
McConachie's bush airline, United Air Transport,
dressed its crew in suits that would not have looked
out of place on the bridge of the *Queen Mary*. TCA
crews wore blue single-breasted uniforms with white
caps. If the pilot was a captain, his sleeve had two
gold rings; his co-pilot's sleeve sported one.

A liveried air crew was meant to reassure passengers and to compete with the service offered on
board the luxury ocean liners. Pan American Airways
was the first to pick up on the nautical theme, making its pilots "captains" of their Clippers. American
Airlines went one better and made their cabin staff
"stewardesses" and "pursers" (both terms taken from

The TCA radio operator had to be versatile, as he was often
the only person at the airport to service the flights. Shown
here is S.D. Leonard at Moncton Airport. AIR CANADA ARCHIVES

Cunard) and all their frequent flier passengers
"Admirals," entitling them to the use of specially
equipped lounges at airports.

The new breed of pilot, as portrayed by Hollywood, was a cool hero who always got the girl,
someone like Clark Gable in *Night Flight*, or Jimmy
Cagney in *Ceiling Zero*. He was endowed with the
sort of reputation that made fathers remove their
daughters hastily from his presence. Newsreels of the
day seemed to be filled constantly with dashing, one-
eyed, daredevil pilot Roscoe Turner (and his pet
lion), or boyish Amelia Earhart bravely crossing the
Atlantic alone, or the enigmatic Howard Hughes,

the moviemaker who flew from Los Angeles to Newark, New Jersey, in seven hours and twenty-eight minutes on February 19, 1937. Every magazine, radio program and newspaper reported altitude, speed and distance records, and it seemed as if the whole population held its breath for the outcome of a record flight. Scientific advancement notwithstanding, the publicity generated by aviators such as Erroll Boyd (the first Canadian to cross the Atlantic) or Jimmy Mollison (who crossed it three times) gave them a status akin to that of the Apollo astronauts forty years later.

In 1931, when Wiley Post and Harold Gatty flew around the world in eight days, their last stop before New York was Edmonton, where heavy rains had flooded Blatchford Airfield. Such was the public's enthusiasm for the aviators that, to keep them on schedule, airport manager Jimmy Bell insisted they use the paved street adjacent to the airport as a runway. The municipality had the electric wires removed from the poles; the streetcars trundled off and Mounties escorted Post's aircraft as it taxied down Portage Street. With what must have seemed like the whole population of Edmonton watching, the pair took off over the Hotel MacDonald (where the entire staff stood waving on the roof) to complete their flight.

A MINISTER'S STUNT

The Trans-Canada Airway was almost complete by 1938, with not only airports every hundred miles but radio stations as well. It was a Canadian, Reginald Aubrey Fessenden, who first successfully transmitted the human voice in 1902, and radio's first use in an aircraft was also by a Canadian—J. A. D. McCurdy on August 27, 1910, over Sheepshead Bay, New York. It was the Germans who discovered that radio waves could be directed, and in World War I they guided their zeppelins along "radio compasses" to bomb British cities. In the mid-1920s, to help airmail pilots at night and in poor weather, the U.S. Signal Corps devised "radio ranges." These were networks of ground units that furnished directional signals to aircraft in the air. The pilot wore his headphones at

all times and listened for the automatic signal sent out by the station, steering according to it. Simply put, the transmitting beacon sent out two signals in a quadrant that sounded "dit-dah," the letter "A" in Morse Code, and "dah-dit," the letter "N." A pilot could pick up either and know what part of the quadrant he was in. When he heard both he pointed his plane along the line where they came in, with the volume increasing until he was directly over the station itself in "a cone of silence." Pilots soon learned to fly from beacon to beacon, using them as motorists might navigate by signs on a highway.

It took practice to use the radio range effectively, and many bush outfits never utilized anything other than the traditional visual reference. But by watching his instruments and listening to the hum in his earphones, a pilot could fly across the country, locating and landing at airports at night and in bad weather.

C. D. Howe, ever the showman, dreamed up a stunt that he hoped would capture the headlines simultaneously for TCA, the Department of Transport and the completed Trans-Canada Airway. Along with a few colleagues, he would stage his own flight from Montreal's St. Hubert Airport to Vancouver's Sea Island, between sunrise and sunset on the same day. The dash over forest, prairie and mountain would demonstrate that transcontinental air travel was no longer only for swashbuckling record-breakers. The combination of the new Lockheeds, Wilson's string of freshly graded airports and C. P. Edwards's ever-vigilant radio operators would make the new mode of transport as easy, as humdrum, as taking a train or bus, Howe predicted. The flight would be a great psychological sop to a public still apprehensive about flying.

Phil Johnson and his Americans, aware of the million things that could go wrong, were horrified at Howe's idea—a circus act such as this was no way to launch an airline. The two TCA Lockheeds conveniently became unavailable. But Howe was determined. Instead, he requisitioned the Department of Transport's Lockheed 12A "CF-CCT" for the flight. DOT officials, taking no chances, had the plane fitted with an extra fuel tank. As symbolic as the completion of the Canadian Pacific Railway in 1885, the flight was scheduled to take place in July 1937, the month of the country's seventieth birthday.

The official party of wellwishers and passengers posed for a photograph in the pre-dawn hours of July 30. Not far away from the assembled party was a relic of another age. St. Hubert's airship mooring tower had cost the Canadian taxpayer $376,000, and it had been used only once, when the British Airship R-100 crossed the Atlantic on August 1, 1930. The tower would be dismantled in 1938, the dreams of the Empire Airship Service ending when the R-100's sister ship, the R-101, crashed on its way to India on October 5, 1930.[3]

With Tuddy Tudhope and co-pilot Jack Hunter at the controls, C. D. Howe, H. J. Symington, C. P. Edwards and J. A. Wilson boarded the Lockheed for Vancouver. Tudhope had just returned from piloting TCA's Johnson and MacLaren on a survey flight across the country in the same aircraft, and he knew the risks involved. The sky was threatening, the weather rainy and forbidding as the plane lifted off at 4:01 A.M. into the gloom over the sleeping city. A thunderstorm enveloped them after Montreal. Given the importance of his passengers to the future of Canadian aviation, Tudhope decided that it was too dangerous to continue and returned to St. Hubert. The aircraft was taxied to the hangar, but Howe insisted that Tudhope try once more. They left again at 5:18 A.M., and this time made it to an emergency airfield at Gillies, Ontario, near North Bay.

Bad weather followed them across the continent. Radio reports told the crew that all of western Ontario was blanketed in low cloud, and they couldn't find their next two stops, at Kapuskasing and Wagaming. The plane ploughed on across the unknown, the gas tanks draining alarmingly. After Kapuskasing, radio reception from the new beacons was poor, and Tudhope tried to calculate their position by dead reckoning. Edwards, who had been trained in wireless by Marconi himself, used Morse Code to hail the operator at Sioux Lookout. The aircraft had a range of about four hours between refuellings. Just as the reserve tank was ready to hit

empty, Tudhope's navigational skills put them into a break in the clouds directly above the town of Sioux Lookout. There were three more stops—Winnipeg, where they met a disapproving Johnson, Regina and Lethbridge—before the Rockies loomed. By now the thunderstorms had been left behind, and Tudhope took the little airliner above the cruising altitude of 8,000 feet to get over the mountains. Throughout the turbulence, Howe made a show of calmly reading his papers and smoking away. Seventeen hours and ten minutes after they had left St. Hubert (fourteen hours in actual flying time), they touched down at Vancouver in a rainstorm.

Howe disembarked from "CF-CCT" (now in the National Aviation Museum in Ottawa) beaming to the assembled press. It had been a close call, and there was no avoiding that, had they run out of gas and crashed at Sioux Lookout, it would been a serious blow to Canada's nascent aviation industry. On hearing of the narrow escape, the CPR's Beatty would say that Howe's power had gone to his head. But the publicity garnered was pure Hollywood, as Howe well knew. He understood that airlines would never become profitable until they could entice travellers away from the upholstered luxury of Pullman railway coaches and promise them as much in the air. The "dawn to dusk" flight proved that transcontinental air travel was no longer just for macho pilots or the idle rich. It was on the verge of becoming a family affair, if not yet for the masses, then at least for middle-income executives.

TCA TAKES TO THE AIR

TCA's inaugural flight was every bit as professional as Johnson had hoped it would be. On September 1, 1937, "CF-AZY," one of the two Electras bought from Canadian Airways, flew from Vancouver to Seattle, a distance of 122 miles. Maurice McGregor, who then flew with Canadian Airways, remembered the day years later:

On September 1, when Billy Wells and I had completed the daily run from Seattle to Vancouver, we were informed that with effect from that day, we

would be with Trans-Canada Airlines. The aircraft had been sold to TCA—that is the two Lockheeds, the Stearman mailplane and two trucks, plus a miscellaneous assortment of tools and equipment. So we and two or three mechanics and, I think, one helper were automatically at TCA. The name "Canadian Airways" was removed from the aircraft and in its place was painted "Trans-Canada Air Lines." TCA didn't have ticket stock, so we used Canadian Airways tickets. We just stroked out "Canadian Airways" and wrote in "TCA." We didn't have enough personnel. Billy Wells and I had to help load the baggage, we helped do the documentation, the customs declarations and so on. I remember very well that Percy Baldwin, who was the first auditor or comptroller for TCA, was looking in askance at us handling the tickets in this fashion. He said, "That isn't correct." We said, "It may not be correct but this flight must depart on time to Seattle."[4]

Waved off at Sea Island Airport by members of the Vancouver Board of Trade and curious on-lookers, the metallic bird flew into bright sunshine with Billy Wells and Maurice McGregor in the cockpit. Guest passengers were the mayor of Vancouver, George C. Miller, and the CNR's W. T. Moodie and

The Dawn to Dusk Flight: Members of C.D. Howe's party and officials who saw them off from St. Hubert Airport, Montreal, on July 30, 1937. From left to right: D.W. Saunders; L. Parmenter, engineer; F. I. Banghart, airport manager; W.H. Hobbs, secretary of TCA and CNR; H.J. Symington, TCA director; C.D. Howe; Squadron Leader J.H. "Tuddy" Tudhope, chief pilot; Commander C. P. Edwards, chief of air services, Department of Transport; J.D. Hunter, co-pilot; J. A. Wilson, controller of civil aviation; George Wakeman, federal inspector of air services; and D. R. MacLaren, TCA. AIR CANADA ARCHIVES

P. W. Baldwin. Representing the airline was Don MacLaren. Fifty minutes later, the Lockheed landed at Seattle Airport "with not a breath of wind, a perfect flight from everyone's point of view." The next morning the Seattle *Post Intelligencer* splashed news of the aircraft's arrival across the front page with "Elaborate ceremonies greet Canadian plane." The one-way air fare between the two cities was $7.90.

STAYING ALOFT

Three more Lockheed 10As, "TCA," "TCB" and "TCC," were delivered in October. Of the original two bought from Richardson, one was kept in Winnipeg for pilot training. The prairie city, with its surround-

ing flat terrain, was chosen as the training and maintenance base. Montreal remained the airline's administrative headquarters.

Rene Giguere, one of the original TCA pilots, recalled that there were nasty rumours circulating about the Lockheeds. They were all that bush planes weren't: twin-engined and faster than the DC-3, with flaps and retractable landing gear. They required different take-off and landing techniques as they tended to "balloon" out. For example, unlike bush planes, which floated down to a three-point landing, the Lockheeds had to be landed on their main undercarriage first. Until they learned the technique, trainee pilots bounced around the Winnipeg Airport runways like yo-yos.

Then there was the infamous Lockheed "stall," when the aircraft would suddenly nose-dive because the wings had lost their lifting capabilities. It took Jack Dyment, a mechanical genius hired by TCA as its chief engineer, to figure out a solution to this; he tried first cutting "slots" into the wings, then de-icing boots, and finally—successfully—moving the navigation lights on the wingtips back.

The Lockheeds were unpressurized and leaked very badly, especially in the cockpit. Many times, after flying through a rainstorm, the pilots would disembark soaked. Bill Norberg remembers one entry in the pilot's log: "Slight precipitation outside—raining like hell inside."

What really separated the bush outfits from the airlines was the new-fangled idea of flying on instruments alone—achieving an Instrument Flight Rating (IFR). To be profitable, airlines had to fly at night, on a schedule, in both good and bad weather, and this meant depending on instruments. To aviation pioneers who had navigated for decades by following the railroad or the contours of the ground and landmarks below, who had flown by the instinct that laypeople called "the seat of their pants," having to rely on an array of instruments was frightening. Most bush planes of the day had an airspeed indicator, a turn and bank indicator and an oil temperature gauge. Now there was a proliferation of indicators to monitor—an artificial horizon, a directional gyro, gauges for each engine, flap positions, landing gear positions and hydraulic pressure—and radio direction beacons to listen for. The pilot's senses told him to orientate himself by looking outside the aircraft, but his mind forced him to disregard that and fly by what was on the dashboard and in his headphones. Many bush pilots could not make the transition to "blind" flying and quit.

Most maintenance engineers were recruited from bush operators and flying clubs. Stan Knight was an old hand at aero engines by 1937. His first job had been as an apprentice air engineer, beginning on Christmas Day, 1926, when the Ontario Provincial Air Service hired him at Sault Ste. Marie to work on their flying boats. Later he joined Western Canada Airways and was posted to the Mackenzie River area. He began TCA ground training at Winnipeg, moving shortly to Regina and working on the night flights. Bruce Saunders was still at aeronautical school in New Jersey when his principal was approached by Johnson, who was looking for promising students. Sam Reid got into aeromechanics in Vancouver through a correspondence course in 1928 and spent the next nine years fixing bush planes with the most primitive of tools and usually in uncomfortable places. Once he repaired a broken aileron on a flying boat with an old piece of brake cable from a motorcycle while bobbing around in the water. He transferred from Canadian Air Lines when TCA took over the Vancouver-Seattle route and then moved to Winnipeg to service the Lockheed 14Hs.

The airline was a simple hierarchy then, recalled Jack McDougall, the vice-president of maintenance and engineering, half a century later. "There were people who sold tickets, people who flew airplanes and people who fixed them. It was expected that an experienced hand knew his aircraft inside out. He was often able to fix any part of it." The early TCA air engineers were expected to know how to do every-

thing, and frequently did. Before take-off they did the ground check, called "flight dispatch," calculated the fuel load and filled the tanks. Then they rolled the passenger stairs up to the aircraft, loaded the baggage on, called the stewardess and told her to bring the passengers out. Once everyone was on board, the engineer shut the door and stood by with a fire extinguisher while the engines started up. He watched the aircraft taxi off and then returned to the hangar to begin his real job of fixing engines. The monthly salary for all of this, Duncan McLaren recalled, was $120, and it was an eight-hour rotating shift.

For Bill Norberg, one of the apprentices at the Winnipeg "shop," there was a great sense of pride in working for TCA and on the Lockheeds. "The tools and equipment were all new and shone like bright, shiny nickels. And so did the aircraft. I remembered being impressed by that when I first started. Those aircraft had dignity . . . and personality as they represented a whole new industry for Canada. I can still see the landing gear 'wobble' up into the retracted position after take-off, just like a bird tucking its feet up."

But what were they like to fly? Captain Rene Giguere, who would retire flying DC-9 jets, thought that the 10As were well designed, reliable and comfortable. The cabin, however, did not have the full headroom of later aircraft, and one had to bend almost double to move about. In fact, that was a running joke: you could always tell a 10A pilot by the way he walked bent over. To Giguere, the aircraft was the "Silver Bird," because the pheasants used to chase it at Vancouver airport on take-off and landing. It flew so beautifully, he felt, maybe they were jealous. As a new pilot, George Lothian watched the first of the bigger Lockheed 14s arriving at Winnipeg on May 10, 1938: "The word was out to get plenty of speed on the ground before take-off in case of engine failure. The practical types said get 110 mph on the clock before take-off or take-off before the runway was used up, whichever comes first."

A wholly new airline profession was that of the flight dispatcher. The World War II movies that show bomber pilots being briefed before they take off on missions are good examples of what dispatchers did before the computerized age. In the early days, an airliner that took off was like a nineteenth-century sailing ship. Until it physically landed at its destination, no one knew its exact whereabouts, and the pilot himself had little idea as to what weather he might encounter. Dispatchers gathered all the information they could about the weather that the pilot was going to fly through and plotted the flight's course. Then they briefed the crew, going over the route and designating alternate airports in case of poor weather. After the aircraft had taken off, they checked with its captain until he was out of range.

Ted Larson and Steve Stevens set up the dispatching office at Winnipeg with two former Canadian Airways pilots, Fred Stull and Frank Barager. Stull and Barager guided the pilots by radio on take-offs and landings. Al Took was a civilian army radio operator in Regina when he heard that the government airline was recruiting. He was hired on December 10, 1937, as the airline's seventy-fifth employee. He lived at the Winnipeg YMCA while working at the airfield. "We worked out of the old Canadian Airways Hangar," Al said. "It was a tin hangar, consisting mainly of a radio room, a weather office, with enough room inside it to house an old Junkers aircraft and the two Lockheed Electras." One of Al's first assignments was to accompany TCA pilots Walt Fowler and Lindy Rood on a training flight between Winnipeg, Regina and Lethbridge. He was paid $95 a month and lived in barracks-style accommodation for many of his eleven transfers, which began three weeks after joining TCA.

The dispatcher, Al said, "did just about everything." He refuelled the aircraft with wobble pumps, assisted the mechanics in the subzero temperatures and, in one of the most memorable daily exercises, "went remote." This consisted of keeping the pilot informed of local weather, traffic and airfield conditions by breaking off ground-to-air communications, dashing to the roof of the radio shack, having a quick look around and then breathlessly dashing back, to report in time for the pilot's final approach and landing. "We had to move pretty fast when we went 'remote'—and often went up top in shirt sleeves with the winter wind biting through us."

Ches Rickard had been a pharmacist before becoming involved in setting up the Trans-Canada Airway radio communications system in 1935. He joined TCA in 1937 as a "radio man" and discovered that this meant doing everything else as well. "Everyone did whatever was necessary to create and keep our budding airline running," he said. "It was not unusual in a day at one of the smaller stations to act as a radio operator, weather observer, passenger agent, ground equipment maintenance man, snow shoveller, assistant to the aircraft mechanic, as well as address a dinner group on the future and operation of Canada's 'big' airline."

SELLING THE SERVICE

At 10:00 P.M. on July 31, 1937, Wally Courtney received a phone call in Victoria. It was Don MacLaren. "You better get the midnight boat and turn up at the CN office in Vancouver first thing tomorrow. We're going to be in business in the morning." Courtney had worked in sales for Alaska-Washington Airways, the Northern Pacific Railway and Canadian Airways. Appearing at the CN office as instructed, Courtney introduced himself to the railway agent, a Mr. Hay, who didn't know anything about sharing his office with an airline. Later that day, Hay received a telegram from the CNR headquarters in Montreal. It read: "Move over and make room for Mr. Courtney." And that was how TCA hired its first sales staff. At forty-three, Courtney was older than his boss MacLaren. With D.H. Bunch, he was the airline's total sales force until George Wakeman was hired in Montreal in 1938.

Knowing they could never equal the Canadian Pacific trains or Cunard ships for comfort, or Greyhound buses for convenience, the TCA sales staff concentrated on the aircraft's advantage—speed. They hit businessmen's clubs and Rotary luncheons. Banks, law firms and media offices were targeted with promotional material and personal calls. They pointed out the advantages to company managers—

the sales territory that could be covered in days rather than weeks, the prestige of arriving at a client's city by air. "Flying," as one magazine advertisement shouted, "was for the Man on the Make."

Very few women flew, and this was a market that the sales department would have liked to open up. An imaginative airline sales traffic manager in the United States hit upon the idea of giving free tickets to the wives who accompanied their husbands on trips. The result was that his aircraft were filled with happy couples for the first time in aviation history. A month later, he sent out letters of appreciation to the wives, expressing the hope that, as they had liked the flight so much, they would fly again. He was surprised by the angry tone of their replies. It seems that few of the travelling companions had actually been wives after all.

What the TCA salesmen didn't need to emphasize was that flying was also the preferred method of travel for the famous. The top level of aero royalty were the movie stars who were regularly photographed on aircraft stairs. American Airlines made sure it carried Clark Gable and Vivien Leigh to Atlanta for the opening of *Gone with the Wind* and, later, Orson Welles to New York for *Citizen Kane*. In fact, legend had it that Hollywood mogul Howard Hughes actually bought TWA to fly his studio starlets about.

Pat Maxwell was one of TCA's first stewardesses, and in 1938 she had what she remembered as one of the biggest disappointments of her life. The Lockheed 10 being used on the Seattle-Vancouver route had ten seats, nine for the passengers and one for the stewardess. One day as they were getting ready to leave Seattle with five passengers, movie star Robert Taylor arrived with a party of four to catch the flight. To make room for the tenth passenger, Maxwell was left behind.

C. D. Howe hopped on his TCA Lockheeds whenever he had a chance. Russ Bulger remembered one flight when Howe and TCA President Phil Johnson arrived unexpectedly, and the only food on board was Bulger's own lunch. "They helped me with it," he said, "and radioed ahead for some more."

The company's entire accounts department consisted of Bill Harvey and Percy Baldwin. If Harvey worked late at the old tin hangar and missed his chance of a ride on the firetruck back into town, he slept on a table, surrounded by files to keep himself from falling off. He would take "a yard of sandwiches to work and stay there for days." Accounting was the first TCA department established outside the jurisdiction of the CNR. "The CN thought TCA was just a pesky fly they couldn't get rid of and that it was being run by a bunch of kids who didn't know up from down," Harvey recalled. As one of the kids, he ended his career in the airline as senior vice-president of finance.

PILOT TRAINING

With Howe and Hungerford's approval, Johnson designated 1938 as a training year. Ten Lockheed 14H Super Electras were added to the fleet and used on practice runs that took the mail and freight between Montreal and Vancouver. On November 18, one of these, "CF-TCL," crashed as it took off from Regina, killing pilots Dave Imrie and Jack Herald. Lockheed and TCA investigators speculated that a fire in the cockpit had been caused by the proximity of the fuel lines to the electrical controls of the engine fire extinguishers. Aircraft were modified by trial and error, and it sometimes took a tragedy to bring a serious problem to light.

Flying practice flights across the prairies was one thing, but crossing the Rockies was another. Usually TCA flew at levels of between 5,000 and 8,000 feet, but over the Rockies, the Lockheeds would have to climb to 11,000 or 12,000 feet. Without pressurization, flying in such a rarefied atmosphere meant anoxia, or oxygen deprivation, which led to eventual unconsciousness and death. After Maurice McGregor had a near crash flying a 14H between Vancouver and Winnipeg, oxygen became mandatory for flights over 6,000 feet—for crew and passengers alike.

Then there was icing. If enough ice builds up on an aircraft wing, tail or propeller, it destroys the air flow around the plane. Heavy accumulation on the upper surface of the wing soon results in loss of lift, and even if the engines are run at full power, the wing's angle of attack increases until a stall occurs. The best defence against icing is to climb higher, into colder, drier air, or to avoid flying through clouds at all—both of which were impossible for the TCA Lockheeds in the mountains. The airlines developed mechanical de-icers, long pneumatic tubes stretched along the leading edge of the aircraft wing. These were effective only some of the time. "The only cure-all for ice was to get the hell out of it," one veteran of the Rockies crossing recalled. Herb Seagrim had a narrow escape from icing on the Vancouver-Lethbridge run. He and Captain Bill Barnes had picked up a heavy load of ice over the Rockies that they could not shake off. As they began their descent into Lethbridge, radio reports warned that the temperature on the ground was below freezing, so there was no hope of losing the ice once they got to the airport. Reducing speed on final approach with ice on the wing increased the risk of stalling. They could only stay in the air "by coming in like a rocket." They radioed this to the ground staff at Lethbridge, and fences were taken down at either end of the runway in case of an overshoot. But as they made a circuit of the airport, Seagrim and Barnes saw, to their relief, that the ice was disappearing in large chunks from the wings. They had run into one of the region's famous Chinooks.

PASSENGER COMFORTS

Comfort for Canadian air travellers before the arrival of the TCA Lockheeds was nil. Only masochists flew. Before take-off, pilots on Fokkers and Fords might pass out chewing gum, wads of cotton wool and "erp" cups to the travellers. The gum was to equalize pressure during take-off and landing, the cotton wool so that the passenger would be able to hear after the flight, and the cup to be used in case of turbulence. Because the Fokkers and Junkers had an engine mounted to the fuselage—as did the Ford Trimotor—vibrations and oil fumes made passengers' lives miserable. And it wasn't only the proximity to the engine. Early in the Second World War, defence engineers discovered that what caused the

most noise was actually the propellers. Conversation was impossible, and in any case, the passengers sat too petrified and sickened by turbulence to converse.

The first Canadian family to travel across the country by TCA were the Findlays. W. O. Findlay, a CBC executive in Ottawa, was on his way to attend the 1939 Royal Visit in Victoria. Accompanying him were his wife and their two sons, six-week-old Donald and one-year-old Billy.[5] The airfare from Ottawa to Vancouver was $145 one way. Mrs. Findlay remembered the snow-covered Ottawa runway very well. She was struck by the number of male passengers on the flight. "I looked back at the men," she recalled, "and they looked a bit nervous. When they realized that there was a young mother on board with her family, it gave them some confidence." The plane touched down and took off eight times, in places she had never heard of. "North Bay was under water so we had to fly on to Kapuskasing. We landed and were taxiing down the runway when all of a sudden the ice crust broke and we nosed downward to an abrupt halt." Fortunately, no damage was done.

At Regina, curious onlookers came to pay their respects in the wee hours of the morning . . . in cocktail dress! Mrs. Findlay remembered holding up the sleeping baby, wrapped in his father's christening gown, to the window. From outside came a chorus of cheers. Then it was off again and over the Rockies.

"The airplane was noisy . . . and it seemed flimsy. From time to time we would hit an air pocket and whoosh . . . our hearts were in our mouths," she remembered. But overall, it was a smooth trip. A crisis arose when Mrs. Findlay went to the tiny washroom: "I pressed the toilet pedal. You could see houses down there! I didn't want to run the risk of landing a diaper on someone's head, so I stuffed them in a bag I had brought with me."

Initially the only concession to aircraft passengers had been a packet of sandwiches thrown into one's lap by the disgruntled co-pilot, who made everyone aware that he hadn't taken all those flying lessons to become an airborne waitress. But the flying boats of

Imperial Airways and Pan American were large enough to have well-equipped galleys in which stewards prepared five-course meals and served them in a dining room complete with tablecloths and fresh flowers. Once their flights became longer than three hours, American Airlines and United began using giant jars specially designed by the Thermos company to keep food warm, and the contents were ladled out onto plates by the stewardess during the flight. Food was cooked at the airport restaurant; this was convenient, as no one really knew how many passengers were going to show up. As part of Canadian National Railways, TCA was able to rely on CN's kitchens.

As flights increased in length and aircraft had the capability to carry ten or more passengers, what was called for was not just an airborne waitress but a nurse, a mother, a luggage handler and, ideally, someone who could hose vomit off the cabin floor, fit everyone with oxygen masks and, in a pinch, help push the aircraft out of the hangar.

The TCA Lockheed cabins were low-ceilinged and, as "tail-draggers," the planes were on an uncomfortable angle while on the ground. So members of the cabin crew had to be less than 5'4", yet strong enough to carry people's bags, seal the door shut (and restrain drunks from mistakenly trying to reopen it under the impression it led to the toilet), and balance hot coffee while the aircraft pitched about. Imperial Airways used only male stewards, fostering, they hoped, the ambience of the best clubs and officers' messes. American Airlines considered hiring Filipino males until United Air Lines got the idea of using nurses. What better way to convince the hesitant public of the safety of flying than with the sight of a petite young woman who flew daily for a living? United even made their first stewardesses wear nurses' uniforms while serving meals.

STEWARDESSES GET ON BOARD

Pat Eccleston (now Maxwell) was a nurse at St. Paul's Hospital in Vancouver in June 1938 when she saw Trans-Canada Air Lines' advertisement for stewardesses. "I wasn't interested in this new glamorous

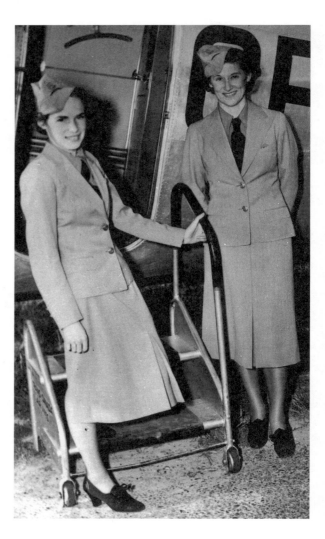

Lucille Garner (*right*) and Pat Eccleston were the first stewardesses TCA hired. Until 1957 all stewardesses had to be registered nurses. AIR CANADA ARCHIVES

job. Things were going fine where I was. But one of the nurses said to me, 'I'll bet you $5 that you wouldn't dare to apply.' With that challenge, I put in my application and three days later I had a phone call saying I was hired. I had never even been to an airport before."

Lucille "Luke" Garner of Regina, a registered nurse trained at Montreal's Royal Victoria Hospital, was working for a doctor in Vancouver that year. Her entry into the career was less conventional. In Montreal, Captain Bob Bowker, who had been flying in eastern Canada for American Airlines, met Killby Harding, one of Luke's nursing classmates. When Bowker joined TCA and came out to Vancouver to crew with George Lothian, he thus had an introduction to a single nurse. Over dinner, Bowker suggested that Garner apply for a stewardess position by calling Western Division assistant superintendent Billy Wells. With transcontinental flights

Bay store, where "the staff came up with what appeared to be an appropriate cap and uniform." After a few flights with Garner, Crispin (who would marry George Lothian) began as the stewardess on the Vancouver-Seattle run. The Lockheed IOA did not have a galley, and in-flight service was basic. There was a tiny cupboard in the rear that contained the food. The meals consisted of box lunches and

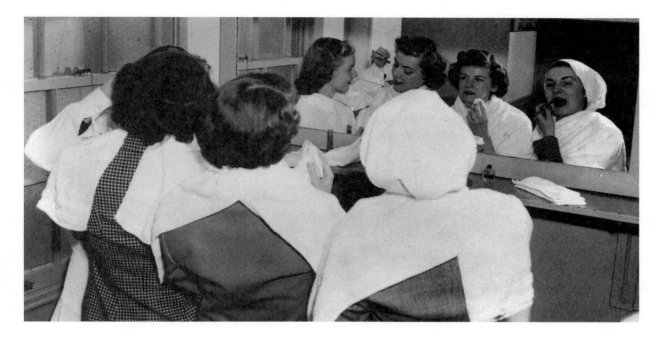

There were strict regulations governing stewardesses' personal appearance. Only approved lipstick and nail polish colours were allowed, and hair was not to be worn below the collar. AIR CANADA ARCHIVES

looming, Wells was looking for someone to organize TCA's in-flight service. Many years later, Lothian would write in his memoirs: "She impressed Wells so much that he sent her for a final interview to P. G. Johnson." Garner set to work. She had never seen a stewardess in action and had very little information to base her requirements on other than "a pilot's manual and a borrowed copy of a United Air Lines stewardess manual." But before going to Winnipeg with Pat Eccleston, where the first stewardess class was to be held, she needed someone in Vancouver for the Seattle run. So in November 1938 a third stewardess—Rose Crispin— was hired.

Rose was given a pilot's manual and told to get a navy-blue suit. Her aunt took her to the Hudson's

coffee from a thermos. "It was always a piece of cake and an apple," another stewardess recalled. "It wasn't much but at least it was food, even if it was served on a pillow on the passenger's lap."

As chief stewardess, Garner, with Eccleston as her assistant, sifted through hundreds of applications, bringing successful applicants to Winnipeg by air for an interview. The graduating class consisted of Evelyn Allan, Margaret Beeber, Margaret Brass, Annette Brunelle, Geralde Brunelle, Killby Harding, Constance Haibeck, Ruth Leslie, Marcelle Levac, Pat

McNamara, Sheila Neill, Dorothy Price, Florence Shanahan, Norah Wallace and Margaret Wilson.

A description of what a TCA stewardess should be appeared in the November 1939 issue of *Canadian Nurse.* "The TCA stewardess must be a girl of good education and she must have a pleasing and courteous manner. These things naturally follow when she is a nurse. It follows too that she will be in excellent

Sam J. Hungerford and Lucille Garner in front of a Lockheed 14. As the president of the Canadian National Railway, Hungerford also became TCA's first president in 1937, but he wisely allowed Howe and his team of Americans to run the airline. AIR CANADA ARCHIVES

physical condition. TCA is strict about this and stewardesses report for medical examinations every three months. The regulations say that a girl must not wear glasses and they add definite specifications about her height and weight. She may weigh as little as 95 but not more than 125 lbs. She must not be under 21 nor over 26 years of age. Married women are not acceptable as TCA stewardesses, even if their husbands are dead or divorced. Only Canadians are engaged." The article noted that "stewardesses must be practical and poised women, cheerful and tactful and experienced in the art of helping people forget their nervousness and helping them feel at ease."

Regulations were strict on appearance. The airlines wanted stewardesses to remind passengers more of the girl next door rather than a femme fatale. Only certain colours of lipstick and nail polish were allowed. Hair was not to be below the collar; girdles were mandatory, as were stockings, except in summer during the war, when leg paint could be worn if properly applied. A *Globe and Mail* reporter summed it up best that year when he wrote: "Girls seeking to become stewardesses must combine the comeliness of Venus with the capabilities of Florence Nightingale to qualify."

Not mentioned in the requirements were versatility and a good sense of humour. Eccleston remembered a passenger who travelled two or three times a week from Vancouver to Seattle. On his way to Sea Island Airport he was regularly stranded on the wrong side of the water when the old Marpole Bridge opened. His secretary would phone the airport, begging them to hold the flight. Alone in the office, Eccleston made an executive decision: "He was our only passenger, so I said okay." The pilots used to call the run the Maple Leaf route—"Maple we'll leave and maple we won't."

One of Garner's graduates, Margaret Wilson, was designated to be the stewardess on the VIP Parliamentary Press Gallery flight from Ottawa to Vancouver on March 20, 1939, since she was the only one with a full uniform. Wilson was sent from Winnipeg to Toronto by mail flight and overnighted at the Royal York Hotel, where she discovered she was responsible for her own room and phone bill.

Pat Maxwell spoke for every TCA employee when she remembered those early days: "Every take-off was an adventure. It was thrilling, and you had to have an eye for the people who looked apprehensive. You had to relieve their fears, and that's where our nurses' training came in handy. I remember once when flying at night, a passenger became anxious when the red and green navigation lights located on the wing tips disappeared in the fog. She had been told that the pilot had to fly between those two lights."

"The perfect flights are all forgotten," said Ross Smyth, one of the first radio operators hired by the airline, "but the crowded waiting room crammed with thirty passengers from three weather-grounded Lockheeds are still remembered . . . along with the night we used the local hospital for stranded passengers." The radio operator was often the only TCA employee at the airport when the flight came in, and as a result "was a jack-of-all-trades. During the ten minute stopover, he put the passenger loading steps in position, greeted the stewardess, gave her a thermos of water previously heated on a hot plate in the office. It was for the instant coffee.

"He also opened the cargo compartment, removed the pouch with company mail, juggled a couple of bags of Royal Mail and occasionally some baggage, hastened back to his office to complete the load and balance clearance for the captain, then sent one or two telegrams for the passengers. All within ten minutes."

The decade of the 1930s is sometimes referred to as the age of heroes, and certainly Erroll Boyd, Wiley Post and Amelia Earhart were heroes. But no less heroic were all those who pioneered the first scheduled airline operations for Trans-Canada Air Lines, the airline created by an act of God.

A TCA Lockheed Lodestar over the Rockies. A civil version of the Hudson bomber, the Lodestar allowed the airline to spread its wings during the war, flying to New York and to Torbay, Newfoundland. AIR CANADA ARCHIVES

CHAPTER SEVEN

The Shape of Things to Come

Even as C. D. Howe was shepherding his Trans-Canada Air Lines bill through the House of Commons in April 1937, Prime Minister Mackenzie King was on his way to London to attend the annual Imperial Conference. King's seven-day voyage on the *Empress of Australia* was not a pleasant one and only underlined the need for trans-Atlantic travel by air.

THE NEXT FRONTIER

It would be King's first Imperial Conference since 1926, when he had returned enthusiastic about committing Canada to the Empire's globe-girdling airship scheme. This time, as prime minister and secretary of state for external affairs, he looked to keep out of Old World entanglements. Europe seemed to be sliding towards war, and King's view was that the less Canada became involved in London's plans to join all of the Dominions by air the better. Thanks to far-sighted men like Wilson and Howe, King arrived in London with a firm national aviation policy: however rudimentary, Canada now had a Department of Transport, a string of airports from coast to coast and a government airline.

The prime minister cast himself as an elder statesman at the conference, relishing his role as a conciliator between Britain, Germany and the United States. His speeches made it clear that he had moved his country's destiny—in the air at least— closer to the United States and away from the Mother Country, and cooperating with the British on commercial air services, especially over the Atlantic, would mean antagonizing the Americans. King's refusal to be drawn into any cooperative agreement on Empire air services forced the new British prime minister, Neville Chamberlain, to search for other ways of dealing with the German threat. Thoroughly enjoying his power, King then left for Germany to chat with Adolf Hitler and give the Germans permission to overfly Canada on their Berlin–New York flights.

On July 5 of that year, both Pan American and Imperial Airways began experimental flights across the Atlantic Ocean, using flying boats. First crossed by air on June 14, 1919, from St. John's, Newfoundland, by John Alcock and Arthur Whitten Brown, the Atlantic was not only a physical hurdle for aviators; it had a diplomatic significance for their governments as well. But at a time when aero engines were consistently unreliable, when taking on the necessary fuel meant dangerously overloading the aircraft for take-off, when the chances of being rescued after a "ditching" were nil, flying over so much water seemed to be sheer stupidity.

The first Canadian to fly the Atlantic Ocean did so on the proverbial shoestring. Perhaps the penniless Erroll Boyd caught the bug during the First World War, when his instructor in the Royal Flying Corps was John Alcock himself. In 1930, Boyd borrowed a secondhand Bellanca, christening it the *Maple Leaf* in the hope of getting sponsorship for a trans-Atlantic flight from Toronto businessmen.[1] But the Depression had bitten hard into the country, and no sponsorship was forthcoming. Boyd flew the *Maple Leaf* to Montreal to try his luck there but couldn't collect enough to even pay his hotel bill.

The Atlantic crossing might have been abandoned there and then had not some McGill University students smuggled Boyd, disguised as a waiter, out of the hotel through its kitchen. At St. Hubert Airport, the Bellanca was impounded by police because its landing fees had not been paid. The manager of the local Canada Dry Ginger Ale company came to Boyd's rescue and paid the fine, and when the hat was passed around to fill the gas tank, apparently even the police constable guarding the aircraft contributed. Boyd and his American navigator, Harry P. Conner, left for Newfoundland on September 13. There storms delayed them, and it would not be until October 9 that they could take off from Harbour Grace Airfield into the wintery Atlantic weather.[2] Twenty-four hours later, a blocked fuel pipe forced them down on a beach on the Scilly Islands near Cornwall. It had been a near thing, but a Canadian had flown the Atlantic. Between 1927 and 1936, sixteen more aircraft took off from Harbour Grace, four of which disappeared completely.

But there were those, such as Pan American's Juan Trippe and George Woods Humphrey of Imperial Airways, who saw the great expanse of water not as a threat but as the most lucrative passenger route on the planet. The millions who travelled annually between the Old World and the New, crammed aboard ships, could one day be crammed aboard airplanes. As early as 1931, Trippe began manoeuvring Pan American into a favourable position by operating a daily flight between Boston and Halifax, hoping to extend this one day to St. John's, Newfoundland. Given airliners with suitable range— and strategically placed refuelling points along the route—he felt that Atlantic air travel was commercially viable.

The "stepping stones" across the Atlantic were the Azores, Bermuda, Newfoundland and Ireland—all colonies (or former colonies) of European powers.

Without refuelling stops there, gasoline posed a problem. Deutsche Lufthansa stationed liners like the *Bremen* permanently in the mid-Atlantic to refuel its flying boats on their way to South America. The British were even more ingenious. In addition to in-flight refuelling, they used a Short-Mayo composite aircraft—a large flying boat with a smaller one on its back that could be launched to complete the journey. On July 21, 1938, Imperial Airways Captain Don Bennett completed a trip from London by landing in Montreal with the upper half of the Short-Mayo component, completing the trip in twenty hours. But at best these were stop-gap measures until long-range airliners could be developed.

Canada, like Ireland, figured in the race to fly the ocean only by virtue of its geographic location. A highly organized American expedition had flown from New York to Southampton in Navy Curtiss flying boats, refuelling at Newfoundland, the Azores and Portugal. They used the southern staging route which, due to the curvature of the earth, meant more flying time over the open sea than the shorter northern one used by British pilots. New York might be the ultimate terminal of oceanic flights, but on the Great Circle, Montreal was closer to Europe. Because of this, Canada assumed an importance in early trans-Atlantic travel that far outweighed its technical capability to participate.

THE JOINT OPERATING COMPANY

In 1935, in anticipation of imminent flights, the governments of Britain, Canada, Ireland and the colony of Newfoundland had met in Ottawa to discuss Atlantic air services. They formed the Joint Operating Company, which optimistically agreed to cooperate on trans-Atlantic flights and to construct flying-boat bases for impending flights at Botwood, Newfoundland; Shediac, New Brunswick; and Longueuil, near Montreal. Rather sportingly, they allowed the competition, Pan American's Sikorsky s-42 Clippers, to use Shediac (an old RCAF anti-rum smuggling base) between Foynes, Ireland, and New York, which was a longer trip over water. Imperial Airways chose Longueuil, which was near St. Hubert

Airport, as its North American terminal. The arrangement, examined from this distance, seems to weigh heavily in favour of the British and the Americans, whose aircraft would attract the traffic and the glory, while Canada supplied meteorological and wireless services. But with no Canadian aircraft capable of flying the Atlantic, it was all Ottawa could hope for.

As luxurious as the flying boats were, with their three-tiered bunks and stewards, they had their limitations. The public might feel that they were safer because, if forced down, the plane could float until help arrived. But the leviathans were enormously heavy, unpressurized and difficult to service, and they could only fly in the summer, when the ice at Shediac had melted. Imperial Airways had high hopes for landplanes, including their sleek de Havilland Albatross wooden airliner—an ominous name for an aircraft if ever there was one—and in anticipation the British Air Ministry completed a huge airport in 1938 at a railway stop in Newfoundland called Hattie's Camp, later renamed Gander. But by the time the Albatross prototype was ready, all British aircraft production had been switched over to military purposes for the approaching war, and Gander was deserted—becoming an early version of Mirabel Airport in the present day.[3]

Pan American had no landplanes at all, and needed none. Its mammoth Boeing 314 Clippers, which had a range of 4,000 miles, were just then coming on stream.[4] In any case, once the war began, the United States Neutrality Act prevented Pan American from using Shediac, and it switched to the southern route via the Azores instead. One of the last to transit through Shediac was future prime minister Lester B. Pearson, who was in Ottawa when Germany invaded Poland in September 1939. As the First Secretary at the High Commission in London, he felt his presence vital enough to secure a berth on the very next Clipper leaving New York for Europe. Canadian diplomats then customarily travelled to their posts by sea, and Pearson must have very persuasive to justify the added expense to Under-Secretary of State for External Affairs O. D. Skelton.

Pearson would later write that he shared a cabin on board the Clipper with two reserve army officers, German and Polish, who were going home to probably kill each other.

CANADA GOES TO WAR

With Canada's entry into the war in 1939, commercial aviation was seriously affected. Gordon Ballentine, a Canadian Airways pilot in Vancouver, remembered the early days of the conflict:

We had to black out the aircraft's windows going over Esquimault. The Department of Transport and the military required that we black out the plane within ten minutes of there. When we said, "Why?" they said, "Well, a passenger could drop an incendiary out of the back door and you couldn't stop them."

There were lots of things you couldn't buy during the war. The military needed it. We commonly ran out of oxygen, and flying at 16,000 or 18,000 feet without oxygen was a very tiring business. But the military got it—fair enough. We weren't getting shot at. They deserved it. And you couldn't buy flying boots—you know, these fuzzy-lined things. Felt slippers and prairie overshoes were the best you could do, because the military were getting the flying boots—quite rightly. They deserved it. Well, the front end of a Lockheed 14 is a bloody cold place to be. You might leave Vancouver at 40 above in the wintertime and end up in Whitehorse at 40 below! What sort of clothes would you wear? If you put on your Stanfields you'd be clammy before you got to Hope, and then cold from then on because you were wet. I finally evolved my own system. I could always wear a sweater, that's easy to dispose of. For the bottom, I used to wear flannelette pajamas, instead of underwear. Nobody knew I had them on. Somewhere around Prince George, I would tuck my pajama bottoms into my socks, take off my uniform shoes and put on a pair of felt slippers and my prairie overshoes. It was pretty comfortable . . .

A great deal of our passenger load [on the Vancouver-Victoria run] was for government business, of course . . . because of the war, there was a

hell of a lot of travel to the capital. One of our most constant passengers was the then Attorney General of British Columbia, Gordon Wismer. One day I was down to the dock a little ahead of time and he was looking at the airplane, a de Havilland Dragon Rapide which carried about seven passengers. Twin engined thing. The pilot's compartment was one little greenhouse-room for one person, period. Anyway, he was looking at it and he said, "Where's the machine-gun?" It just rocked me on my heels. I said, "What machine-gun?" He said, "You mean to say there's nothing up there? You're going over Esquimault drydock, which is a very sensitive area." And I said, "Hell, there's hardly room for me up there." Then he said, "Well, of course, you can carry a gun yourself, or a pistol or something." And I said, "No, I have no licence to carry a pistol." So he just said, "We'll see about that."

The next day, we had orders to equip all pilots with sidearms. I was chief pilot then, so I had to go around all the shops on the Lower Mainland for pistols. I carried mine in a shoulder holster so nobody knew I had it on. Actually it was a ridiculous requirement. The only time I ever had the faintest possible use for it was when I had a drunken passenger who was all by himself on the airplane and insisted on doing things which I thought were dangerous. I was over water and couldn't get out of the seat or land to stop him. I was on the point of pulling out this damned pistol I was wearing. Fortunately, before I did it, I thought, "Well, if I pull it out, there's only two things I can do with it. I can either shoot this guy or put it back. In either case, I'm in trouble!" So I shot him with the fire extinguisher instead and radioed ahead for the police to meet me.[5]

The war improved commercial air communications in British Columbia. The vulnerability of Alaska to Japanese attack and the need to ferry aircraft to Soviet allies caused the United States to build highways, gas pipelines and airports in the North on a priority basis. Suddenly, bush outfits that had been dying for lack of spare parts, and whose pilots had enlisted in the RCAF, were in demand.

Grant McConachie's Yukon Southern Air Transport was given unrestricted permission by the Pentagon to purchase scarce fuel, tires and, best of all, the latest Lockheed Lodestars, right off the assembly line at Burbank. Unfortunately, the Lodestars came off the line drenched in sombre camouflage paint, forcing McConachie's staff to spend days scraping it off to a shiny aluminium finish.

The transformation of commercial aviation on the other side of the country was even more dramatic. Though Pan American and British Overseas Airways Corporation (BOAC), as Imperial Airways was renamed, continued to operate flying boats through Shediac until 1945, the Second World War ushered in the era of landplanes. Added now to the other hazards of flying was the danger of being shot down by enemy aircraft, but incredibly, from 1940 onward, everyone of any importance flew the Atlantic. It was quicker and safer than taking a ship.

THE ATLANTIC FERRY ORGANISATION

The ocean suddenly seemed to be infested with U-boats, as C.D. Howe discovered in 1940 when his ship was torpedoed on its way to England. Canadian newspapers were getting ready to print Howe's obituary, and the prime minister was beginning to look for a successor, when the minister was rescued at sea.[6] Aware of Howe's importance to the Canadian war effort, Churchill sent him home in one of His Majesty's battleships.

The German occupation of France in 1940 forced the British to consider an immediate massive airlift of American-built aircraft across the North Atlantic. The British government placed the largest single order in history with American manufacturers; they ordered a total of 26,000 planes and expected delivery in England at the rate of a thousand a month. Most critically needed were 177 Lockheed Hudson patrol-bombers, and these began to collect at St. Hubert Airport, a situation that was in violation of President Roosevelt's neutrality policy. U-boats were sinking an average of two ships a day, making conventional shipping unreliable.

Churchill's minister of aircraft production, the hard-driving Canadian Max Aitken (who became the press baron Lord Beaverbrook), had a reputation for singlemindedness and enjoyed overriding bureaucracy. Beaverbrook phoned his old friend Sir Edward Beatty, president of Canadian Pacific Railway, for help in flying the Hudsons over. Beatty saw the opportunity to win one over C.D. Howe and TCA after the Richardson affair, and he agreed that Canadian Pacific would organize the airlift from Montreal. The CPR Air Services Department was created, and bush pilots such as Punch Dickins were brought in to help administer it. ATFERO, the Atlantic Ferry Organisation, was administered by the British government and operated by the CPR. It began to recruit volunteer air crew of any nationality (the CPR referred to them as the Foreign Legion), offering to pay them $1,000 for each aircraft delivered.

Canadian government officials watched the Beaverbrook-Beatty arrangements with some annoyance, but, now compromised, agreed to make radio and meteorological facilities available for the ferrying. Pilot Don Bennett would lead a trial convoy of seven bombers, flying at night so that star bearings could be taken, from Newfoundland to Northern Ireland. If four made it, the operation would be considered a success. The aircraft were fitted with extra gas tanks and their wings were smeared with antifreeze solution. Crewed by nine Americans, six Britons, six Canadians and a single Australian, the planes were to fly in formation led by Bennett; only he and one other pilot had any Atlantic navigational experience at all.

They began by flying the Hudsons to Gander on November 9, where they spent the night in three CPR railway carriages. The next day, the legendary Department of Transport meteorologist Dr. Andrew McTaggart-Cowan briefed them as to weather conditions. As one pilot later reported, although McTaggart-Cowan had had no weather reports from outside North America to go on (all the Atlantic weather ships had been sunk), he predicted what the planes would encounter with complete accuracy.

Gander afforded few amenities for pomp and

circumstance, but it had recently acquired a fully equipped band—the Queen's Own Rifles of Canada had been posted to Newfoundland to guard the airport in case German parachutists fell from the sky. So in the gathering darkness of the wintery November night, the band assembled before the bombers as the crews boarded. It became too dark to read the music on their song sheets, so the bandsmen chose to play a piece they knew by heart from church parade. Thus it was, before Bennett started his engines, that the mournful strains of *Nearer My God to Thee*—the "Titanic hymn"—filled the air.

The seven aircraft were helped by a full moon and a tail wind, but airsickness and lack of oxygen took their toll. Exactly where McTaggart-Cowan had said they would, the Hudsons hit a storm, and they vainly tried to climb to 22,000 feet to get above it. By dawn they were scattered across the ocean, their engines and controls icing up dangerously. Bennett touched down at Aldergrove Airport near Belfast eleven hours after take-off, and the other six crews eventually made it too. The fact that they had initiated the age of mass trans-Atlantic air travel was probably the last thing on their minds. Bennett left ATFERO soon after to form his Pathfinders for Bomber Command.[7]

LIBERATORS AND FLYING FORTRESSES

The following summer, when ATFERO became swamped by the flood of aircraft from American factories, the RAF took over from the CPR, setting up Ferry Command and moving the whole operation to the new Dorval Airport on the west island of Montreal. The rows of waiting Hudsons were augmented with four-engined giants like the B-17 Flying Fortress and the B-24 Liberator, the first true trans-Atlantic aircraft. Ferry pilots were returned to Dorval to pick up their next Hudson by Liberators flown by BOAC air crew. The flight back to Canada was an uncomfortable journey, memorable to passengers for the acute frostbite and temporary deafness they suffered. The only passenger "comforts" were the long wooden benches lining the cabin walls. Sleeping bags were scattered about, conversation was impossible, and there were no windows to gaze out of. But the operation, called the Return Ferry Service, cut the crossing time to fifteen hours and soon began to assume the reliability (and boredom) of a bus service.

It was a Liberator that carried the first Canadian prime minister ever to fly. Mackenzie King crossed the Atlantic in August 1941 to meet with Churchill. A month before, King's dog Pat had died and the prime minister was devastated, relying on his seances more than usual. His diary records that at one such table-tapping session, he was visited by the spirits of Sir Wilfred Laurier, W. E. Gladstone and his own mother, all of whom advised him to make the flight.[8]

Vincent Massey, the Canadian High Commissioner to London, was a passenger on a trans-Atlantic Liberator flight from Dorval to Prestwick, Scotland, in March 1944, and his memoirs give a wry look at the trials of the Return Ferry Service:

We took off at 11:30 A.M. and were flying over Montreal itself on our way east when we were told by the Flight Engineer that an engine was vibrating and that we would be returning to the airport. Another aircraft, without seats, would be ready for us so we lunched at the airport and spent the afternoon waiting for it to be ready. After tea we assembled for the second take-off . . . but this time the engines were short 150 revolutions of the required power and we did not leave the runway. It was later decided that it would be safe to leave on the same aircraft and we took off at 7:30 P.M., just about dusk. We flew for two hours and then were told by the Flight Engineer that we were going back, and that it would be four hours before we could land. This estimate was entirely correct and we touched down at 1:30 A.M. We were all driven in to Montreal. At lunch with the McConnells the next day . . . the only other guest was a Transport Command pilot, the Comte de la Roziere. When I mentioned the delays, he observed with Gallic candour that the engines of the Liberators were getting quite old and were beginning to go wrong—a most comforting comment.[9]

With its long range, the Liberator was the first true trans-Atlantic aircraft. It was widely used by both Coastal Command and the Return Ferry Service, in both of which TCA air crews participated. NATIONAL DEFENCE CANADIAN FORCES PHOTOGRAPHIC UNIT PL 2729

After lunch, Massey was driven out to Dorval and put, sardine fashion, on a third aircraft, which made a perfect non-stop flight to Prestwick in fourteen hours. He was further cheered by the good fortune of having the movie director Alexander Korda on board. Korda, who had directed the prewar utopian aviation epics *Things to Come* and *The Conquest of the Air*, must have regarded the experience of flying across the Atlantic during a war with a mixture of annoyance and wonder.

Military personnel, diplomats, prime ministers and presidents crossed and recrossed the once-feared Atlantic, on a scale inconceivable a few years earlier, making Big Power conferences routine. The multi-staged ferry route—from factory to Front—soon included Goose Bay in Labrador and, after the United States entered the war, Narssarssuaq (better known and more easily pronounced as "Bluie West 1") in Greenland and Reykjavik in Iceland.

TCA LOOKS TO EUROPE

Trans-Canada Air Lines had begun a second trans-continental service in April 1940, and flights to New York in May 1941. When Torbay, Newfoundland, became part of its network a year later, no one could doubt that TCA was looking to Europe. The little Lockheed 10s were sold off and twelve Lodestars—the civilian version of the Hudson—were added to the fleet. TCA engineers at Dorval were also called on to service BOAC's Return Ferry Liberators.

Inevitably, the battles raging in the air over Europe and the Pacific had repercussions for airline personnel. With the attractions of aerial combat and

TCA added 12 Lockheed Lodestars to its fleet in 1943. By now 35 per cent of its staff were female, including this air engineer at Winnipeg. AIR CANADA ARCHIVES

the Commonwealth Air Training Plan's need for instructors, many of the men on TCA's staff tried to join up, requiring the permission of TCA president H. J. Symington to do so. The shortage of male staff forced the airline to recruit more women and, by 1943, 35 per cent of the airline was female.

The war was a boon for both British and American airlines. The British, concentrating on fighter production, had access to superior American transport aircraft such as the DC-3, the Lodestar and the Liberator. The Americans did even better: President Roosevelt traded fifty old destroyers for British bases in the Atlantic, giving American airlines access to the stepping stones in the Atlantic and to British colonies in Africa and the Caribbean. The U.S. airlines seized the chance to spread their wings. Northeast Airlines flew to Newfoundland, Greenland and Iceland; Pan American, using landplanes, to Trinidad, Ascension Island, Accra in Ghana, and all the way to Cairo. Northwest Airlines flew through Edmonton to the Yukon and Alaska. The outcome of the war might still have been in question in 1942, but no one could doubt that the airlines of the United States, with their vast resources, were jockeying for position in the postwar world.

None of this was lost on Howe and Symington, who realized that the Return Ferry Service could provide TCA with Atlantic experience and, in October 1942, offered to lend Ferry Command three TCA air crews. The RAF, desperate for experienced pilots but not wishing to offend BOAC, agreed to take them, but made it clear that the aircraft flown by TCA crews were to remain RAF property; they were to be flown on Ferry Command orders, and no TCA insignia could be displayed on them. Captains George Lothian, M. B. "Jock" Barclay and Lindy Rood were transferred to Ferry Command along with First Officers W. R. Bell, H. I. Hayes and A. H. Palmer, Navigator Harold Thomae and Radio Officer A. Blackwood. Together, they became the

Canada's
National Air Service

first Canadians to achieve one hundred crossings of the Atlantic.

In September 1943, Rood and Lothian were loaned to 10 Squadron RCAF at Dartmouth and Gander to convert air crews from their twin-engined patrol aircraft to Liberators. Frank Young, another TCA pilot, was named chief of the TCA ferrying operations, and he instructed and "checked out" Americans applying to fly the Atlantic, as did Walt Fowler. Romeo Vachon, TCA superintendent of maintenance, was loaned to the Aircraft Productions Branch of the Department of Munitions and Supply. Z. Lewis Leigh, the IFR instructor who had flown the first official TCA westbound flight from Winnipeg to Vancouver in 1939, joined the RCAF as a flight

"Canada's National Air Service": A Trans-Canada DC-3 over Niagara Falls. AIR CANADA ARCHIVES
Right: The Douglas DC-3 cockpit sports the latest in 1930s avionics. Recognizable here are the rudder pedals with the fuel tank selectors and the throttles directly above. The manifold pressure gauges and RPM indicators lead to the magnetic compass at the apex of the dashboard.
CANADAIR ARCHIVES

lieutenant in 1944. With his expertise in instrument flying, Leigh was soon given command of 164 Transport Squadron to airlift freight to Goose Bay—where U-boats had been prowling—and later organized 168 Transport Squadron to carry Canadian forces mail to Scotland, Italy and Egypt.

Pilot F. E. W. Smith's experiences were common to many TCA crew:

> In August, 1942 I was sent to 12 Communications Squadron at Rockcliffe in Ottawa. On arrival I was met at the Station by "Lewie" Leigh . . . My job, he told me, was to teach Service pilots to fly the way TCA did. I knew nothing about IFR, but Leigh and former TCA captain Marlowe Kennedy who commanded 12 Squadron taught me the rudiments of IFR and eventually I became marginally competent to teach it. Their aim was to make Transport Command fully IFR and the first thing they started was a scheduled service between Ottawa and Halifax, calling enroute at Montreal and Moncton. We called this the "Blueberry" and even used two of TCA's original Lockheed 10As on it. The run operated to TCA's IFR standards of 300 feet and ¾ of a mile of visibility and TCA ran its despatch service, ticket counter service, all communications and ground handling.
>
> The RCAF officers were all experienced pilots who were to be qualified as captains. They were put on the run to get them used to an airline type of operation; its emphasis on instruments, flying in cloud using the radio range, and airline communications—all foreign to a Service trained pilot. Then they were given the course, which consisted of putting them under the hood for about five hours a day, during which they had all the drills TCA pilots had in company training.[10]

HOWE STEPS IN

By 1942, having TCA man the three BOAC Liberators wasn't enough for Howe. The British and the Americans seemed to be carving up the world, particularly the Atlantic, into, as one journalist put it, "empires of the air." What brought matters to a head were the U-boats, which continued to send Allied ships to the ocean bottom with Teutonic regularity, sinking forty-two off the American coast in the month of May 1942 alone. There were now two tons of mail addressed to the Canadian troops stationed in England piled up at the Shediac flying-boat base, because the British and American flying boats that

came through had other priorities. In London, Vincent Massey bore the brunt of the military's complaints of an inadequate mail service from home, and saw at first hand the poor morale of the soldiers, some of whom would soon be in battle. High Commission staff were also harassed by requests from Canadian civilians and military VIPs for seats on the Return Ferry Liberators. Massey begged the prime minister to alleviate both situations with an independent Canadian trans-Atlantic airline. Cabinet minutes outline his concerns over American encroachments across the Canadian North and over the Atlantic. These projects might be part of the war effort now, Massey warned, but once it was over "all they [have] to do [is] repaint their planes and change the clothes of their crews and they will have their civil routes in being directly peace is declared."[11]

Howe informed London that, as a wartime emergency measure, TCA was going to launch its own trans-Atlantic service. He now had three TCA crews who had logged hundreds of hours with the Return Ferry Service—but no suitable aircraft for them to use. As "Minister of Absolutely Everything," he tried to buy some Liberators, but was told that all had been slated for the United States war effort. Douglas had built a four-engine airliner called the DC-4 in 1938, but all of those had been requisitioned by American Overseas Airlines for military charters. It gradually became clear that neither the British nor the Americans were going to provide a future competitor with trans-Atlantic aircraft.

The only aircraft being manufactured in Canada that could be considered long-range were the Catalina flying boats being built by Boeing in Vancouver and Vickers at Cartierville. Howe had TCA's O. T. Larson look into obtaining some, as they could also be landed in Shediac to pick up the mail, but he was told that the planes didn't have the necessary range to fly the Atlantic. That left Victory Aircraft Ltd. at Malton, Ontario, which in March 1943 was gearing up to manufacture Avro Lancaster bombers. Victory Aircraft Ltd. had been formed in 1942 when C. D. Howe nationalized the Malton plant of National Steel Car at the instigation of plant

manager David Boyd. After obtaining the contract to build Lancaster bombers in Canada, Boyd had realized that his plant's ability to do so would be hampered by the necessity of clearing all decisions through the NSC head office in Hamilton. Howe sent in one of his "dollar-a-year" men, J. P. Bickell, to take over the facility, making it a Crown corporation.

It would be many months before one of the Avro Lancaster bombers would be ready to use, but the British had sent over a Lancaster bomber for the Victory Aircraft engineers to use as a "pattern," and when they were finished with it, Howe exercised his authority to have the British bomber kept at Malton.

A timely pretext was provided by the torpedoing of a ship carrying construction material for Goose Bay airport by a German submarine. The urgently needed supplies were steel beams too bulky to fit into the RCAF Lodestars. Howe is credited with the idea of having them loaded into the hold of the "pattern" Lancaster and getting Rood and Lothian to fly it to Goose Bay. This was the excuse he needed to hijack the Lancaster permanently, and in May 1943 the aircraft was flown by TCA to the Avro factory in England to be modified.

Victory Aircraft Ltd. removed the nose turret and bomb bay of the Lancastrians to make room for ten passengers and cargo. AIR CANADA ARCHIVES

On June 16, 1943, Howe told the House of Commons that the government was going to establish a trans-Atlantic air service to carry the military mail and VIPs on war duty. The service was to be neither permanent nor commercial; no fares would be charged, and seats would be allocated by the deputy minister of transport and, in London, the High Commissioner. Massey negotiated with the British for landing rights to Prestwick, all the while emphasizing that the operation was entirely a wartime measure. Thus was born the Canadian Government Trans-Atlantic Service (CGTAS), the forerunner of all TCA (and Air Canada) flights across the ocean. The British Lancaster, now designated "CF-CMS," began operations on July 22, 1943, between Dorval and Prestwick, carrying eight passengers and 2,600 pounds of mail on its first flight. Howe and Symington would travel on it to England in October, crossing the ocean in under twelve hours.

THE LANCASTRIANS

Eventually, there were eight Lancasters used by CGTAS, the other seven built at Victory Aircraft. The planes were called Lancastrians. Unlike the uncomfortable Liberators, the Canadian aircraft were outfitted with the best passenger amenities that Victory Aircraft could provide. The nose turret and bomb bay were removed to allow ten passengers to sit in insulated, soundproofed comfort, their hot meals served by a white-jacketed steward from a well-equipped galley. Each passenger had a reading light, a call button, an ashtray and a personal oxygen outlet. An interior decorator was hired to design the aircraft's interior; the yellow-and-rust-coloured walls and roof contrasted with a brown carpeted floor and green seats. Cargo space was sacrificed for cabin height—unlike in the Lodestars, the cabin was "stand-up" size.

By the summer of 1944, Lancastrians with the TCA insignia were flying three times a week to Prestwick, and by December, they had carried 2,000 passengers and more than a million tons of mail. As Howe had promised, no fares were charged until 1945, when the price of a Montreal-London ticket was $572.12

George Lothian returned from the RCAF to fly the Lancastrians for TCA, capturing the Atlantic speed record in January 1944, when he made the Montreal-Prestwick crossing in 11 hours, 16 minutes. Lothian is also remembered for nursing a Lancastrian across the Atlantic on one engine. What Howe hadn't known was that the Lancaster's Merlin engines were notorious for failing in mid-flight. Designed by Rolls-Royce in 1931 to power the British entry for the Schneider air racing trophy, the Merlin gave an aircraft quick, short bursts of speed, making the engine ideal for fighter aircraft like the Spitfire and the Hurricane, and the Merlin had been a major factor in allowing the RAF to "scramble" fighters during the Battle of Britain. In 1940, when the British needed a

Canadian Government Trans-Atlantic Service passengers were served hot meals by a white-jacketed steward in insulated comfort. The Lancastrian's interior was yellow and rust, with brown carpeting and green seats. AIR CANADA ARCHIVES

long-range bomber to hit deep into the industrial heart of the Third Reich, Avro developed the twin-engine Manchester bomber, but when Rolls-Royce's Vulture engines tested as unreliable to power it, Avro's chairman, Sir Roy Dobson, personally secured a supply of Merlin engines and convinced the British Ministry of Aircraft Production to put four of them into his Manchester airframe, creating the classic Lancaster bomber. In a war that consumed aircraft with wasteful fatalism, few Lancasters survived even two "tours" (or fifty bombing missions) over Germany. The spark plugs on Merlin engines made to cruise for prolonged lengths of time coated over with lead and stopped firing. Engine overhaul in the air force was hardly a problem, but in airline service, where regular schedules had to be kept and the bottom line watched, the Merlins were a liability.

There were accidents with the Lancastrians. In

December 1944, "CF-CMU," on an eastbound flight, sent out a distress call over the Atlantic and then disappeared. The original "CF-CMS" crashed at Dorval in a training flight in July 1945. Whether either incident was a result of engine failure was never conclusive, but because of their suspicions TCA pilots almost mutinied, preferring to fly the Liberators with their Pratt & Whitney engines. But Howe would have none of it. He wanted Victory Aircraft to keep turning out Lancasters with Merlin engines, providing employment for thousands of Canadians and making the country independent of the United States. He also had his eye on the Avro York, a Lancaster derivative being made at Malton. What frightened TCA pilots was that this plane too used Merlin engines.

The Second War ended as it had begun, by aircraft dropping bombs on civilians. But by this time the Luftwaffe Stukas that had originally frightened Polish refugees seemed like antique toys compared to the B-29 Superfortresses. By war's end, no one could doubt that aircraft had triumphed over all other weapons. The British may have invented radar and the Germans the jet turbine, but the sheer scale with which Boeing, Lockheed, Douglas, North American and Consolidated churned out airplanes transformed warfare—and the world—forever.

The war jump-started aviation technology and forced it to leap ahead. The wood and canvas aircraft that most airlines had begun with were now elegant aluminium tubes with electronic controls, upholstered seating, soundproofing, room for twenty passengers and—best of all—the capacity to operate efficiently enough to make company accountants happy. Pilots no longer relied on "the iron compass," the intercity railway line, to navigate but had access to radio ranges and radar. Bennett's seven Hudsons feeling their way across the Atlantic had been followed by more than nine thousand other aircraft. The watery grave between the Old World and the New had been subjugated, the public's fear of flying assuaged, the stratosphere explored. A new world was about to dawn.

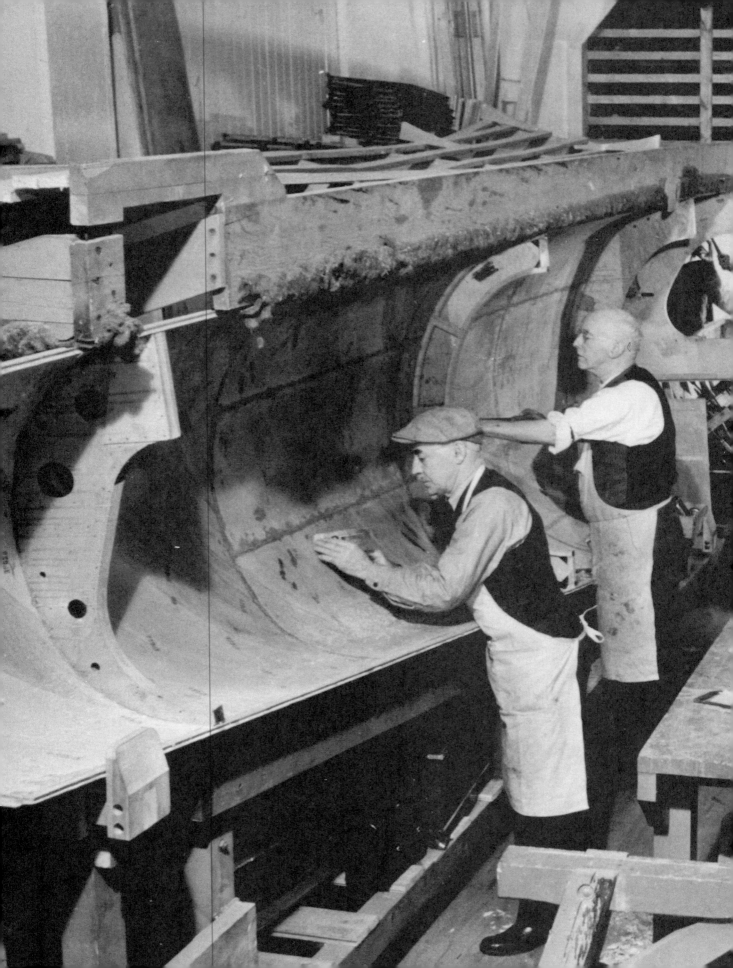

CHAPTER EIGHT

War without the Shooting

In the years between the First and Second World Wars, there were 678 aircraft made in Canada. Most of the companies that made them, like the shipbuilder Canadian Vickers, did so as a sideline to their main business. The airframes were made in Canada—the country had wood and canvas enough for that—but the engines were imported from Britain and the United States. The few brave firms that had no wealthy parents, such as Reid Aircraft

Company, were run by aviation enthusiasts, and they were commendable efforts doomed to bankruptcy. For the meagre commercial market in Canada, it made poor economic sense to support an indigenous aviation industry when cheaper aircraft could be purchased "off the shelf" from the United States and Britain.

CANADIAN FIRMS BRANCH OUT
In 1909, millionaire-to-be William "Max" Aitken

had merged a trio of railway carriage makers into Canadian Car and Foundry Ltd. (CCF), in recognition of which *Busy Man's Magazine* (soon to be called *Maclean's*) christened him the "Napoleon of the Financial World." A friend of prime ministers Robert Borden and R. B. Bennett, Aitken believed all his life in an empire that encompassed the English-speaking peoples of the world, with London

Canadian Vickers struggled on through the Depression until 1936 when Ottawa ordered it to build Supermarine Stranraer flying boats for coastal patrol, allowing the company to stay solvent until the Second World War. NATIONAL DEFENCE CANADIAN FORCES PHOTOGRAPHIC UNIT PL 2728

at its heart. He left for England in 1910, and almost as soon as he got off the ship ran as the Conservative

The prewar Canadian Vickers plant on the Montreal water-front typified the country's limited ability to mass-produce aircraft. With the contract to build Cansos in 1941, the company sought new facilities at Cartierville in the city's suburbs. CANADAIR ARCHIVES

candidate in a Manchester suburb. Amazingly, he won. He took his seat in the British House of Commons and for the remainder of his life returned to Canada only to visit. Family members back home took over CCF operations.

Profiting from munitions contracts in the First World War, by 1937 CCF owned several plants around Montreal and one in Fort William, Ontario. The Fort William plant was run by David Boyd, a McGill University–trained engineer who had left Dominion Bridge Ltd. for CCF. Boyd was far enough away from company headquarters to dabble in the aircraft manufacturing business, and in 1936 CCF (Fort William) took the risk of building Grumman Goblin biplanes, in the hope of exporting them to the Spanish Republicans. When an arms embargo prevented this, the Goblins were dumped onto the RCAF as front-line fighters.[1]

Then, in 1938, the talented Elsie MacGill became

CCF's chief aeronautical engineer, and with designer Michael Gregor produced the first Canadian fighter, the FDB-1. Constructed solely of metal, it had flush riveting, a retractable undercarriage and gull-wings. But the day of the biplane was over—the German Messerschmitts being tested in the Spanish Civil War demonstrated this—and the DB-1 project was cancelled. MacGill then turned out a more mundane aircraft, the very basic Maple Leaf Trainer. The plane received its certificate of airworthiness within eight months of its conception. But here too events conspired against MacGill. De Havilland and Fleet had cornered what market there was with their own

The DH-60 Tiger Moth, the most successful British trainer of all time, was designed by Geoffrey de Havilland to compete with Avro's Avian. In Canada, Phil Garratt adapted it to suit winter conditions. BOMBARDIER/DE HAVILLAND ARCHIVES

aircraft. The failure of the DB-I and the Maple Leaf were signals to Canadian aircraft manufacturers of the risks involved in indigenous designs.[2]

By 1939, Aitken was the press baron Lord Beaverbrook, waiting in the wings for his friend Winston Churchill to assume power. Aitken himself was looking to become minister for aircraft production. He had left his brother-in-law Victor Drury to run CCF in Montreal, and it came as no surprise when the company suddenly received a lucrative contract to produce Hawker Hurricane fighters. The Fort William plant made 1,451 of the famous flying gun platforms; some Hurricanes took part in the Battle of Britain, and many flew in defence of the Soviet Union. The following year, the CCF factory at Verdun was awarded the contract to build the British Hampden bomber. It was a second-rate aircraft with little potential, but company managers hoped that the experience gained would allow the plant to make four-engined Short Stirling bombers in the near future.

The Ottawa Car Manufacturing Company, as its name implied, built trams and buses at its factory at 301 Slater Street. It was owned by the Thomas Ahearn family, who were generous Liberal Party supporters. In 1936, the RCAF was talked into purchasing worn-out Westland Wapiti fighters from the Royal Air Force. With the Liberals in power, the Ahearns were given their reward. The Wapitis had been well used by the RAF in the Middle East, and Ottawa Car Manufacturing was contracted to refurbish them, cleaning out the scorpions and desert sand. For years after, the luckless pilots who flew the Wapitis—nick-named the "What-a-pities"—claimed that the aircraft still smelled of camel dung. The contract gave Ottawa Car a taste for aviation, however, and the company looked for more business.

In Winnipeg, the sheet metal company that brothers Jim, Grant and Edwin MacDonald had

Once the Mosquito's halves were bonded under infrared
light, the "glued and screwed" fuselage was trucked to the
main assembly plant for the wings and engines to be fitted.
BOMBARDIER/DE HAVILLAND ARCHIVES

Right: With the Mosquito, de Havilland achieved the impossible: tools, jigs and drawings were sent from Britain in
September 1941, and the first Canadian-built Mosquito was
flown on September 23, 1942. BOMBARDIER/DE HAVILLAND
ARCHIVES

begun on the shores of the Red River in 1914 was well known among the bush-flying fraternity for its metal floats. Prodded by James Richardson himself, in 1930 the brothers opened MacDonald Bros. Aircraft Ltd. in a two-storey building on Robinson Street, employing two hundred workers to repair the Canadian Airways fleet. Anticipating more business because of the hostilities in Europe, the Richardson family invested heavily when the company expanded to larger quarters at Stevenson Field, where MacDonald Buildings No. 1, 2 and 4 were erected in

record time. (Building 3, built across the street, was sold to Midwest Aircraft when its location was found to be inconvenient.)

The National Steel Car Corporation of Hamilton, Ontario, had built only railway rolling stock until Robert Magor, the brother of its president, thought to diversify into making aircraft under licence. In 1938, National Steel Car's Aircraft Division put up a small factory in a hay field at the corner of the recently opened Malton Airport and secured a contract to build Westland Lysander air-

A swarm of de Havilland Mosquitos at wartime Downsview awaiting delivery. In September 1942, the founder's son, Geoffrey de Havilland, Jr., came to Downsview to test-fly the first Canadian-built Mosquito, giving the factory workers an impromptu aerobatic display. BOMBARDIER/DE HAVILLAND ARCHIVES

craft for the RCAF. A year later, the first Lysanders were flying.

Other Canadian aircraft manufacturers owed their beginnings to the drive and vision of aviation-minded foreigners. By 1937, at Longueuil, Sherman Fairchild was building the Bristol Bolingbrooke bomber for the RCAF and sharing in the Hampden contract as well. Robert Noorduyen, a talented aeronautical engineer who had come to the United States in 1920 to work for fellow Dutchman Anthony Fokker, in 1934 obtained financing from Montreal backers to begin Noorduyen Aircraft Ltd. and rented space at the Curtiss-Reid factory at Cartierville. His sturdy Norseman was the first bush plane designed specifically for the North. Between 1935 and 1945, 903 Norsemen would be built.

The impetus for Fleet Aircraft of Fort Erie, Ontario, literally fell from the sky. In September 1929 an American aircraft manufacturer, Reuben Fleet of Consolidated Aircraft, was flying his own plane from Detroit to Buffalo when he decided to take a short cut across Ontario rather than risk flying over Lake Erie. The aircraft lost power and crashed near London. Fleet was badly injured (his passenger was killed), and he was taken to Victoria Hospital. Jack Sanderson, an instructor at the local London Flying Club, visited Fleet there out of professional courtesy. The two men impressed each other so much that Fleet decided to manufacture his light planes at Fort Erie,

hiring Sanderson as the company's president and chief demonstrator.

Fleet Aircraft of Canada Ltd. came into being in March of 1930. But the few orders for its Fleet Model 7 trainers could not justify a full-time staff of more than eleven. By 1932 this was reduced to eight, with the company president living on the premises to save money. Not until 1937, with the world plunging into war, would the market improve and Fleet begin exporting its aircraft to China, Argentina, Portugal, Venezuela, Iraq and New Zealand. In 1938, a British trade mission touring the United States to place orders for aircraft decided to stop off at Montreal on their way home. With the hope of siphoning off some of those orders, Canadian aircraft manufacturers like Sanderson met with members of the mission. And once Sanderson got wind, along with other manufacturers, of a rumour that Canada would be asked to participate in an air training plan for RAF pilots, he immediately laid plans to expand Fleet's facilities and had his staff design a training aircraft called the Fort.

When Canada declared war on September 10, 1939, its air force was barely able to muster ninety-two aircraft, a motley collection of Stranraers, Wapitis and Goblins. The first RCAF casualties resulted not from enemy action but from poor equipment. On September 14, an air force Northrop Delta flown by WO2 J.E. Doan and Cpl. D.A. Rennie disappeared on patrol over New Brunswick. When the plane's remains were discovered in 1958, many in the RCAF recalled the unsavory reputation of the Delta aircraft.

In the face of the United States' observance of strict neutrality, the British must have looked on their nearest Dominion with some despair. Canada was not turning out the arsenal of airpower that the beleaguered RAF needed to face the Luftwaffe. All aircraft engines in Canada were imported and, worst of all, there was no ready source of aluminium.[3]

What put the aviation industry in Canada on a more secure footing was the British Commonwealth Air Training Plan, an agreement signed by Britain, Canada, Australia and New Zealand on December 16,

1939, to set up a joint training program for air crew. Each country would run elementary training at home, but for more specialized skills, each Dominion would pay into the scheme as follows: Canada $287 million, Australia $40 million, New Zealand $29 million. The training aircraft to be used were de Havilland Tiger Moths, Fleet Finches, North American Harvards, Avro Ansons and Fairey Battles. Britain would supply the Ansons and the Battles, and Canada would construct the airfields. Specialized air-crew training for air observers, navigators, wireless operators, air gunners and multi-engined pilots would be conducted in Canada, where there were appropriate facilities and sufficient space.

Elementary trainers like the Tiger Moths and the Finches were simple to produce, and both de Havilland and Fleet had already expanded their plants to do so. When the supply of British Gypsy engines used in the Tiger Moths was in danger of being cut off, American-made Menasco engines were substituted.

The speed of the German advances in 1940 and the fall of Norway, Belgium, the Netherlands and

Using specially designed 200-gallon fuel tanks, 646 Mosquitos were ferried across the frigid Atlantic, with the loss of only 28. One of the most outstanding aircraft of World War II, the "Wooden Wonder" served as a night and day fighter and also in anti-shipping, bombing and photo reconnaissance. BOMBARDIER/DE HAVILLAND ARCHIVES

France prompted the mass ferrying of aircraft across the Atlantic and also forced the British aircraft manufacturer Avro to transfer complete production of the Anson to Canada. The twin-engined Anson was a docile, forgiving plane, descended from the Fokker F.VII of 1928 vintage, and construction should have been relatively easy. But such was the elementary state of aircraft manufacturing in Canada that no single company had the capability to produce even so simple an aircraft in its entirety. C. D. Howe spread the contracts among five companies (dealing them, his critics said, like a pack of cards), creating Federal Aircraft Ltd. in Montreal to administer them all. Federal Aircraft made the single prototype Canadian Anson, called MK.II, but Canadian Car and Foundry at Amherst, Nova Scotia, built 341, de Havilland at Downsview 375, MacDonald Bros. at Winnipeg 319, National Steel Car at Malton 736, and Ottawa Car Manufacturing 60.

Cut off from their British suppliers, Canadian companies looked for ingenious solutions. Supply of the British-built Anson engines became irregular with the U-boat sinkings. Ralph Bell, federal director general of aircraft production, felt that Canada did not have the expertise to manufacture aircraft engines. Undaunted, Howe located the Jacobs Aircraft Company in Pottstown, Pennsylvania, which made 330-hp aero engines and agreed to give the Canadian government 2,300 of them for $10 million.[4] While these engines were not as powerful as the British Armstrong-Siddeley 395-hp Cheetahs, at least their supply was assured. The Anson's original nose, wing and tail had been made of aluminium but, without a supply in Canada, moulded plywood was substituted. The Anson MK.V, using the completely moulded fuselage and more powerful Wasp engines, became the ultimate model. Three hundred MK.Vs were built by Canadian Car and Foundry at their Amherst plant, and 748 by MacDonald Bros. at Stevenson Airport, Winnipeg.

By 1940, 17,000 Canadians were employed in the aviation industry, turning out Hurricanes, Hampdens and Ansons. A year later, the figure had climbed to 42,000, and by 1942 almost doubled to 71,000. By the time Robert Magor died in mid-1942, National Steel Car had two assembly lines producing three aircraft daily, its pace attracting the attention of C. D. Howe. Magor had lured David Boyd away from CCF to make his company more efficient, and with an educated labour force available from nearby Toronto, the NSC plant had enormous expansion possibilities.

THE LANCASTER AND THE CANSO

The NSC Anson program was to be followed in December 1941 by a contract to build the famous Lancaster bomber. When the Malton division of the company was nationalized by C. D. Howe, Boyd stayed on as manager. Nicknamed "the Great White Father," he was popular with his workers. He knew

them all by their first names and he walked the assembly lines in his shirtsleeves, even taking over occasionally from a welder if he thought the job wasn't being done to his standards. Like Howe, Boyd had little love for bureaucracy. Once, when he received a tedious list of dos and don'ts from a defence production bureaucrat in Ottawa, he took a black marker, scrawled "BALLS" across the list and threw it in the garbage.

The Lancaster program was the most politically sensitive of the war. Despite British opposition, Ottawa had pushed to have its own bomber group equipped with Canadian-built aircraft. A dormitory was installed at the Malton factory, and Boyd instituted two nine-hour shifts running six days a week. The Lancaster prototype KB700 was rolled out on August 1, 1943, with much fanfare before crowds of workers, invited guests and the media.

The first Canadian-made Lancaster was christened the *Ruhr Express*, and its RCAF crew were filmed flying it off to war. But not before the aircraft was sent to Dorval to have its electrical system fitted.[5] Soon Victory Aircraft was turning out 50 Lancasters monthly, to a total of 430 by the war's end.

Not far from Malton, de Havilland's Downsview facilities had also been transformed. Tiger Moth production ended in 1942, and de Havilland then retooled to turn out one of the war's most phenomenal aircraft—the "Wooden Wonder," the Mosquito. The high-altitude fighter-bomber with Rolls-Royce engines and a plywood exterior could climb to 30,000 feet and fly at 425 mph. Between 1942 and 1945, 1,033 Mosquitoes came out of the Downsview plant, including one that was christened by the actress Joan Fontaine, sister of screen star Olivia de Havilland and a cousin of the company's founder.

To meet the U-boat menace, the RCAF needed a more rugged, more powerful seaplane than the Stranraers that Canadian Vickers had turned out in 1937. The Consolidated Catalina or, as it was known in the RCAF, the Canso, was chosen, and Canadian Vickers was given the initial order for 39 of them. The dockyard facilities where the Vedettes had been

built were too cramped for such a large program, so the Department of Munitions and Supply moved the Canso operation out to Cartierville Airport, where Noorduyen was building his Norsemen and CCF the Anson. There, in the summer of 1942, the federal government built a sprawling wooden complex where the Cansos could be moved quickly down the line, parts rivetted together and the wings and engines added by a work force increasingly made up of women. The first Canso left Cartierville within three months of the factory's foundations being laid. The planes were then taken to St. Hubert for testing. In 1943, the United States military ordered 230 variants of the Catalina, and, including the Boeing factory in Vancouver, the PBY program employed 19,000 Canadians.

Other advances in aviation, in areas such as radar, radio communications, wing-loading, meteorology

Canadian Vickers built 369 PBYs at Cartierville during the war, some for the U.S. military. The RCAF called theirs Cansos after the strait between Cape Breton Island and the mainland of Nova Scotia. CANADAIR ARCHIVES

and Ground Control Approach, were all war babies destined to influence how humans would navigate the skies in the decades of peace to follow. One of the most underrated products of the Second World War was the 100 octane fuel developed for military purposes, which would make possible a new generation of superchargers and compression ratios in engines. It might have been the greatest contribution of all.

At its peak in 1944, the Canadian military-industrial complex employed 116,000 people in aviation alone. Nineteen hundred combat aircraft were built that year; Canadian Car alone employed 15,000 people in aircraft production, followed by Victory Aircraft with 9,500. The seismic shift created by the war gave Canada's aviation experts, engineers, designers, entrepreneurs and managers a chance to demonstrate their capabilities, and those of the nation.

THE FIRST INTERNATIONAL AVIATION CONFERENCE

In November 1944, when C.D. Howe flew to Chicago for the first international conference on aviation, he changed the course of Canadian aviation forever. It was forty-one years since the Wrights had flown, and certain locations had come to be associated with the defining moments in aviation: the sands at Kitty Hawk, a frozen lake in Nova Scotia, Le Bourget, the site of Lindbergh's landing, and even the little-known airfield in Marienehe, Germany, where, under the supervision of Dr. Han-Joachim von Ohain, the first jet aircraft flew. In 1944, these illustrious locations were joined by Chicago's Stevens Hotel, which became for six weeks the unlikely centre of international commercial aviation.

For two centuries, seafaring nations had encouraged the notion that the oceans of the world were open to whichever nation wanted to ply them. For most of those years, the Royal Navy had generously ensured that even British mercantile rivals such as the Dutch and the Germans could carry cargo and passengers wherever they liked, calling at any port, picking up any nationality. With the founding of the United Nations in 1944-45, could the freedom of the seas be extended to the air? During the war, the British had allowed thousands of American civil aircraft to land on their island, and to use any other real estate they owned around the world. The other colonial powers, depleted of aircraft and needing American aid, had done the same. But it appeared the old rivalries had only been put aside for the duration. In October 1944, the Allies had accepted the surrender of the German forces in Calais. With several European capitals liberated and complete victory in sight, Harold Balfour, the British minister for air, had announced in the House of Commons that "After the war, all bets are off."

But the other nations attending the Chicago conference knew that an overwhelming majority of the civil aircraft in the world were by now American. By the time the Japanese bombed Pearl Harbor in December 1941, Douglas had already turned out 800 DC-3s. By August 1945, this total had risen to 11,000; the Santa Monica factory produced one DC-3 every five hours.[6] The British airline BOAC was making do with converted bombers, and in 1945 it was forced to press captured Luftwaffe Junkers 52s into service. No one had anything to compare with the new generation of American airliners. The Lockheed Constellations and the Boeing Stratocruisers were graceful, pressurized, four-engined giants, able to cross the Atlantic with sixty passengers in complete comfort. If Britain had ruled the waves in the previous century, America was master of the air in this one.

The Canadian government feared American influence in the postwar commercial aviation world. The United States military had built hundreds of airports in Canada along the Mackenzie River, on Hudson Bay, and at Mingan, Quebec; Goose Bay, Labrador; and up the whole Northwest Staging Route to Alaska. Prime Minister Mackenzie King wanted to make sure that all these airports would now belong to Canada. He did not want American bureaucrats to suddenly claim ownership or landing rights at some time in the future. Not all of the airports would ever be used; some were useless in peacetime. But despite a looming postwar recession, King found the $111 million to pay for all of them. It was a down payment, he said, on Canadian sovereignty.

President Roosevelt had stated in 1943 that he favoured freedom of the air, a rudimentary "Open Skies" concept. Under pressure from his aggressive airline lobby, he contemplated allotting geographic zones around the world to American airlines. But by late 1944, Roosevelt was very ill, and many feared the growing influence of others in his circle. Roosevelt's under-secretary of state, Edward R. Stettinius, was Juan Trippe's brother-in-law. The president had needed Pan American's resources to build airstrips throughout South America and Africa early in the war, which had allowed Trippe considerable licence in air routes and landing rights. By now, Pan American was so powerful that in certain areas of the world it not only dropped off passengers but transported them from one place to another, stifling what little local competition there was. Freedom of the air in peacetime seemed to most Americans what they had fought for. Clare Booth Luce, the American congresswoman, told Congress in February 1943: "We want to fly everywhere. Period."[7]

Fifty-four nations attended the conference in Chicago. (The Soviet Union, which refused even to contemplate foreign air traffic within its borders, did not participate.) The Stevens Hotel swarmed with delegates, advisors, secretaries, clerks and journalists; the bazaar-like atmosphere caused one Canadian diplomat to sniff about the long wait for elevators and telephones in this "mammoth second-rate hotel."[8]

The Americans and the British dominated the agenda. The British approached the Chicago convention as they had the Congress of Vienna, ready, as Lord Beaverbrook biographer A.J.P. Taylor wrote, to carve up the world.[9] With the increasing importance of Gander to Atlantic air travel, the colony of Newfoundland was their trump card. The actions of the British delegation were orchestrated from London by Lord Beaverbrook, who saw the convention as an opportunity to reassert the 1927 globe-circling imperial (or Commonwealth) air routes. Canada, Australia and New Zealand were to be part of a British scheme that would effectively check the American influence. The British had even built the aircraft to use on these routes.[10]

But as they would one day do with the de Havilland Comet and the Concorde, the British overreached themselves, creating imaginative but economically unfeasible status symbols that had little chance of being mass-produced as airliners. In 1943, while the Americans were turning out the Constellation and the DC-4, the British had begun work on the immense Bristol Brabazon aircraft, which was designed to ply the imperial routes in regal splendour.

The smaller nations were equally self-serving. The Irish wanted no part of the 1935 agreement of cooperation with the British now that Shannon Airport had become a critical link in trans-Atlantic flights. The Latin American countries voted as a block to take back their air space from Pan American. And the Dutch and the French, whose airlines had been decimated by the war, looked to regain their colonial monopolies.

The Canadian delegation consisted of C.D. Howe, Herbert Symington and J.A. Wilson. The public lives of all three had been inextricably linked with the development of commercial aviation in Canada. But none represented the country's aeronautical progress as much as the delegation's RCAF advisor, Wilfrid Austin Curtis. Curtis had been a bank clerk before joining the Curtiss Flying School at Hanlan's Point in 1915. Over the course of two world wars and twenty-one years of peace, he had risen to the rank of air vice marshal. During the span of Curtis's career, Canada had gone from harbouring a few forest protection flying boats to becoming the third most powerful manufacturer in the world.

Howe emphasized to conference delegates that competition in the air should be controlled by a strong international authority. He wanted a guaranteed minimum of routes and frequencies for airlines of all nations, large and small, with the absence of discrimination or exclusive landing rights. Canada, because of its size and position, could not grant landing rights on an unlimited scale. But equally, he said, his country had responsibilities to the international community. To its bewilderment, the Canadian delegation found itself thrust into the role of conciliator between the superpowers.

In committee, technical matters such as rules and regulations were hammered out, including the adoption of the metric system. A major coup for Canada occurred with the universal acceptance of a system for air traffic control developed by the Department of Transport for use in their Trans-Canada Airway program. But over the issue of "escalation"—regulating the frequencies of plane landings according to the numbers of passengers that used them—the two superpowers remained deadlocked. With so many of the world's crucial air refuelling points located in British colonies, the Americans were hamstrung. It was rumoured that they offered to give the British 50 DC-4s if Beaverbrook would acquiesce to the escalation clause. The mayor of New York, Fiorello La Guardia, who was part of the American team (and soon to have his city's new airport named after him), pointed out to British delegation head Lord Swinton that it was useless to have all those airports around the world without aircraft to land at them. But despite his and Symington's efforts to push for an equitable solution, the conference failed to arrive at one. While it provided a starting point for the safe development of air travel in the years to come, the Chicago conference reflected the political balance of the postwar world. Freedom of the skies was never achieved, and, as they do today, participants resorted to negotiating bilateral air agreements with each other. The dream of philosophers and poets, to achieve worldwide peace and prosperity through unfettered air travel, was not to become a reality.

In any case, the postwar world changed faster than anyone predicted. The British Empire would soon melt away, and the resurgence of Germany and Japan as major commercial air powers would make the passions of the Chicago conference seem irrelevant half a century later. After Roosevelt's death, the U.S. began to resist foreign aircraft flying into the country. Churchill was voted out of office, Trippe's brother-in-law was replaced by Cordell Hull, and Newfoundland became part of Canada. And new Lockheed and Douglas aircraft were able to fly from New York to London without using the stepping stones across the Atlantic.

But the conference had been a success for Canada. Praise was heaped on Howe—who had to rush back to Ottawa to deal with the second conscription crisis—and on Symington for their mediation between London and Washington. As the third largest aviation power in the world (a position that would of course be temporary), Canada had been wooed by other countries. In recognition of

Montreal's importance as the Ferry Command terminus (and, since that summer, of TCA's own Atlantic service), both the Americans and the British approved that city's acceptance as home for a permanent authority on regulating international air transport. The birth of the International Civil Aviation Organization (ICAO) at Montreal coincided with that of the International Air Transport Organization (IATA), the association of airline operators. This last was wholly Symington's project, and he was elected its first president.

For a single, crowning moment, Canada held centre stage in world commercial aviation. The failure of Beaverbrook's Commonwealth scheme meant that TCA was free to pursue its own agenda. Using its Commonwealth ties as a bargaining chip with the Americans, Canada was assured entry into the huge market below the border.

Between 1939 and 1945 Canada had built 16,418 aircraft—trainers, fighters and bombers. There was now a transcontinental airline that flew the Atlantic on a regular schedule. Through the British Commonwealth Air Training Plan, Canada had trained 131,553 air crew, of whom 80 per cent were Canadian. Most of all, there were a huge number of ex-servicemen and -women who had travelled abroad and expected to continue to do so with their families. Howe and Symington (with Mackenzie King lurking in the wings) wanted to ensure that, as the government's "chosen instrument," Trans-Canada Air Lines would go from strength to strength on both the domestic and the international scene. The nation was on the threshold of a new era in commercial aviation.

CHAPTER NINE

Another Ocean, Another Aircraft

The early years of the war that would
transform the Canadian aviation
industry and Trans-Canada Air Lines
severely curtailed the operations of
small bush-flying outfits. The German "blitzkrieg"
might have been a hemisphere away, but it upset the
equilibrium of bush communities forever. Most bush
pilots were of the generation trained by the Royal
Flying Corps and were too old for the armed forces.
Some taught in the flying schools, others tested air-

craft or ferried them to Britain. But even in the best
of times, the industries that serviced the fur trade and
prospecting operated close to the margin. If before the
war it had been a case of too many operators vying for
too few customers, now there were no customers at
all. Men left the mining and lumber camps to join
up, and spare parts and aviation fuel were requisitioned for the war effort. New planes were unavailable
from either American or Canadian manufacturers,
and unless bush pilots were somehow deemed to be

doing work connected with the defence of the continent, most went bankrupt as their aircraft rusted.

BUSH PILOTS TO THE RESCUE

Then, on December 7, 1941, the Japanese attacked Pearl Harbor and the chessboard changed abruptly. The United States had been forced into the war. Winston Churchill would later write of his response to the news: "Being saturated and satiated with emotion and sensation, I went to bed and slept the sleep of the saved and the thankful."[1] His euphoria must have been felt by many bush pilots as well, but none more than Grant McConachie. The shiny Barkley-Grows and snappy crew uniforms notwithstanding, Yukon Southern Air Transport was deeply in debt to the Royal Bank at the time and unlikely to survive another week.

The United States Navy knew that the Japanese had a base in the Kuriles, near the Aleutians, and Pentagon strategists concluded that if their enemy wanted to land troops in Alaska there would be nothing to stop them. The Canada United States Joint Defense Board recommended that a northwest route through Canada to Alaska be developed into an all-weather gravelled road so that troops could be rushed from the south. In March 1942, work was begun on an inland highway of 1,600 miles from Dawson Creek to Fairbanks. Sites for airstrips, fuel dumps and construction camps all had to be surveyed, and the Canadian bush pilot fraternity suddenly found that their unique skills and knowledge of the terrain were much in demand by Washington and Ottawa. It was the biggest construction project since the building of the Panama Canal, and McConachie's YSAT, flying in engineers and supplies, was suddenly deemed vital to national defence.

The Canadian Pacific Railway had taken the plunge into the airline business as early as 1919 and then retreated in the wake of the Richardson affair. When war broke out, Sir Edward Beatty assigned his treasurer L. B. Unwin the task of buying up all the bush air companies he could. With the upheavals caused by the war, these companies would be going at bargain basement prices, and by merging their

resources, aircraft and routes, Beatty hoped the CPR just might be able to compete with the CNR/TCA.

THE FOUNDING OF CPA

Like the Ruler of the Queen's Navy in Gilbert & Sullivan's *HMS Pinafore*, Unwin had applied himself to the company's ledgers all his life only to discover one day that he was running airlines. He left the CPR head office at Windsor Station with the equivalent of a sack full of money, and called in at bush airline offices across Canada. He bought W. Leigh Brintnell's Mackenzie Air Services for $658,000, Ginger Coote Airways for $63,000, Prairie Airways for $528,000 and Starrat Airways for $425,000. (Two years later, he also bought Wings for $190,000.) Then he met with James Richardson's widow and purchased her controlling interest in Canadian Airways. Unwin knew better than most that YSAT was still in financial trouble, and on January 31, 1941, he bought it from McConachie for $1,057,000. As part of the sale, McConachie was made manager of the western region, based at Edmonton, at a monthly salary of $500. The new corporation was to be called Canadian Pacific Air Lines (CPA) and run as part of the CPR from Windsor Station.

With so many experienced bush pilots now under him, Beatty could afford to choose the best to run his CPA—and he did. Punch Dickins was made general manager of the airline and brought to Montreal to help with the Return Ferry Service at St. Hubert. Dickins had a reputation for being meticulously careful. He had learned long ago that the bush was an unforgiving environment. Now his attention to detail would extend to the airline's expenses—any invoice over $100 would have to be authorized by him. That he would clash with McConachie, whose dreams did not include such details, was inevitable.

Wisely, Beatty informed Howe of the acquisitions and asked his blessing. Then the CPR president retired in May 1942, making Unwin Canadian Pacific Air Line's first president. Howe had no objection to the CPR's purchases but warned the new president to forget any idea he might have of expanding on routes that would bring CPA into conflict with TCA. On April 2, 1943, Howe made a statement in the House of

TCA STEWARDESS MARGUERITE BREZENSKI — graduated as Registered Nurse from Ottawa Civic Hospital—joined TCA in 1941 and flew as Stewardess on Inter-City flights—in 1943 was appointed Supervising Stewardess for TCA services out of Moncton — transferred to "North Star" Trans-Atlantic service when it was inaugurated in 1947. Now Station Stewardess, she makes frequent check flights to Britain and to the West Indies, seeing that TCA's high standards of courtesy and attentive service are constantly maintained.

Your HOST AND HOSTESS aboard TCA's great Skyliners are the Purser-Steward and Stewardess. Your comfort is their business.

The Purser-Steward helps passengers on all matters regarding customs and immigration procedures and foreign exchange regulations, with which he is thoroughly familiar. A trained caterer, he also assists the Stewardess in the care of passengers—including the serving of delicious hot meals.

Every TCA Stewardess is a Registered Nurse. Her training and experience enable her to give a constant, courteous and helpful service appreciated by all passengers—and especially by those travelling with small children.

TCA PURSER-STEWARD B. W. FOGGO—had both hotel and banking experience before the war—joining the RCAF, completed a tour of operations a Navigator with Bomber Command—upon discharge joined TCA—served for a time as Passenger Agent—became a Purser-Steward in September 1945—is now Station Purser-Steward for Trans-Atlantic and Caribbean flights, supervising the various phases of "North Star" cabin service which is one of the most important factors in making a TCA flight the pleasantest —as well as the fastest—of modern means of travel.

TRANS-CANADA *AirLines*
INTERNATIONAL · TRANS-ATLANTIC · TRANSCONTINENTAL

Commons on Canada's postwar airline policy. Trans-Canada Air Lines was to be the sole Canadian agency allowed to operate international air services, he told the House. Within Canada, TCA would continue to operate all transcontinental services. And competition between air services over the same route would not be permitted, whether between a publicly owned service and a privately owned one or between two privately owned services.

If this did not leave much room for CPA, in 1944 the Air Transport Board stated that the Canadian Pacific Railway would have to divest itself of its airline within a year of the war's end. It was a battle that Unwin had no heart to face, and he was succeeded in 1946 by W.M. Neal, who successfully appealed the ruling. With the war's end, CPA rationalized its fleet and personnel by selling off most of the bush planes and acquiring army-surplus DC-3s. In 1947, it even succeeded in getting Howe to allow it to operate a Vancouver-Calgary route.

Postwar Trans-Canada Air Lines advertisement. AIR CANADA ARCHIVES

All his adult life, Grant McConachie had dreamed of flying over the pole to Europe or across the Pacific to the Orient. To anyone who would listen, he demonstrated the Great Circle route with a piece of string and an inflatable plastic globe. With aircraft like the Lockheed Constellation and the DC-4 now available, and backed by the deep pockets of the Canadian Pacific Railway, he could theoretically afford to do both. But there were obstacles. Only TCA was authorized to operate outside Canada, and Punch Dickins controlled the pursestrings at CPA.

UNION BROTHERS

Then fate (or McConachie's famous luck) stepped in to change all of that. Neal was made president of the whole Canadian Pacific system, and Dickins left the company to act as head of sales for de Havilland's

CPA president Grant McConachie in a classic pose. Probably the best description of him was made by rival Gordon McGregor, who called McConachie "charming, disarming . . . but yielding nothing in return." CANADIAN AIRLINES ARCHIVES

conditions: that McConachie purchase Canadair North Stars for the route, and that, before China, McConachie serve Australia "to demonstrate Commonwealth solidarity."[2]

The wily old minister was gambling that CPA would never be able to make such long flights economical, and that the Australians, who already flew between Sydney and Vancouver, would turn down any request for landing rights. McConachie, unaware of this last, caught a Pan American Clipper (it was a DC-4 landplane now) to Sydney in November 1948, bursting with enthusiasm. In Canberra, Howe's assumption proved correct. The Australians had just elected Ben Chiffley as prime minister, with his staunchly socialist party. There was no sympathy for a privately owned airline, and McConachie was viewed as a capitalist on par with the Rockefellers. Every minister's door was closed to him, and everyone he tried to see in the Australian government was out. The Canadian High Commissioner assured McConachie that he had exerted all the diplomatic pressure he could for landing rights, right up to the prime minister's office, but the prejudice against anything that smacked of private enterprise was too strong. A former locomotive driver, Ben Chiffley was proud of his climb to the prime minister's office and suspicious of anything that represented high-flying privilege. However, the High Commissioner said, being the good fellow he was, the prime minister had invited McConachie to a farewell luncheon.

At the lunch, flanked by the Canadian High Commissioner and Chiffley, McConachie thought fast. His airline's future was at stake. As he and Chiffley talked, it became apparent that the Australian prime minister had the idea that the young man next to him was the president of the entire Canadian Pacific Railway. Grant's father had worked for the CPR all his life, but the closest his son got to a similar career was in high school, when he had slaved as a stoker on a freight locomotive during the summer holidays. For some reason, however, McConachie still kept the railway union card that had been issued to him then in his wallet. Between courses, he produced it for the amazed Chiffley. Then, as only McConachie

bush plane project. On February 7, 1947, Grant McConachie was appointed president of Canadian Pacific Air Lines.

A lesser man might have rested on his laurels and enjoyed the view from the executive suite, but President McConachie immediately showed up at C. D. Howe's door with his inflatable globe and piece of string. He demonstrated to Howe the Great Circle route from Vancouver to Shanghai, and asked permission to fly it. Howe and Symington had their hands full negotiating TCA's landing rights in Europe and getting Canadair North Stars to fly on these routes. In a decision that would return to haunt the government airline four decades later, Howe gave the whole Pacific region over to CPA in 1948. He did make two could, he regaled everyone with stories of his railway and bush-flying days, concluding by marvelling at how he, a humble stoker, had risen through the ranks to become president of the mighty Canadian Pacific. The prime minister was known to be a shy man, but he leapt to his feet and almost embraced his Canadian brother of the tracks, saying with emotion that "all this put a different complexion on the landing rights altogether."[3]

AN OLD PAL

Securing the permission to fly to Australia was dramatic enough, but the proving flight to Shanghai almost cost the airline most of its pilots and navigators. In January 1949, McConachie and his manager Wop May went to Tokyo to meet with the man who at that moment in history ruled all of Japan and the Far East: the Supreme Allied Commander, General Douglas MacArthur. The Canadian ambassador managed to get McConachie a fifteen-minute audience with MacArthur so that the sales pitch could be made. To McConachie's dismay, the Great Man, upon hearing the words "Canadian Pacific," spent the precious fifteen minutes reminiscing about taking a CPR train to Banff and Lake Louise.

However, just meeting MacArthur must have been sufficient, for the military government immediately gave the Canadians permission to land in Tokyo. Then McConachie and May went to Shanghai to meet with Chinese leader Chiang Kai-shek. They found the city in complete chaos as the People's Liberation Army moved daily closer. At the audience, the Generalissimo seemed preoccupied with his own future, and landing rights into Shanghai were the last thing on his mind. All seemed lost until May recognized Chiang Kai-shek's bodyguard from his bush-flying days in Edmonton. Morris "Two-Gun" Cohen was an Englishman whose family had exiled him to Canada. He had worked as a cowboy on the prairies, becoming a hired gun and something of a Robin Hood to Edmonton's Chinese community. He had protected Sun Yat-Sen when the leader came to Canada on a fund-raising tour. Cohen and Wop May swapped stories. The meeting of these two legendary

figures from Canada's frontier days clinched the landing rights in Shanghai, and McConachie returned to Vancouver well satisfied.

Three months later, on April 19, a Canadair North Star borrowed from the RCAF and filled with CPA air crew left Vancouver for Anchorage, Shemya, Tokyo, Shanghai and Hong Kong. A spare Merlin engine was carried in the cabin. The party landed at Shanghai's Lungwha Airport on April 25, just as the Communist armies entered the city. Chiang Kai-shek and Two-Gun Cohen were long gone. But the Canadian embassy was glad to see the flight, and threw on board packages of confidential documents. With the advance Communist units only ten miles from the airport perimeter, the North Star took off. The CPA plane was the last departure from Shanghai before the airport was overrun and China closed itself off to Western airlines for almost three decades.

ACROSS THE PACIFIC

The Orient in turmoil, McConachie tried to salvage what he could from the Australian route. The inaugural CPA flight to Sydney left Vancouver Airport on July 10, 1949, stopping at Honolulu and Fiji. It was packed with thirty-two guests, including McConachie; Clarence Campbell, president of the National Hockey League; Roy Thomson, the influential newspaper tycoon; and various journalists who were urged to write about the swish of Fijian grass skirts and moonlight over Waikiki for their Canadian audiences. In Sydney, the wife of the Australian minister of the air christened the North Star *Empress of Sydney*, a tradition of naming aircraft that has continued through to the present days of 747s.[4]

But Howe had been right. The thirty-seven-hour flight across the Pacific cost the airline $18,500 one way, and to break even, the aircraft would have to carry a minimum of twenty-one passengers on each flight. On the next trip, which was supposed to be the revenue-making one, only a single passenger boarded. The one-way fare to Australia was $685, well out of the reach of most Canadians. Besides, with the short range of the North Star, the Vancouver-Honolulu flight had to be routed through San Francisco,

In July 1949, at Sydney's Mascot Airport, Grant McConachie addresses invited VIPs at the ceremony marking the inaugural CPA flight from Vancouver. The Canadair 4 CF-CPI behind him is the "Empress of Sydney." CANADIAN AIRLINES ARCHIVES

making for a longer flight. Through the 1950 winter season, when it flew every fortnight, CPA carried only 150 passengers to Hawaii.

It became no secret to the board of directors that the airline was losing large amounts of money in its first year of operation. The Australian run was half empty, and China had retreated into seclusion. The Tokyo stopover could not generate any traffic, as no tourists were allowed into Japan and no Japanese were allowed to leave. The CPR's accountants knew it was only a matter of time before the board at Windsor Station pulled the plug on McConachie and got out of the flying business. But the bush pilot had survived worse, and he kept his grin confident and his cigar burning. Something would turn up. It always did. Sydney, Shanghai and Tokyo were disasters. That left the British Crown Colony of Hong Kong.

In 1949, Hong Kong was a large refugee camp with little food and no water, about to be swallowed up by the battle-hardened millions of the People's Liberation Army, who were held back, it seemed, only by the stiff upper lip of the British Army garrison.[5] Unable to feed or protect so many, authorities encouraged the columns of refugees who flooded through the border

to immigrate overseas as quickly as possible. Hong Kong had traditionally been a transit station for Cantonese emigrants, and an established network of "compradores" or middle men flourished to facilitate the procuring of tickets and travel documents for any ship or aircraft that called.

As McConachie's luck would have it, most refugees had relatives in Canada who were willing to sponsor them on the next available CPA flight. It was an arrangement made in heaven. Canadian dollars flowed in from Chinese restaurants in Canada, and the Canadian government immigration office ensured that each refugee had his or her airfare of $798 paid in full. The CPA North Stars took off from Kai Tak as packed as Wanchai trams in rush hour, each load representing a profit of $29,000 for Canadian Pacific. The gold mine that was Hong Kong yielded the airline $17 million in the next five years, more than paying for the prestigious (but empty) Australian flights.

When the Korean War broke out in June 1950, McConachie wheedled permission out of Ottawa to operate a charter service for U.S. military personnel from Vancouver to Tokyo. He reasoned that the North Stars could take U.S. troops to Japan, then fly on to Hong Kong to pick up the refugees, ensuring a captive payload both ways. For once, the federal government was willing to help Canadian Pacific Air Lines. Ottawa had limited its military involvement in Korea to two patrolling destroyers and a few regiments. Paying for an airlift of American troops was a bloodless way of demonstrating Canadian support—especially if the money went to a Canadian airline. More 39,000 American military personnel enjoyed

cpa's first-class cuisine on the way to Tokyo. As word spread, officers pulled rank on G.I.s just to fly out of Vancouver on cpa. The contract for 700 military charter flights to Tokyo ended in 1955, netting cpa $16 million.

Canadair's founder was the dynamic former salesman Ben Franklin. At the war's end, Franklin bought up carloads of C-54 spares and fuselages at bargain prices. From them the first North Stars were made, one of which glistens behind him. CANADAIR ARCHIVES

THE NORTH STAR

For McConachie, the Hong Kong and Korean routes were a gamble that had paid off. He planned to use the profits for a payment on a fleet of DC-6Bs and, most of all, as legal ammunition with which to fight the TCA monopoly. But first he had to sell off the North Stars. Designated Canadair Fours in Canadian Pacific service, the cpa North Stars were heavier than the TCA version, making them expensive to operate on long routes and limited in payload. It wasn't just the noise of the four Merlin engines that made them unpopular. The exhaust flames from the Merlins, invisible in the daylight, blazed eerily away at night. To customers who had never flown the Pacific before, it looked as if all four engines were on fire.

Management at Trans-Canada Air Lines had always thought of their Lancastrians as a stop-gap measure until the war ended and a more suitable air-craft—preferably one built in Canada—could be found. The two candidates to replace the converted bomber were the C-69 Constellation, which Lockheed had launched in 1943, and the DC-4. The DC-4 was revolutionary when it appeared in 1942. It was the first airliner to require power-boosted controls and to have flush riveting and a steerable nose wheel. But what those ferry pilots during the war really appreciated were the aircraft's four Pratt & Whitney R-2000 Twin Wasp engines. They were so powerful that even if two engines gave up, the plane could still fly.[6]

The first airliner assembled in Canada, the North Star was much like C. D. Howe himself. It was noisy and unpretentious, and its idiosyncrasies were either loved or hated. Its windows and pressurization were modelled on those of the latest DC-6. Howe had initially wanted Boeing in Vancouver to build the Lancastrian replacement, but in March 1944 Canadian

A North Star cockpit in 1949. Little has changed from the 1930s DC-3 cockpit; still recognizable are the throttles, the RPM indicators with the fire extinguisher controls, and the generator gauges (above the windscreens). The hoses on the far right were for oxygen. CANADAIR ARCHIVES

Vickers, personified by its general manager Ben Franklin, convinced Howe to give Canadian Vickers the contract. Howe's first priority was to keep the aviation industry in Canada going, and companies like Fairchild, Federal Aircraft Ltd., Ottawa Car and Noorduyen were grinding to a halt. The RCAF wanted twenty-four of the aircraft, unpressurized, and TCA wanted twenty pressurized planes. The contract stipulated that the first would have to be ready by July 1947.

Canadair's critics have said that Franklin obtained war-surplus aircraft parts from scrap dealers at bargain basement prices and cobbled them into a passenger aircraft that he called Canada's first airliner. He did go to Parkridge, Illinois, to buy up a complete Douglas C-54 plant made surplus by the war's end and have it shipped home to Cartierville. The United States was disposing of its great arsenal of fighters, bombers and transports, which had been made before VJ Day at astronomical expense and now sold for a few hundred dollars apiece. It was the same in Canada, where the sale price of a CCF Hurricane was $100, an Anson $50, and a new Victory Aircraft Lancaster $600. Scrap merchants, aircraft brokers and representatives from third-world air forces went on buying binges across North America.[7]

It remains a mystery today why, in spite of the

Lockheeds it had in use, TCA opted for the Douglas DC-4. It was slow—200 mph compared with the Constellation's 280 mph—and unpressurized. The North Stars had to be expensively modified before the airlines could use them regularly. On the positive side, the DC-4s had flown the Atlantic regularly during the war and their design was a masterpiece of simplicity and sturdiness, allowing Douglas to stretch into the DC-6 and the DC-7. The DC-4 was also seen as a simple project suited to a Canadian workforce.

The airframes were married to four British-made Merlin engines. But Merlins were never made to be throttled back (which happens when an airliner loses altitude to land), since lead deposits would build up on their spark plugs, shutting them down. While it was true that Canada did not have an aircraft engine industry then, Pratt & Whitney in Longueuil had been assembling and servicing aircraft engines since 1928 for Fairchild, Fokker, the RCAF and Canadian Airways. The TCA Lockheeds used P&W Wasps, as did hundreds of Harvard trainers in the British Commonwealth Air Training Plan. After their sterling service during the war, Pratt & Whitney must have expected a contract to supply their R-2800s to Canadair, and they were disappointed when the British-made Rolls-Royce Merlin was chosen instead.

As the main customer for the new airliner, Trans-Canada Air Lines had been given their choice of engine. Considering the trouble the company had already had with the Merlins used on the Lancastrians, their decision is puzzling. Fifty years later, it seems to have more to do with politics than with engineering. The impoverished condition of the Mother Country—as many Canadians still thought of Britain—and the prestige associated with Rolls-Royce might have played a large part in TCA's decision. In Ottawa, the Opposition attacked the North Star assembly as subsidized obsolescence, but history has proved that the aircraft served both TCA and the RCAF well, and the plane was destined for a special place in the national psyche.

Canadair had come into being on November 11, 1944, when the federal government, acting on C.D. Howe's recommendation, purchased the Cana-

dian Vickers plant at Cartierville. Ben Franklin was made its president, and Howe made it clear that Franklin should look for another company to buy Canadair as soon as possible.

Like Boyd at Victory Aircraft, Franklin is remembered as a hard-driving manager who possessed boundless energy. A former farm machinery salesman, he knew little of aircraft before coming to Vickers but was experienced at negotiations. When the war ended, so did the PBY program, and he hustled to find work for his employees by "civilianizing" hundreds of war-surplus C-47s for the new airlines sprouting up around the world. Franklin convinced the American submarine makers, Electric Boat of Groton, Connecticut, to take a 10 per cent interest in the company (and later to buy it all). By early 1946, the North Stars began to take shape, and the first complete aircraft were ready by July. On a sunny Saturday afternoon, the aircraft was put through its paces for assembled spectators and dignitaries.

The first North Stars completed were unpressurized, as they had been ordered for the RCAF, but both TCA and CPA borrowed the aircraft from the air force until their more comfortable, pressurized versions were ready. Trans-Canada Air Lines put its first North Star on the trans-Atlantic route on November 19, 1946, cutting the flying time to an average of eleven hours. Howe himself travelled on one of the first North Stars to London to attend the ceremonies marking the betrothal of Princess Elizabeth to Philip Mountbatten. Eventually, the noise problem with the Merlins was solved by putting in a cross-over exhaust system designed by a TCA engineer named, by coincidence, Merlin McLeod. Gordon McGregor was galled that the government then gave the contract to install the system on all aircraft to Canadair.

Howe had great hopes for an export market for Canadian aircraft after the war, at least until the British and the French industries could catch up, but this was not to be. The Douglas licence forbade the selling of its DC-4, whatever its new name, to anyone except Britain. British Overseas Airways Corporation, waiting for their own aviation industry to turn out the de Havilland Comet and the Bristol Britannia,

H. J. Symington (*left*) and C. D. Howe with the first North Star. Canadian aviation owes much to both men. Symington accepted no salary while he was president of TCA from 1941–47, and Howe's proudest possession was always his TCA pass. AIR CANADA ARCHIVES

did buy twenty-two North Stars and called them Argonauts. The sale was made at the time Britain allowed its colony of Newfoundland to join Canada, giving rise to speculation that Newfoundland had been traded for Canadair aircraft.[8]

In all, Canadair made 71 North Stars, and one C-5, a VIP version with Pratt & Whitney R-2800s, as a personal aircraft for Prime Minister Louis St. Laurent. The RCAF used their North Stars in the Korean War, the Congo and Cyprus, and flew them to Vienna in 1956 to bring back refugees during the Hungarian uprising. The TCA North Stars in commercial service were supposed to be phased out by 1956, but they soldiered on into the turbo-propeller era, the last one retiring on April 30, 1961. Several were put out to pasture at Dorval before being sold to airlines in Mexico and Cuba. Today, the only example of the first Canadian airliner sits quietly deteriorating outside the National Aviation Museum in Ottawa.

C. D. Howe, the American immigrant who had been hell-bent to drag Canada into the Air Age, was voted out of office in 1957 and died in 1960. By then, the Canada that he had helped change did not want him any more. Political campaigning now depended on a good television "image" and Kennedy-like charisma, and Howe had neither. He had become a symbol of what the country wanted to forget—the paternalistic, old-fashioned ideals of the Depression and war. Like another American immigrant, William Van Horne, C. D. Howe had committed himself wholly to his adopted country. At his funeral service, his wife Alice chose the hymn "Ten Thousand Times, Ten Thousand." Howe would have approved its sentiment.

CHAPTER TEN

Gordon McGregor and His Airline

When asked how he fell in love with aviation, Gordon McGregor used to relate the story that, as a boy, he had the good fortune to spend his summers on the lakeshore of Montreal's west island. He was there when the first aerial meet took place in 1910, and the impression it made on the eight-year-old remained with him throughout his life. In his memoirs, he said he stayed on the fields "from dawn to dusk, supervising the preparation of the ground, the erection of small grandstands, and the arrival and assembly of the aircraft. The men of those days must have been a patient lot, because as long as I kept my hands off the aircraft, I was allowed to be near them, and even under them . . . and I don't ever remember being asked for a ticket of admittance." Years later, he remembered "a hot air balloon carried a man aloft, who descended by an unpacked parachute. One night the balloon drifted out over Valois Bay and had to be towed ashore by local volunteer rescuers, amid great excitement."[1] He also witnessed de Lesseps taking off in his Blériot to fly over the city of Montreal.

After taking a degree in engineering from McGill University, McGregor joined Bell Telephone. He was posted as a district manager to Kingston, Ontario, where he learned to fly at the local club, soloing in a Tiger Moth in August 1933. Typically for McGregor, nothing was done half-heartedly. He won the Webster Trophy—which is awarded to the best amateur pilot in Canada—not once but three times, in 1935, 1936 and 1938.

A WAR HERO

When the newspapers reported that Trans-Canada Air Lines was recruiting pilots, McGregor wrote to S. J. Hungerford, the president of the Canadian National Railway, and asked him for a job. His letter was acknowledged, but no more was heard of it. War was on the horizon then, so it seemed natural for McGregor to join 115 Squadron RCAF. As soon as the conflict began, he was sent to England to fly operationally. At thirty-nine, he was the oldest pilot to take part in the Battle of Britain, and the youngsters who flew with him were barely out of school. They called him "Old Gordie." But F/L McGregor showed them: he shot down five German aircraft, had seven "probables" and damaged eight. Along with S/L Ernie McNab and F/O Dal Russel, McGregor was presented to King George V at Buckingham Palace to be given the first award to Canadian airmen for courage. In 1976, when the remains of a Junkers Ju-88 were discovered in an English bog, one of McGregor's "probables" was confirmed as a "kill," and he became the highest scoring RCAF ace in the Battle of Britain.

McGregor was posted to Alaska in 1942, where he commanded a Wing. In 1944, he returned to Britain as a Group Captain to take command of 83 Group in the Second Tactical Air Force. After the D-Day landings, the Group was the first Allied unit to be permanently based on the European mainland. For organizing eighteen squadrons of Spitfires and Typhoons, of which fifteen were Canadian, to fly

from the rough, makeshift airstrips to harass the enemy, G/C McGregor was awarded the Order of the British Empire. He stayed on the Front, his 126 Wing strafing anything that moved behind German lines. At about this time he acquired a captured Luftwaffe Messerschmitt Bf 108 to fly as his personal aircraft, his initials "GRM" painted on its fuselage.

When the war ended, McGregor was asked by a journalist what his plans were. He said, "I'll be back to prewar standards, back to being a Sunday pilot with the hometown flying club. But I'm all set. Got a desk to fly in Montreal with the phone company." However, the next three decades of his life were to be quite the opposite.

TCA COMES CALLING

Herb Symington, the president of TCA, had other ideas for the air ace. Symington had his eye on three RCAF Group Captains, and he recruited McGregor, along with the other two, into TCA. McGregor's old employer, Bell Telephone, gave him leave to join the airline "until he came to his senses." He started as general traffic manager with TCA in Winnipeg on December 1, 1945.

The TCA board of directors probably first heard of McGregor in 1947, when he took part in the International Air Transport Association (IATA) conference outside Rio de Janeiro. His organizational skills there so impressed the delegates that he was elected chairman of the association. He returned to Winnipeg, where in January of the following year, Symington phoned to tell McGregor that he had been appointed president of Trans-Canada Air Lines. Symington told McGregor to go immediately to Ottawa and speak to C. D. Howe, which he did.[2] Howe, in his infamous brusque manner, asked McGregor what he wanted. Taken aback, the new president said, "I expect I need some terms of reference for my new job." Howe growled: "Most people who come here want more than that; but I'll give you one term of reference. You keep out of the taxpayer's pocket and I'll keep out of your hair." It was an oft-repeated story that well described the relationship between the two men.[3]

McGregor soon discovered what Howe meant. The airline was a public service, and no one expected it to be run at a profit. As the chosen instrument of the government, it had no competition. But McGregor, who had made a point of travelling on the Canadian Pacific Railway before the war because it was privately owned, summed up his management philosophy thus: "There isn't a reason in the world why a corporation financed by taxpayers shouldn't be as well managed as one financed by private capital." By the time he took the helm, Trans-Canada Air Lines had suffered through a decade of poor management.

THE BOTTOM LINE

For the first two years of McGregor's presidency, TCA ran a deficit. In 1948, Trans-Canada's fleet consisted of converted Lancaster bombers and war-surplus DC-3s. The company had maintenance bases at both Dorval and Winnipeg, and the only new aircraft ordered were the untried Canadair North Stars. It did not help when, in the ensuing federal election, the leader of the Opposition, George Drew, called the North Stars "obsolete white elephants." McGregor might have privately agreed with some of the criticisms, but as company president he could say nothing.

Another reason for the deficit was that several of the routes flown were wholly impractical. The British Commonwealth Air Training Plan had given most small communities in Canada their own airport, and because TCA was a government airline, every member of Parliament wanted his constituency served by it. An example of this was the daily round-trip flight between Lakehead, Ontario, Howe's own riding, and Duluth, Michigan. The passenger load varied between two and zero, averaging at a single passenger, yet an aircraft and two crews were stationed at Lakehead permanently.

McGregor went to see Howe about stopping the Lakehead flight altogether. Howe was politician enough to know that cancelling the air service in his own constituency would cost him votes in the next election, but if it helped Trans-Canada Air Lines, it

should go. The incident told McGregor that the often irascible Howe cared more about the financial welfare of the airline than his own chances for reelection.[4] Howe, for his part, left McGregor alone as he had promised, explaining that "Either you have faith in the men who have been given the job, and back their judgement, or you get rid of them."[5]

McGregor's transfer of company headquarters from Winnipeg to Montreal in 1949 was unpopular with Westerners, especially Manitobans. Montreal was the headquarters of ICAO and IATA; it was where the CNR had its head offices, and it was the logical choice for an airline with routes across the Atlantic, the eastern United States and the Caribbean. But that did not stop a furore from erupting in the media and in Parliament. McGregor remained adamant.

McGregor set out to remedy other shortcomings too. When he first took over, the company's phone reservations system was open only during business hours. As a former Bell man, McGregor was appalled, and he proceeded to have calls answered twenty-four hours a day seven days a week. Reservations were handled at Toronto, Moncton and Edmonton, and seat sales were coordinated from these locations by teletype.

Streamlining the fleet was next. By the end of 1949, TCA operated twenty-seven DC-3s and twenty North Stars and, besides its North American routes, flew to London, the Caribbean and Bermuda. Crossing the Atlantic in the North Stars still meant refuelling at Gander, Goose Bay and Shannon Airport. Pan American, BOAC and Trans World Airlines were about introduce the Lockheed Constellation, which would fly New York to London with a single stop. Being saddled with the North Stars and their unreliable Merlins meant that TCA would always be in the red, and McGregor hunted around for replacements.

In 1950, to McGregor's joy, a modest budget surplus was recorded. He was enough of a realist to know that it had been caused in part by a CNR strike and a government-sponsored immigration scheme, which assisted the passage of over 10,000 British immigrants to Canada, but it was, as Churchill said, the end of the beginning. McGregor's reforms were achieving results.

Bill Harvey, the TCA accounting clerk who had often slept at the old tin hangar at Winnipeg, was appointed comptroller when TCA headquarters moved to Montreal. As a means of self-preservation, he learned to deal with McGregor. "I always asked myself how 'G.R.' would approach this problem. You had to think that way because you always had to face him with answers." Harvey remembered that the president used to say of him: "I wouldn't work for Harvey for twice my salary. He's a bloody slave driver."[6]

Because TCA was a Crown corporation, each year members of Parliament would grill senior management witnesses after the annual report was tabled in the House. McGregor became an expert at gauging the mood of the tribunal his team was to face. Members of Parliament would ask questions about everything from their lost luggage to why pipe-smoking was banned on board TCA but not on American Airlines to what the criteria were for selection of particular aircraft. The length of these sessions averaged at three days, though the 1949 session stretched out to ten. Bill Harvey learned to read McGregor. If G.R. leaned forward during a question it meant that he had the answer and everything was under control. If he leaned back, it meant that Harvey had better produce the reply—quickly. McGregor was adamant that all questions concerning his airline be answered immediately, unlike CNR officials, who would sometimes mail replies to questions asked by MPs during their hearing. "Ninety-nine per cent of our answers were given on the spot," said Harvey.[7]

Both the DC-3s and the North Stars were reaching the end of their commercial lives, and the perennial Merlins were still costing the struggling airline dearly. McGregor informed Howe in July 1949 that it cost TCA $80 per aircraft hour to maintain its Merlins, while it cost $18.40 an hour for an American operator to maintain the Pratt & Whitney R-28000 engines on his DC-6. McGregor then selected the Lockheed Super Constellation L1049 to

replace the North Star on the overseas runs and ordered five to be delivered by 1953.

The Constellation brought TCA into line with the giants on the Atlantic, Pan American and BOAC. It seated sixty-three passengers (forty-eight in first class and fifteen in tourist) or eighty-two (four in first and seventy-eight in tourist) and required three flight attendants. It cruised at 310 mph, had a range of 4,820 miles and was the first TCA aircraft to have weather radar installed.

Deliveries were delayed because Lockheed was backlogged with orders for military aircraft for the Korean conflict, and it was not until May 14, 1954, that the first TCA "Connie" flew. Designed by Lockheed's Kelly Johnson of "Skunk Works" fame (who would also turn out the U-2 and SR-71 spy planes), the concept owed a lot to Johnson's P-38 twin-boom Lightning fighter. The distinctive three fins, which allowed the aircraft to fit into hangars, made it the most beautiful airliner of its day.

No one could forget the clouds of smoke that poured out of the engines when a Connie started up. The Wright Cyclone RB-3350 Turbo-Compound eighteen-cylinder radial engines (nicknamed "corn-cobs" because of the concentric rows of cylinders), were very complicated after the Merlins, highly susceptible to "hot spots" and propeller-blade failure. Maintenance staff complained that there were 144 sparkplugs to change in a single aircraft. The Constellation engines were finicky enough that a flight engineer became an essential part of the cockpit crew, monitoring the propeller control switches, throttles, controls to feather the engines, mixture controls and a cowl flap control to position the cowls on each engine.[8]

The technology of the Constellation meant that the days of a captain's absolute authority over an aircraft were through. The airline's public relations office now also required that the captain make the announcements about the flight, the route and the weather over the intercom. One pilot recalled that many senior captains were tongue-tied, and TCA had to hire a Canadian Broadcasting Corporation radio host to give them lessons.

TCA President Gordon McGregor (*left*) greets Sir George Edwards, the president of Vickers, in June 1959. An anglophile, McGregor bought both the Viscount and the Vanguard for his airline from Vickers. AIR CANADA ARCHIVES

The Connie was infamous for oil leaks—hydraulic, engine and fuel—and oil consumption was a constant problem. It was said that you could recognize anyone who worked on or near a Connie because their clothes had permanent spots on them. But it was the first airliner you could walk under without bumping your head.

THE VISCOUNT

With the TCA insignia on the Constellations hardly dry, McGregor surprised the board of directors in October 1952 by telling them that he had ordered fifteen Vickers Viscounts from Britain to replace DC-3s on short-haul routes. After the North Star experience, he never allowed Ottawa to interfere with the airline's purchasing policy, choosing what in his

opinion were the most suitable aircraft for the job.

The former Battle of Britain ace had been seduced by the Viscount at the Farnborough Air Show where he met George Edwards, Vickers' chief designer. The two became firm friends, and a trial flight in the Viscount followed, with McGregor taking the controls himself. As he later wrote, "It felt like one of the later Marks of Spitfires. Neither on the ailerons, elevators or rudder was there the slightest hint of heaviness, which is the hall-mark of a four-engined aircraft." McGregor knew that after the noisy, uncomfortable DC-3s, the Viscount would have great passenger appeal. There was a complete absence of engine sound and vibration from the Viscount's four Rolls-Royce Dart engines, and the aircraft's cabin windows were—and remain—the largest ever installed on an airliner.

As a turboprop aircraft, the Viscount was far ahead of anything that the United States then made. But to avoid the kind of disastrous experiences TCA had had with the Rolls-Royce Merlins, McGregor made sure that the Viscounts came with a good engine maintenance warranty. Even so, the TCA maintenance department was not pleased with McGregor's decision. After a visit to Vickers, Senior Projects Engineer Clayton H. Glenn wrote:

> Although George Edwards was very congenial and open to suggestions, the Vickers people were very hostile. They knew we had ordered the aircraft contingent to a number of sales being made and as far as they were concerned the airplane was perfect and required no sales at all. . . . The cabin interior reminded one of an American suburban bus of the mid-thirties. The baggage rack consisted of lace webbing into which you threw your parcels and clothes. The electrical control system for the propeller feathering was extremely complicated . . . Similarly, the air conditioning and pressurization system were such that it took two pilots to operate them. The structure of the plane left a lot to be desired. The wing had basically one spar with the ribs more or less hanging from it like limbs from a tree. A very serious design deficiency existed in the fuel system. Although

the Viscount was a four engine airplane, the fuel system was designed as if it were a twin. This meant that a single failure in the fuel system could cause the shutting down of two engines on the same side.[9]

Herb Seagrim thought the Viscount "too advanced for TCA."[10] Used to the layout of American avionics, others found the Viscount's cockpit poorly designed and unnecessarily complicated. However, Vickers was so desperate to break into the North American market that George Edwards was willing to make whatever changes TCA wanted at his company's expense. The price for fifteen aircraft was a bargain $15 million, and the TCA pilots agreed with McGregor that the aircraft were light on the controls and flew like fighters.

In October 1952 McGregor called Howe to tell him of the planned purchase. After worrying about the maintenance of British-made equipment, Howe said: "I suppose it's the right thing." Then he thundered, "Your blood will be on your head! You'll never get them delivered on time."[11]

The TCA Vickers Vanguard, with its Rolls-Royce Tyne engine, proved unreliable, making it unpopular with maintenance staff. Like British European Airways, the other major Vanguard operator, Air Canada converted several to freighters. AIR CANADA ARCHIVES

That a North American airline should buy other than a North American aircraft was seen as traitorous by many in the United States and Canada. McGregor was an Anglophile and his friendship with George Edwards was well-known; these things made his decision suspect. But his pilot's intuition proved the naysayers wrong. The Viscounts were delivered on time, and TCA became the first airline in North America to use turboprops. In a welcome reversal of fortune for the British aviation industry, Capital Airlines in the United States bought British aircraft in 1955 and within a year had tripled its business. Howard Hughes, the 1930s aviator and owner of Trans World Airlines, also recognized a winner. George Lothian trained Hughes to fly the Viscount at Dorval Airport and wrote about that strange episode later. The eccentric millionaire avoided contact with everyone else as much as possible, and for ten days lived in his own 1649 Constellation parked on the ramp at the airport.

By the time it ended the aircraft's production run in 1964, Vickers had made 444 Viscounts (of which TCA took 52), and the little airliner was the most successful British commercial aircraft ever exported, with a dozen still flying in 1996.[12]

THE VANGUARD

The choice of a medium-range aircraft to ply the short, high-density routes such as Toronto–Montreal–New York was harder to make, and McGregor's decision was met with a storm of criticism. While Boeing and Douglas were gearing up to mass-produce jet airliners, in 1957 Lockheed brought out the turboprop Electra. Their popular C-130 Hercules military transports used Allison 501-D 15 turboprop engines, and the company hoped to buy time until they could develop their own jets. American and Eastern Airlines both bought Electras, as did KLM, QANTAS and Ansett. Knowing that TCA was looking to supplement their Viscounts, Lockheed hoped that the aircraft's name would evoke for the airline the romance of its early days.

But they had not reckoned on TCA's ties to the Mother Country. British European Airways (BEA) wanted to replace its Viscounts with an aircraft that had greater passenger-carrying capacity on its London-Manchester-Belfast-Glasgow runs. Both BEA and TCA wanted a wider cargo space under the cabin floor, capacity for up to a hundred passengers and a maximum range of 2,600 miles. So Vickers tailored the Vanguard to the needs of both airlines, giving the aircraft a curious "double-bubble" body that hurt its sales to other airlines. BEA bought twenty Vanguards, and on January 31, 1957, TCA signed an order for twenty-three. To drum up more sales, in 1959 Vickers sent Sir George Edwards in a Vanguard on a tour of North America.

Once more McGregor had chosen well. At $2.7 million, the Vanguard was cheaper than the Lockheed Electra—and, it turned out, a lot safer. In March 1960, the Federal Aviation Authority issued an order to ground all Electras. Two had lost their wings in flight, and subsequent testing determined that successive landings had damaged the aircraft's engine mounts, causing total structural failure. By the time the modified Electra was returned to airline service in 1962, the aircraft had lost the market and was too late to be an effective airliner. It evolved into the P-3C Orion maritime patrol aircraft that several air forces of the world (including Canada's) continue to use.

By the end of 1961, all the TCA Vanguards were in service, flying, in addition to the Montreal–Toronto–Ottawa link, to the Maritimes, Vancouver, the Caribbean and the United States. Two and a half years after taking delivery of its last Vanguard, TCA (now Air Canada) began to withdraw the aircraft from their passenger routes and convert them into freighters. BEA did the same, selling them off as Merchantmen. Passengers now preferred to fly jet aircraft, and the Electra and the Vanguard became dinosaurs.

ON THE HOT SEAT

The Vanguard's replacement caused McGregor the worst moments of his presidency. In 1963, there were three contenders for a small twin-jet airliner to replace the Vanguards—the Douglas DC-9, the British BAC 1-11 (Vickers had metamorphosed into the British Aircraft Corporation, run by Sir George Edwards), and the French Sud Aviation Caravelle. The French plane was five years older than the other two, but there was hope that its purchase would bring subcontracting work to Canadair at Cartierville. French President Charles de Gaulle personally lobbied for the Caravelle, and Quebec Premier Jean Lesage, looking for a few cheap votes, told the media that Air Canada shouldn't reject the aircraft "just because it was French."[13]

McGregor had his technical team study the three aircraft on the basis of cost, upkeep and efficiency, and he accepted their report that the DC-9 was the most suitable. When he had to explain this decision to a House of Commons committee, he whispered

to an aide "that the Caravelle is no good for TCA, not that I think it's any great shakes either." Unfortunately, a microphone amplified his remarks, and the French media exploded his words into headlines.

University of Montreal students paraded outside the airline's offices, the riot police were called and Prime Minister Lester Pearson was pulled into the fracas. McGregor, as usual, took the most direct approach, meeting with a student delegation from the university to explain his remarks. The whole situation was eventually defused, and Vice-President Herb Seagrim accepted Air Canada's first DC-9 from Donald Douglas himself the following year.

The size of TCA had increased greatly with each decade. In 1939 it had 500 employees. By 1950 this had risen to 5,512, and ten years later to 11,284. When Trans-Canada Air Lines became the first carrier to use the DC-8 jet aircraft in 1960, McGregor

invited J. A. D. McCurdy as an honoured guest aboard its first transcontinental flight. Years before, McCurdy had accompanied McGregor to the historic site at Baddeck. The old man pointed into the clear water of the lake where the engine of his *Silver Dart* had been abandoned. After the Aerial Experiment Association disbanded, the most historic aeroengine in Canadian aviation history had been used to power a motor launch. When that disintegrated, the engine sank into the lake bed. McGregor urged McCurdy to "do something about that" and, with McGregor's encouragement, the Bell Museum opened at Baddeck a few years later as a historic landmark.

As Delta Airlines is said to have made Atlanta an international city, so Trans-Canada Air Lines did for Montreal. TCA started flying to Paris in 1951, and since Berlin was still under military occupation, to Dusseldorf the following year. Brussels followed, then Zurich, and by 1958 Rome. McGregor wanted Cairo, New Delhi and Rio de Janeiro in the immediate future. He turned down the opportunity to fly to Mexico City, thinking it unprofitable and allowing Grant McConachie to grab the route in exchange for CPA's Quebec network. When McGregor later asked McConachie how the route was working out, the CPA president is supposed to have said, only half in jest, "Not so good—it's costing me two or three Cadillacs a year."

A NAME CHANGE

As early as 1953, McGregor had applied for permission to change the airline's name to Air Canada. With Canadian Pacific Air Lines now flying interna-

tionally, McGregor felt that TCA needed to assert its official status. In 1964, he received help from an unexpected quarter. A new name would also be more acceptable in Quebec, figured a young Jean Chrétien, then a novice Liberal member of Parliament. "The old name," he later wrote, had become "a hateful symbol because it didn't translate easily into French."[14] Chrétien resolved to have it changed. But as a junior backbencher, he knew that he had little chance of getting a private member's bill passed. So he went to see as many friendly Conservatives as he could and asked for their help, in Quebec's name. Then he lobbied the only NDP member who spoke French, and did the same for Social Credit MPs. Officially the Tories were strongly opposed to changing the airline's name, but the French-speaking ones were prepared to help.

When Chrétien's bill came up in the House of Commons, the future prime minister emphasized that the name "Air Canada" was shorter, that the airline was no longer flying just in Canada and that there were now two other TCAs—Trans-Caribbean and Trans-Continental. All those he had lobbied then got up and agreed with the young man, and his bill passed the second reading. The government wasn't pleased about the change, reasoning that the cost of repainting the fleet would be high. But the bill received Royal Assent on January 1, 1965. The prime minister later thanked Chrétien for solving what could have been a thorny problem in a painless way.

When a princess, Queen Elizabeth II had flown in the North Stars, so it seemed appropriate that she should inaugurate the Air Canada DC-8 bearing the new company logo. McGregor would later write of the occasion:

> In October 1964, Air Canada flew Her Majesty Queen Elizabeth II nonstop from Ottawa to London in the first DC-8 to be painted in the new company livery and carrying the name AIR CANADA. It is probably not generally known that a second DC-8, fully fuelled and provisioned but still carrying the name Trans-Canada Air Lines because there had been no

time to repaint it, was waiting unobtrusively behind in a nearby hangar, in case on start up, one of the several hundred instruments on the aircraft flight deck did not show the exact reading that was expected of it.

McGregor's presidency was coming to an end. He had groomed his vice-president, Herb Seagrim, to take his place. But this was not to be. After the publicity surrounding the Caravelle affair, the government airline was increasingly viewed in some circles as a club for former RCAF officers, all of whom were Anglophones. The new prime minister, Pierre Trudeau, knew that the preponderance of English Canadians in the airline's management would not go unnoticed from the Opposition benches in Ottawa or in Quebec City. He suggested Yves Pratte, a Quebec City lawyer, to replace McGregor.

THE END OF AN ERA
Always immaculately dressed, reserved with strangers to the point of shyness, Gordon McGregor had served his airline well. He was an innate administrator who made sure TCA's ledgers stayed in the black as much as possible. He had no time for management consultants and enjoyed telling the story of a lusty bull who, seeing a field full of cows, charged forward but didn't quite make it over the fence. "So he became a consultant," said McGregor.

His frankness often got him into trouble. He said publicly that the Department of Transport's estimate of what it would cost to build Montreal's Mirabel Airport was only half of what it would eventually cost—and he was correct. As early as 1961, he predicted that the Anglo-French Concorde would be an unprofitable venture, that in the future, its epitaph would read, "Never in the history of human endeavour has so much money and effort been spent in producing something that the purchaser didn't want."

His personality was in direct contrast to that other giant of the airline industry, Grant McConachie, who drank champagne, was never happier than when he was entertaining, and substituted pizazz

Gordon McGregor, Mrs. J. A. Grant, the former Lucille Garner (*right*), and an unidentified well-wisher commemorate the airline's 25th anniversary in 1962. By then, Trans-Canada Airlines had grown to 11,719 employees and was the eighth largest airline in the world. AIR CANADA ARCHIVES

and theatrics for a successful bottom line. McGregor conceded that McConachie was the best sales manager he ever knew, that he used his string and inflatable balloon to good advantage. "On the slightest provocation," he would say, "Grant fills it with hot air and cigar smoke. Then he sits on it."

McConachie retaliated with this reference to his rival: "Actually, Gordon and I are good personal friends. The only flaw in our friendship is the fact that I envy him. I would envy any man who can eliminate his competition by losing money, and the more money he loses, the more secure his monopoly."

In 1967, the Pointe Claire Chamber of Commerce on the west island of Montreal commissioned a sculpture on the site of the aerial meet that had taken place at Lakeside fifty-seven years earlier. As president of Air Canada, the main employer in the region, Gordon McGregor was asked to unveil the

marker and talk at the luncheon held afterwards. His speech paid tribute to the early aviators "who took off reasonably certain that their engines would fail and that they had no idea how to fly. It is astonishing that under these circumstances anything ever got airborne and I think it right and fitting that their courage be commemorated. Certain it is that none of the participants in 1910 had the slightest inkling of what they were starting, and it is equally true today that none of us can envisage what the next half century will do for Canadian aviation."[15]

When he retired in 1968, McGregor and his wife devoted themselves to travelling the world. In his nineteen years as its president, Air Canada had grown to 16,656 employees with a network that stretched from Los Angeles to Moscow, ranking among the world's seven great airlines. It was always McGregor's firm conviction that some form of merger of both Canada's airlines was the only practical solution to the problems of each. He also predicted that the federal government's financial investment in Air Canada would be decreased in the future and that stock would be sold to the airline's employees, giving them a personal stake in the company's financial well-being.

Gordon McGregor died on March 8, 1971. He was named to Canada's Aviation Hall of Fame in 1973. Throughout his life, McGregor had enjoyed quoting poet Rudyard Kipling. The first verse from Kipling's "The Song of Diego Valdez" is a fitting tribute to McGregor's career:

The God of Fair Beginnings
Hath prospered here my hand—
The cargoes of my lading,
And the keels of my command.
For out of my many ventures
That sailed with hope as high,
Mine own have made the better trade,
And Admiral am I![16]

CHAPTER ELEVEN

The Alphabet of Industry: Avro, Bristol, Canadair, de Havilland

The 1950s in Canada were memorable for two major trends in aviation: the introduction of jet aircraft and the achievements of the aviation industry. Both developments laid the roots for the aerospace industry four decades later.

TROUBLED SKIES

The end of the Second World War and the delivery of an atomic bomb by a B-29 bomber had both posi-tive and negative effects on North Americans. The research and development that made the bomber (and its bomb) possible would influence civil avia-tion in the form of advanced aerodynamics and elec-tronic control systems. At the same time, German war booty yielded secrets that would allow the Allies to produce swept-wing jet turbine aircraft, which the United States, the Soviet Union and Britain would develop into the jet fighter and, ultimately, the jet airliner. In Britain, Geoffrey de Havilland had begun building the Comet, the world's first passenger jet, in 1945. In Canada, interest in turbine power had begun as early as 1942 when Ralph Bell, the federal head of aircraft production, sent Canadian engineers to England to study the work of Frank Whittle, the RAF officer who had built the world's first jet engine. When the engineers returned to Canada they formed the country's first jet engine company, Turbo Research Ltd., in July 1944. The war's end and the expense involved in pure research prompted the federal government to look for a parent company for Turbo Research.

As beneficial as these advances to commercial aviation were, they also ended the protection that the North American continent had enjoyed since the sixteenth century, surrounded as it was by an ocean moat. The enemy was now the Soviet Union, and the threat of a nuclear attack from over the pole prompted the biggest arms build-up in history. An electronic Maginot Line of concentric radar networks, the Distant Early Warning Line, extending from Alaska east to Baffin Island, was built to detect incoming aircraft or missiles and deploy interceptors to destroy them. If it rained Soviet bombs and missiles—and the surprise performance of the Soviet MiG-15 in the Korean War made this look entirely possible—Washington and Ottawa wanted the battle to take place over the uninhabited wastes of northern Canada. An aircraft capable of operating in the harsh climate above the pole and able to carry sufficient fuel and sophisticated weaponry did not exist in the Canadian armoury, and would have to be built. The euphoria of the Trans-Canada Airway and the industrial build-up of the war still lingered with C.D. Howe, who said that the country needed one large project at all times to keep its economy going.

The decision to build an all-Canadian interceptor also stemmed from the country's "loneliness" complex, to borrow a phrase used by Jim Floyd in a speech given to the Royal Aeronautical Society in London in 1958. Throughout the Second World War, Canadian airmen flying operationally felt that they were low on the list for the latest aircraft. Whether this was true or not, Canadian bomber crews flew slow, vulnerable Halifaxes and slower Stirlings long after their British counterparts had moved on to the Lancaster. At home, the Hurricane fighters made at Fort William, Ontario, to meet a possible Japanese threat to the British Columbia coast had been allocated to the Soviet allies. Thus in 1946, when the RCAF looked to replace its World War II Mustangs, it had two good arguments for persuading the government to finance the design and manufacture of a twin-engined, jet interceptor program.

The British aircraft manufacturer A.V. Roe had sold his company in 1928, but the company's new owners kept the name.[1] A.V. Roe turned out aircraft at Manchester, two of which, the Anson and the Lancaster, were the cornerstones of the aviation industry in Canada. At the end of the war, the managing director at A.V. Roe, Sir Roy Dobson, looked to break into the civil aviation market in North America. Impressed by David Boyd's program for building Avro Lancasters at Malton, in 1946 Dobson negotiated with the Canadian government to purchase both Victory Aircraft Ltd. and Turbo Research Ltd. The two merged under the name Avro Canada Ltd.

THE AVRO JETLINER

The deal promised Canada access to British jet technology and thousands of jobs. The federal government underwrote Avro Canada's start-up costs (which were so high, in fact, that Howe kept the figure secret), and, to make the deal even more attractive, the RCAF prepared specifications for a new all-weather jet fighter to be built by Avro. Turbo Research, as part of Avro's Gas Turbine Division, built the first Canadian gas turbine engine, the Chinook, in March 1948, and then went on to develop powerplants for the first Canadian jet fighters, culminating in the manufacture of the Iroquois engine that was to have powered the Avro Arrow MK.2.

By late 1949, testing on the first of these Avro aircraft, designated the CF-100, had begun. There were problems both structural and operational: no one

had built or tested a jet fighter in Canada before.[2] The peculiarities of the turbine engine, the Dowty hydraulic system and the airframe skin (which buckled at high speed) all had to be gradually learned by Avro and the RCAF. On October 17, 1951, Avro delivered the country's first production jet fighter, the CF-100 Mk.2, to the RCAF at Rockcliffe. It had taken five years from drawing board to production line. At the ceremony, C. D. Howe correctly predicted that the stolid, tubular aircraft before him, called the Canuck, would mark a milestone in Canada's industrial progress. He had little idea of what was to follow. [3]

Dobson had other fish to fry. Parent company A. V. Roe was already involved in the British civil market, building Lancastrians, Yorks and Tudors. Trans-Canada Air Lines was looking to replace its DC-3s, and "Dobbie" lobbied Howe and Symington for a contract. Talented A. V. Roe designers such as James C. Floyd had come over to Malton with ideas for a revolutionary new airliner. Floyd proposed a twin-jet aircraft that would carry thirty-six passengers, cruise at 450 mph and have sufficient range to service TCA's transcontinental network. The airline expressed an interest but didn't sign a formal contract to purchase the C-102 Jetliner, as the aircraft was called. Floyd originally wanted to power the airframe with two Rolls-Royce Avon engines, developing 6,500 pounds of thrust. But the British refused to declassify the Avon engine, fearing the

An aircraft before its time: designed by Avro's James C. Floyd, the C-102 Jetliner flew on August 10, 1949, the first jet airliner in North America. Sadly, the Canadian government remained indifferent to the aircraft, and only airline magnate Howard Hughes recognized its potential. NATIONAL DEFENCE CANADIAN FORCES PHOTOGRAPHIC UNIT PL 50431A

Jetliner might fly before the de Havilland Comet, jeopardizing British sales. So Floyd was forced to redesign his aircraft using four smaller Derwent 5s instead. This change made the plane 13 per cent more fuel-hungry and increased its weight from 45,000 to 65,000 pounds, limiting its range to 700 miles at a time when TCA wanted to reduce its refuelling stops across the country.

On August 10, 1949, the Jetliner prototype made its first flight at Malton. The de Havilland Comet had flown two weeks before, but this was the first flight of a passenger aircraft powered by jet engines in North America—and it was made in Canada! Two years later, Floyd received the Wright Brothers Award for his paper on the Avro C-102 Jetliner, the first non-American to be so honoured. Unfortunately, this recognition did not cut any ice with Howe, who harboured a deep dislike for the C-102, feeling that the money and time would have been better spent building fighter aircraft for the Korean War. Besides, he had made up his mind that the first Canadian airliner was to be made by Canadair in Montreal.

Aeronautical engineer James C. Floyd in 1995. Primarily
responsible for the design of the Avro C-102 Jetliner and the
CF-105 Arrow, Floyd took Canadian aviation to the very
forefront of technology. In 1984, the United States space
shuttle *Challenger* carried into space a plaque commemo-
rating Floyd's achievement. JAMES FLOYD PHOTO

Right: Beloved in aviation lore as "the Clunk" and "the Lead
Sled," the Avro CF-100 Canuck was the first Canadian-
designed jet fighter, equipping RCAF squadrons in 1951.
NATIONAL DEFENCE CANADIAN FORCES PHOTOGRAPHIC UNIT RE 75-931

TCA did not want the Jetliner either. President Gordon McGregor found the aircraft too radical and too expensive, coming as it did at a time when he was trying to get his airline out of debt. Even the RCAF, the first air force to operate jet transports, ordered two de Havilland Comets in November 1951.

Ottawa finally ordered that all work on the Jetliner stop immediately. When Floyd tried to interest airlines in the United States, Howe was reportedly furious, fuming that Canadian taxpayers had been financing an aircraft that might be used only below the border. But only Howard Hughes test-flew the plane. The prototype was all that was ever built of the C-102 Jetliner, and while many Torontonians remember it performing at the Canadian National Exhibition airshows in 1953 and 1954, it ended its days as a "chase" plane for the CF-100. On November 23, 1956, the Jetliner flew for the last time. Floyd desperately tried get the Smithsonian Institution in Washington or the National Research Council in Ottawa to save the aircraft. But here too he was unsuccessful. The aircraft's parts went to technical schools and scrap dealers, and its seats to a charter airline. The wheels were bought by a farmer for his wagon. Today only the nose is housed at the National Aviation Museum in Ottawa.

THE AVRO ARROW

Future generations of Canadians might forgive the destruction of the Jetliner, but the demise of the next Avro aircraft has become a national tragedy of almost mythological proportions. Avro's speed in developing the Canuck encouraged the RCAF to submit specifications for the next generation of fighter, which was to be supersonic. More ink has been spilled about the Avro Arrow than any other aircraft in Canadian history, and it has come to symbolize all that is daring and romantic, and at the same time petty and vindictive, in the national character. While the debate about the effectiveness of the missile versus the manned interceptor raged in Washington and London, the Arrow represented Canada's last grab for the golden ring: independence from the United States in the form of its own fighter aircraft.

In hindsight, the aircraft was too expensive for any one country to build without an expectation of export orders. For this the RCAF must share the blame. The British and the Americans, both with established aviation industries, developed less sophisticated, cheaper aircraft like the Lightning and the F-102 for the same purpose. The RCAF remained impractical and inflexible in their demands for what they wanted a Canadian-made aircraft to do. In May 1953, they issued "AIR 7-3," which specified that the CF-105 supersonic all-weather interceptor must have a range of 6,000 nautical miles, be capable of Mach 1.5, carry a crew of two, use two engines and operate effectively in the harsh northern climate. Its armament would consist only of missiles, stored not under the wing but in a large internal bay. Its nose would hold a radar and fire-control system so advanced that they hadn't been tested yet. Nothing was to be derivative, nothing "off the shelf," and all systems—fire-control, electronic and engine—had to be completed within an allotted time span.

That Floyd and the Avro team were able to build the CF-105 Arrow at all was amazing. That they were able to pull it off while the CF-100 was being modified and the Jetliner put through its paces is beyond comprehension. In a lecture to the Royal Aeronautical Society in London in 1958, Jim Floyd gave some indication of how it was done: "The decision was made to proceed with a number of development aircraft on the basis of a production type drawing release from the outset. In other words it was decided to take the technical risks involved to save time on the programme. Production personnel worked alongside the Design team to check and advise. Detailed layouts were all issued on a full production basis." [4]

On October 4, 1957, at 2:00 P.M.—in time for reporters to file copy for the evening papers—the first Arrow was rolled out of the Avro hangar to the accompaniment of a military band and the delight of 12,000 spectators. The podium was heavy with VIPs: Sir Roy Dobson, four air vice marshals, Air Chief of Staff Hugh Campbell and the minister of defence, the Honourable George Pearkes V.C., D.S.O.

Linking the event with the past were two others whose careers had been central in the country's aviation history: Air Vice Marshal Wilfrid Curtis (now retired) and J. A. D. McCurdy. When the Arrow subsequently broke the sound barrier on March 25, 1958, it was the most important event in Canadian aviation since the *Silver Dart* had lifted off the ice at Baddeck.

But 1957 was an election year, and as the production cost of an Arrow grew from $2 million to $12.5 million, the aircraft had been subjected to intense scrutiny by both the media and John Diefenbaker's Conservative Party in Opposition. Diefenbaker, running on a nationalist platform, was elected in June 1957. If he and his ministers were unaware of the technological consequences of thwarting what might

The Avro Arrow is destined to live forever in Canadian aviation history. When it was rolled out at 2:00 p.m. on October 4, 1957, aerial pioneer J.A.D. McCurdy was a member of the audience. NATIONAL DEFENCE CANADIAN FORCES PHOTOGRAPHIC UNIT PCN 217

be Canada's last chance to develop a fighter, as politicians they knew the labour unrest that the cancellation of the Arrow would cause. So the decision was taken to continue the program for another year. There were, after all, three Conservative MPs from the Malton area.

Avro management had loudspeakers broadcasting radio news rigged up around the Arrow production line to keep the work force informed of what was taking place in Ottawa. The Cabinet bought time by jettisoning some of aircraft's options. On September 23, 1958, the radar and fire-control systems were cut, and in the same announcement, for the first time, the Bomarc missile was introduced as an alternative. Diefenbaker then shelved the distasteful decision until after the Christmas holidays. His biographer would later write that Diefenbaker always hoped postponements might make miracles happen. The prime minister began the new year with a series of Cabinet discussions on the Arrow.

The United States had their own F-106 fighters coming off the production line by then. The Convair F-106 Delta Dart was similar in shape to the Arrow, and also relied on air-to-air missiles. But as a derivative of the Delta Dagger, it was a fraction of the cost of the Arrow to produce and sell, and its computer could process data from SAGE, a ground-based system that guided the interceptor towards the intruder until the aircraft's own radar could pick up the target. The Canadian fighter could not be sold to the U.S. Air Force because its range was limited—the RCAF had not allowed for the Arrow to have in-flight refuelling—and the aircraft was not equipped to use SAGE. Yet the Americans did offer to help. Norman Robertson, Canadian ambassador to Washington, was told that the Pentagon was prepared to buy up the Arrows and present them to the RCAF. This offer was refused on grounds of national pride.

February 20, 1959, has gone down as "Black Friday" in Canadian history. At 11:15 A.M., Prime Minister Diefenbaker announced that the whole CF-105 program was to be cancelled and that all work on the development of the Arrow was to stop immediately. As if to cushion the blow, the prime minister said that the government was examining the option of acquiring Bomarc missiles with nuclear warheads and storing them on Canadian soil.

When Cabinet met on February 23, the irony of the date was not lost on those present. Meeting to prepare for an emergency debate on what would in later years be termed "damage control," Cabinet members were aware that, in an eerie coincidence, it was the fiftieth anniversary of the flight of the *Silver*

Dart. As they sat, a reproduction of the *Silver Dart* was lifting off the ice at Baddeck, piloted by w/c Paul Hartman of the RCAF, with J.A.D. McCurdy as a witness.

At Malton, the final act was about to be played out: the wanton destruction of the six Arrow proto-types. Their jigs and all the tools were cut up by the welder's torch. For many years the story has persisted that this last order came directly from the prime minister's office. There were also rumours that the order had come from the Americans and the British, who had supplied Avro with equipment and advice still on the classified list. In 1997, it came to light that it was actually chief of the air staff, Air Marshal Hugh Campbell, in a memo to minister of defence George Pearkes on April 26, who recommended that all Arrows be reduced to scrap. "Selling it in its original state," he wrote, "could lead to embarrassment and the airframe could conceivably be used as a roadside stand."[5]

Throughout the years, Prime Minister Diefenbaker has been labelled a coward for not standing up to American pressure. In fact, he twice refused to scrap the Arrow for fear of the unemployment it would cause in the Toronto region and the exodus of aviation professionals to the United States. Historians today hold that Pearkes was convinced by his military advisors that Canada could no longer afford the Arrow.[6] The Army needed to re-equip its brigade in Europe, the RCAF wanted to upgrade its Sabres, and the Navy wanted more modern ships. Building indigenous fighter aircraft was an expensive indulgence: each CF-100 cost $750,000 to make, while the North American F-86 Sabre, built under licence by Canadair, was a bargain at $250,000.

The chosen Bomarc missile, meanwhile, was the subject of a series of spectacular test failures at Cape Canaveral, even though it is reputed that Pearkes kept insisting to the press that "it was a vital element in the country's air defence." On May 1, 1960, the Russians shot down an American U-2 spy plane on a photographic mission over Siberia, causing the Paris Summit between President Eisenhower and Russian President Nikita Krushchev to collapse. Two years later, another U-2 spotted Soviet surface-to-surface missiles in Cuba, and the Cold War looked likely to explode. But it was all too late for the Avro Arrow.

One who didn't join in the criticism of Diefenbaker was the old warhorse C. D. Howe, now living in retirement in Montreal. There were limits to government spending, Howe said, and as he had learned with the North Star, the aviation market was a fickle and expensive one. Only the superpowers could afford to risk millions on aircraft development.

On August 1, 1957, Canada agreed to participate in NORAD, the North American Defence Command, which integrated the U.S. and Canadian air defence systems. On August 27, the Soviets launched their first Intercontinental Ballistic Missiles, leading the Western military establishment to believe that ICBMs would have made an aircraft like the Arrow obsolete even before it became operational.

The Arrow's cancellation, following that of the Jetliner, finished off Avro Canada, and all 14,000 of its employees were dismissed. The former Victory Aircraft plant was acquired by de Havilland in 1964 to manufacture components for the DC-9. A year later, Douglas took over the premises themselves to establish a permanent base in Canada, becoming McDonnell Douglas in 1967. Today, because only wings are made there, the scene of so much of Canada's aviation history has a low profile at the edge of Pearson International Airport.

Diefenbaker too became a casualty of the whole affair. By replacing the Arrow with nuclear Bomarc missiles, the Conservatives started down the road to defeat at the polls in 1963. There were other aviation hurdles ahead for the Conservatives, such as the Canadair CL-44 fiasco, but none would be as lethal as the Avro Arrow. Pearkes retired as minister of national defence on October 11, 1960, and reappeared as lieutenant governor of British Columbia. He was replaced at DND by Douglas Harkness, whose career would also be shot down by the Bomarc missiles.

If there was a villain to be found (and all good tragedies need one), it was the RCAF, the organization that had set Avro such impossible standards.

The British Defence White Paper of 1957 had also declared "push button warfare" the way of the future, but the British Lightning program was not cancelled, and the aircraft served until the late 1970s. Manned interceptors continue to be used today, but as Canada learned early on with the Panavia Tornado, the McDonnell Douglas/BAE Harrier and the Sepecat Jaguar, these are usually made by consortiums of nations with firm export orders. Even by the end of the 1950s, fighter aircraft were so expensive to produce that military planners asked for aircraft capable of multipurpose roles as a means of limiting the expenditures. The RCAF, by its very inflexibility, had doomed the Arrow to a single mission. Having paid Avro a total of $967,371,827 between 1949 and 1957, the air force killed off the Arrow and failed to put the related research and technology to any use at all. The next generation of Canadian fighter aircraft were Lockheed F-104 Starfighters and Northrop F-5 Freedom Fighters, both built under licence by Canadair. The only Canadian-designed jet fighters, the CF-100 Canucks, were replaced in 1961 by secondhand F-101 Voodoos from the U.S. Air National Guard.

The demise of the Arrow coincided with the start of the race to the moon, and many Avro engineers were recruited by NASA to work on the Mercury and Gemini programs. Jim Floyd, having seen two of his projects destroyed by political timidity, returned to England and got a job at Hawker Siddeley, where as chief engineer he conducted a feasibility study for a proposed British supersonic airliner. In 1961, the Royal Aeronautical Society awarded Floyd the George Taylor medal for his work on supersonic technology, and he opened his own aerospace company. Undoubtedly, Floyd's proudest moment took place on February 3, 1984, when the United States space shuttle *Challenger* carried into space a special plaque with a citation bearing his name.

DE HAVILLAND CANADA TAKES OFF

Avro had built one last design, the VZ-9V Avrocar prototype, before vacating the premises to de Havilland and its managing director Phillip Clarke

In four decades at de Havilland Canada, the unassuming P. C. (Phil) Garratt influenced a dynasty of legendary Short Take-Off and Landing aircraft. BOMBARDIER/DE HAVILLAND ARCHIVES

Garratt. The unpretentious, unflappable "PCG," as he was called, had begun his flying career at the Curtiss Aviation School in 1915 and joined the Royal Flying Corps at the Western Front, like many of his class. When he returned to Canada after the war he barnstormed for the Bishop Barker Flying Company until 1922, when he instructed at Camp Borden for the newly formed Canadian Air Force. When de Havilland started up in the canning factory at the old de Lesseps Field, Garratt was managing his own chemical business, but such was his love of flying that he offered his services as a part-time test pilot. By 1936, he was running de Havilland Canada. Under his leadership, the company "Canadianized" the British-designed aircraft such as the DH-60 Moth and DH-82 Tiger Moth that it was then assembling.

With war clouds gathering, Garratt retooled the plant to prepare for orders from the RCAF, and when

the British Commonwealth Air Training Plan called for basic trainers, a contract for twenty-five Tiger Moths was awarded to de Havilland. This had become 1,547 Moths by the war's end, even as the plant also made 375 Ansons and 1,135 DH-98 Mosquitos. At its height in 1944, the Downsview factory employed 7,011 workers. After 1945, this fell to 250 people. With other aviation companies closing down, Garratt kept his alive by turning out a batch of prewar Fox Moths and repairing Cansos. The Canadian Moth had a more powerful engine than its British cousin, as well as a strengthened cabin floor and an enlarged left-hand door for freight. It was the prototype for a series of unique bush planes to come. Fifty-three were produced, and their popularity with bush pilots no doubt planted the seeds for the de Havilland Beaver.

In May 1946, under Garratt, the company began turning out its Chipmunk basic trainer, which was destined to become a favourite with air forces around the world. It was also the first Canadian-designed aircraft de Havilland produced, and the initial step to breaking away from its British parent. In August that year, Max Ward, ex-RCAF instructor and future Wardair owner, came to Downsview to buy one of the Fox Moths. With every Bellanca and Stinson of 1930s vintage that disintegrated, the bush-plane market opened up further.

De Havilland's only Canadian competitors in the bush market then were Fairchild and Noorduyen. The Longueuil company that had produced the stalwart 71s and 82s in the 1930s approached the postwar era with two projects—prefabricated houses and a lumpy, underpowered bush plane called the Husky. The Husky flew in 1946 and, given time, might have succeeded, had not the housing venture bankrupted Fairchild, allowing only a dozen to be built. As for the Noorduyen Norseman, it was a victim of its own success. Because of the large number of previous Norseman models still flying, convincing the owners of bush outfits to buy the latest model, the Norseman VII, was a hard sell. In 1946, Noorduyen Aircraft was sold to Canada Car and Foundry, and production of the Norseman ended in 1959.

THE BEAVER

With bush pilots of Max Ward's generation in mind, Phil Garratt designed the Beaver as a high-wing, all-metal, seven-seater utility transport. It was the first of the Short Take-Off and Landing (STOL) planes, and it outdid the Norseman and the Husky in performance. The Beaver first flew on August 16, 1947. British Gipsy Queen engines were fitted to the Beaver mockup, but these were replaced before the planes flew with 450-hp Pratt & Whitney Wasp engines, which the company had left over from production of the Anson. Bush pilots preferred the Pratt & Whitneys for their reliability and simplicity, both assets in the wilderness. So did the United States

The classic bush aircraft in a classic Canadian setting. In 1978, the Canadian Engineering Centennial Board selected the de Havilland Beaver as one of Canada's most outstanding engineering achievements—in any field. BOM-BARDIER/DE HAVILLAND ARCHIVES

Army, which bought Beavers for the Korean War, the first time a truly Canadian aircraft was successful below the border. By the time 1,692 Beavers had been built in 1968, de Havilland knew it was onto a good thing.

The Ontario Provincial Air Service was so impressed with the aircraft that it asked for a "Super Beaver," with twice the passenger capacity and

By 1982, de Havilland Canada was turning out one DHC-6 Twin Otter a month. In worldwide service with twelve air forces, this example, distinguished by its garish orange colour and skis, was used by the British Antarctic Survey.
BOMBARDIER/DE HAVILLAND ARCHIVES

power. A turbo Beaver was produced. After its first flight in December 1963, the OPAS ordered seventeen. De Havilland marketed turbo-conversion kits to other Beaver owners as well, but these did not catch on. So many of the regular Beavers were still in the air that in 1968, after sixty Turbo-Beavers had been built, the model was dropped.

Instead, Pratt & Whitney designed a 600-hp Wasp for de Havilland, and on December 12, 1951, the first Otter took off from Downsview. It received its certificate of airworthiness on November 5, 1952, and quickly made a name for itself. It seated eleven passengers and could fly one and a half tons of freight over two hundred miles. The large freight door on its left side enabled bulky items to be loaded in. The Australian airline QANTAS used its Otters in the jungles of New Guinea. The Belgians and the British flew theirs in Antarctica. The U.S. Army bought 223 Otters, and in Vietnam their versatility and ruggedness earned them the nickname "the Flying Jeep." Beavers were also sold to India, Ghana and Norway. Canadian Pacific Air Lines used two as the last of their bush planes. The Ontario Provincial Air Service used their fleet as water bombers. By the time the 466th Otter was produced in 1967, de Havilland was firmly established in the aviation scene. Except for an assembly line strike in 1955, the company was thriving.[7]

The high-wing DHC-4 Caribou made at Downsview for the U.S. Army was so successful as a STOL freighter that in 1964 de Havilland enlarged it to build the DHC-5 Buffalo.
BOMBARDIER/DE HAVILLAND ARCHIVES

The company followed its earlier successes with the Twin Otter and, in 1965, the Buffalo, a rugged military transport. In Britain, the company's founder, Sir Geoffrey de Havilland, died in 1965. His company had not recovered after the production of the catastrophic Comets, and in 1960 it was taken over by Hawker Siddeley. De Havilland (Britain) had entered the field of Short Take-Off and Landing with its DH-125, and the new owners incorporated the technology into their Hawker Siddeley 748, and later the all-jet 146. A mockup of a quiet STOL airliner was built by de Havilland Canada and shown to Hawker Siddeley personnel, but, with their own aircraft for sale, Hawker Siddeley did not encourage the Canadian program.

Although conceived after Phil Garratt's retirement, the Dash 7 STOL airliner would not have been possible without his influence and leadership. Awarded the McKee Trophy in 1951 and again in 1965, Garratt had received the McCurdy Award from the Canadian Aeronautics and Space Institute in 1960 and was named to Canada's Aviation Hall of Fame in 1974. PCG died in Toronto on November 16, 1974, at the age of eighty, having been responsible for the most remarkable series of bush aircraft ever produced.

The end of the war hit MacDonald Bros. hard at their Winnipeg Airport plant. The sheet metal company had been a major contractor for the Anson,

In the early 1970s, Hawker Siddeley was trying to market its own HS748 and had little interest in the DHC Dash 7. Fortunately, Ottawa bought de Havilland Canada in 1974, allowing the Dash 7 prototype to be launched on March 27, 1975. It became the most successful STOL airliner of its era. BOMBARDIER/DE HAVILLAND ARCHIVES

and by 1945 two aircraft a day were being turned out. Grant MacDonald died in 1949, at a time when his company was trying to diversify into products that would sell in the civilian market. It reconditioned surplus army trucks, made farm equipment such as crop dusters, sprayer tanks and swathers, and finished tractor cabs. For three years, it refinished heavy aluminium cookware for the Aluminium Company of Canada. What revitalized the company's division was the reappearance of the faithful Anson—this time in civil colours. Of the thousands sold by War Assets Disposal, many required reconditioning. MacDonald Bros. was also awarded contracts to convert RCAF Beech Expeditors into pilot trainers, and in 1952 it installed machine guns in the nose of a Chilean air force Beech Expeditor to serve as an armament trainer in that country.

BRISTOL AERO-INDUSTRIES

The Cold War brought with it some orders especially for the North American Air Defence Scheme. The RCAF purchased 130 Mustangs and 130 B-25 Mitchell bombers from the USAF and had them

reconditioned at MacDonald Bros. Both aircraft had been out of production, and finding surplus parts from the original manufacturers proved difficult. In many cases, components were received at Winnipeg still in their packing, having come from USAF stores overseas. All work was done in unheated hangars, and the Mustang and its liquid-cooled Merlin engine were especially vulnerable to the prairie cold. The engines were warmed up with Herman Nelson heaters, which blew hot air into them prior to starting. Engine oil was preheated in forty-five-gallon drums, then mixed with gasoline to thin it out. Modern components were made for the Avro CF-100, and floats for the Noorduyen Norseman and the de Havilland Beaver. No doubt de Havilland director

In March 1961, Bristol was awarded a contract by the Canadian military to modify 24 Hiller 12E helicopters. The company had hoped that it could manufacture the Bristol Sycamore for the Canadian navy, but the program was cancelled for budgetary reasons. BRISTOL AEROSPACE

Punch Dickins remembered when MacDonald Bros. first began repairing Edo floats on the Red River three decades before.

In 1954, the Bristol Aeroplane Company of England bought MacDonald Bros. for a reported £1 million. Bristol had already bought two other Canadian engine repair operations: British Aeroplane Engines Ltd. in Vancouver and Canadian Wright Ltd. in Montreal. The James Richardson family owned shares in both companies, as it did in MacDonald Bros. In 1959 the Montreal, Vancouver and Winnipeg branches were amalgamated under Bristol Aero-Industries, and when the parent company in Britain was bought by Rolls-Royce Ltd., Bristol (Winnipeg) became a subsidiary.

Through the years the Winnipeg work force had adapted itself so well to so many demands that in 1961, when the RCAF looked for a prime contractor to maintain its CF-101 Voodoos, it selected Bristol. The same year the company was awarded the contract to modify twenty-four Hiller UH 12E helicopters for the Canadian Army, half of which were to be stationed at Canadian Forces bases in Germany. The company took business wherever it found it. When Trans-Canada Air Lines urgently needed to return its Super Constellations to service in 1961, Bristol undertook the 3,000-hour inspections. When the Federal Electric Company's DC-4s, which serviced the DEW Line, needed inspections, they were brought to Bristol. Bristol staff recalled that the DC-4s had high tails, and getting them into the hangar presented a problem. Engineers came up with a special bracket that permitted the nose of the aircraft to be raised by a forklift truck, which lowered the tail sufficiently.

In the summer of 1962 a Canadian S-55 helicopter crashed on Lougheed Island in the high Arctic, far above Resolute. It would need a complete engine change if it was to fly again, and Bristol was asked to help. Louis Mickulan, John Grant, Steve Klem and Luke Lanthier left Winnipeg on June 16 for a 2,000-mile, seventeen-hour flight to Isachsen, the weather station with the landing strip closest to Lougheed Island. From there, they were taken by helicopter to the crash site. In twenty-four-hour sunlight, which the men recalled melted the snow into eight inches of mud over the permafrost, the job of changing engines was begun. High winds and poor visibility sometimes isolated them for days, their only neighbours a herd of curious caribou. Transportation of the damaged engine and its replacement over the quagmire was accomplished by placing it on a toboggan, then moving this on roller conveyors over

sheets of plywood. On June 25, Autair took Mickulan and Klem to service another of their disabled helicopters, this one on the ice near Alert, leaving Grant and Lanthier to finish the engine installation. Then the weather closed in, and the latter two men were isolated until June 30, when a pilot was flown out to test the helicopter. It would not be until July 6 that the party of three left the weather station at Isachsen, hitching a ride on a Canadian Forces C-130 that also picked up Mickulan and Klem at Alert. Twenty-four days and 6,000 miles after leaving home, the Bristol staff returned to Winnipeg.

A more exotic product line for Bristol were radar antennas and rockets. After the launching of Sputnik in 1957, Western aviation companies began entering the field of rocketry. The United States followed with the launch of Explorer 1, but for nations that could not afford such expensive satellite systems, ballistic rather than orbital rockets offered possibilities for exploration. What especially fascinated scientists was the interaction between the earth, the sun and the aurora borealis. The Canadian Armament Research Development Establishment (CADE) was designing a solid fuel rocket to be fired from the Churchill, Manitoba, Research Range, which was directly under the aurora belt. Since Bristol possessed the technological base and was the nearest company to the Churchill range, it was awarded the contract for the development of the Black Brant rocket. On June 15, 1962, as the culmination of four years of research, the Black Brants were launched. This marked the start of Bristol and the federal government's cooperation on a missile program, and since that day, in various modes, Black Brants have been fired in experiments that have supported the Apollo program, the National Research Council and the Skylab. Smaller rockets were made by Bristol for the Canadian Armed Forces in 1971, with the development of the CRV7 missile system leading to cooperation with the German Dornier GMBH to build the CL-89 reconnaissance drone aircraft. In December 1981, the U.S. National Aeronautics and Space Administration honoured Bristol for "a job well

NORTHWEST INDUSTRIES

Aircraft Repair Ltd. of Edmonton had been founded
at historic Blatchford Airport in 1936 by W. Leigh
Brintnell to maintain his Mackenzie Air Service fleet.
In 1940, when the Canadian Pacific Railway bought
out Mackenzie Air, Brintnell continued with Aircraft
Repair Ltd., expanding from two small sheds to
three new hangars for the assembly of aircraft to be
used in the British Commonwealth Air Training
Plan. In 1943, Northwest Industries Ltd. (NWI) was
incorporated into Aircraft Repair Ltd., and, at peak
production, there were 2,500 people working three

Finishing touches: the United States Air Force bought sixty
Canadair Sabre Mk.2s for use in the Korean War. It was
rumoured that, because of improvements Canadair had
made to the aircraft, USAF pilots competed to fly them.
CANADAIR ARCHIVES

shifts to assemble or overhaul Ansons, Oxfords and
Bristol Bolingbrokes. As Edmonton was on the
Northwest Staging Route from the United States to
the Soviet Union, P-39 Airacobras destined for the
Soviet Air Force were also repaired on their way to
Alaska.

The end of the war was a traumatic time for
Brintnell's company, and NWI diversified into
making canoes, duck-hunting boats, skiffs and one

Canadair's chief test pilot Al Lilly talking to Omer Levesque, the RCAF Korean War air ace (*in cockpit*). On August 10, 1950, in a Sabre Mk. I, Lilly was the first Canadian to exceed the speed of sound. CANADAIR ARCHIVES

ject, the F-86 Sabre. The swept-wing concept that made the F-86 so distinctive owed much to the Luftwaffe Messerschmitt P.1101. As had the British and the Russians, postwar American aircraft engineers adapted captured German jet technology to their own needs. The F-86 and the Russian-built MiG-15, designed by Soviet mathematician Mikhail I. Gurevich, were very alike for that reason.

The RCAF chose the Sabre as its NATO fighter, and in 1949 gave Canadair the contract to build 130 F-86Es under licence. The company had already taken over the old Noorduyn building and this, called Canadair Plant 2, became the main Sabre facility. The first of the shark-nosed fighters were built from North American parts and rolled out on July 28, 1950. It was in a Sabre that Canadair test pilot Al Lilly became the first Canadian to break the sound barrier on August 10. Unfortunately, when he did so, his engine "flamed out," and he was forced to land at Dorval Airport, bursting a tire.

RCAF squadrons equipped with Sabres and sent to Europe in 1950 were for a brief period of time the undisputed kings of the air. Nothing the other NATO air forces had could compete against them. The British, waiting for their Hawker Hunters and Swifts to become operational, asked to be provided with Sabres. Canadair and North American Aviation gave the British four hundred Sabre 4s, and the RAF ferried them from Cartierville to Britain between December 1952 and November 1953.

The United States Air Force first used jet fighters in the Korean War, initially as ground support fighters, their pilots delighting that the Lockheed F-80 Shooting Star was free of the engine torque and

aircraft—the Bellanca Skyrocket. With so many war-surplus aircraft available, the Skyrocket had little chance of succeeding, and only thirteen were built. In 1947, F. G. Winspear became president of NWI, and he succeeded in getting an RCAF contract to modify ten of its DC-3s. Little else happened until the outbreak of the Korean War, when overhaul work on T-6 Harvards, B-25 Mitchells, C-119 Packets and the Bristol Freighter put the company solidly on its feet. By 1959, NWI was doing so well that it acquired B.C. Airlines, selling that company to Pacific Western Airlines in 1970. CAE Industries bought NWI in 1962, and the company began building airframe components under subcontract for the Scottish Aviation Jetstream, the Boeing 707 and the Lockheed TriStar. NWI moved to Edmonton's International Airport in 1983 and took over the former Wardair hangar, becoming the maintenance facility for the Canadian Armed Forces trainers and transports. The company's close relationship with Lockheed has existed since the 1950s; the very first T-30 Silver Star built by Canadair is mounted on a pedestal at the company gates, and in the 1960s NWI began to specialize in modifying the CAF's CC-130 Lockheed Hercules aircraft.

THE SABRE

Across the country, at Canadair, the last of the North Stars had left by the summer of 1950, and the company was looking to the launch of its next pro-

An aerial view of Canadair's plant at Cartierville during the CL-44 program. Once a polo field, the airport had been in use since 1911 as the home of such historic manufacturers as Curtiss-Reid and Robert Noorduyen. CANADAIR ARCHIVES

vibration of piston-engined aircraft. But the F-80 was no match for the MiG-15 that the Chinese Air Force threw into the conflict, and for a while Allied air superiority in Korea hung in the balance. Washington rushed squadrons of F-86s to Korea, and these turned the tide.

With the F-86 Sabres, USAF pilots soon shot down MiG-15s at a ratio of twelve to one, and the war deescalated to a stalemate of permanent peace talks. Canada had allocated its Sabre squadrons to NATO, but twenty-two RCAF pilots did see combat in Korea with USAF F-86 squadrons. One was F/L Omer Levesque, who was not only the first RCAF pilot to fly the Sabre but the first Canadian to shoot down a MiG-15 and become a jet-air ace.

The Canadair Sabre had outflown the Russian MiGs, and every air force in the world clamoured to buy them, either new or secondhand. Sabres built by

Canadair served with the Luftwaffe, the South African Air Force, the Colombian Air Force and, in 1967, were about to be shipped to the Israeli Air Force when Ottawa embargoed the sale. After use by NATO allies, many Sabres were given to Greece and Turkey in mutual aid programs. Germany sold its Canadair Sabre 6s to Iran, which transferred them to Pakistan, and the British Sabres were sold to the Yugoslav Air Force which, after many years of use, sold them to the Honduran Air Force. The RCAF retired its Sabre on February 24, 1969, but for a whole generation of pilots and aviation enthusiasts, there was not a more beautiful aircraft.

The CL-84 was Canadair's foray into the Vertical/Short Take-off and Landing field. But the technologically advanced craft could not attract customers either at home or abroad and is now displayed at the National Aviation Museum in Ottawa. CANADAIR ARCHIVES

CANADAIR KEEPS BUSY

With the F-86 program under its belt, Canadair went on to build several military aircraft under licence: the T-33 jet trainer (derived from the P-80 Shooting Star); the Argus maritime patrol aircraft; and the long-range military transport the Yukon, along with its civil version, the CL-44. The Argus, the Yukon and the CL-44 derived from the Bristol Britannia. The CL-44 is remembered for its unique swing tail, which could be opened and closed without disconnecting the controls to the rudder

and elevators. And this aircraft too was embroiled in a national scandal.

In 1960, the United States military offered the Diefenbaker government an exchange of "low-time" F-101 Voodoo fighters for CL-44s. Use by the U.S. Military Air Transport Service around the world would give the CL-44s maximum exposure and open up the American commercial market for Canadair. But the prospect of thousands of jobs for the plant in Montreal caused certain Ontario members of Parliament to criticize the deal, coming as it did a year after the cancellation of the Avro Arrow and the resulting layoffs of Avro staff. Diefenbaker vacillated until the USAF, supposedly disgusted by the wrangling, bought KC-135s from Boeing instead. Much later, the media discovered that the American generosity had had a sting in its tail—the F-101s came equipped with nuclear weapons, a detail that the prime minister did not reveal even to his Cabinet.

Canadair did manage to export some CL-44 freighters to the U.S. freight airlines Flying Tigers, Seaboard World Airlines and Slick Airways. As many university students of the 1960s will recall, passenger versions of the CL-44 were also sold to Loftleidir Icelandic Airlines, which operated them between New York and Luxembourg as the cheapest way to visit Europe.[9]

Canadair developed only one original design. Knowing that the RCAF would need a jet trainer soon, a pair of Canadair aerodynamicists, Keith Matheson and Jim McManus, built scale models of what they considered the perfect "spin" aircraft in the early 1960s. The stabilizer and elevator were put on top of the fin and rudder for good spin recovery. It was designated the CL-41 Tutor, and the first of 190 jet aircraft was delivered to the RCAF in December 1963. The Royal Malaysian Air Force bought twenty Tutors, which they christened Tebuan or "Wasp." For most Canadians the little trainer is associated with the RCAF's 431 Squadron's Snowbirds, the aerobatic team that represents Canadian aerial agility to the rest of the world.

Diversification in products is an expensive venture for any manufacturer, but the promises offered by opening up new avenues in aerodymanics were irresistible. During the Vietnam War, military strategists became keenly aware of the need for flexibility on the battlefield, and the concept of Vertical Take-Off and Landing (VTOL) aircraft took root at Canadair and elsewhere. The Canadair CL-84, called a "convertiplane," could change from conventional flight to vertical when its wing was tilted upward. The high-wing, twin-turboprop plane could fly like an aircraft but land and take off like a helicopter. The first one hovered on May 7, 1965, and subsequent versions were evaluated by the RAF, the USAF, NASA and even the U.S. Marine Corps for the aircraft carrier USS *Guadalcanal*. Unfortunately, the ingenuity that Canadair engineers put into the CL-84's control systems—which automatically adjusted the controls for the pilot depending on vertical or horizontal flight—contributed greatly to the science of aerodynamics but did nothing for the company's ledgers. Odd-looking and boxy, the CL-84 in the end interested no one, not even the Canadian government. Still, the concept did not die. In 1972, Bell Helicopters won a U.S. Army contract to build a tilt-wing demonstrator which it flew in 1977, three years after Canadair ended its CL-84 program and donated the two aircraft prototypes to museums.

Like the Avro Jetliner, the CL-84 was an aircraft before its time. The lessons to be drawn from both innovations were not lost on the Canadian aviation industry. An even more crucial lesson for the industry was to avoid an overdependence on the military market. The Lockheed crisis of the 1970s was an example of what could happen. The company, living off the reputations of its popular C-130 Hercules and C-5 Galaxy military transports, lost its place in the airline market. Even though it regained some standing by designing the TriStar, which Air Canada bought, Lockheed came close to bankruptcy in 1971 and was saved only by an emergency loan from Congress. Canadair must have seen the Lockheed troubles as a warning to jump off its own military gravy train.

The economics of aircraft design and production, the complexities of aircraft construction and the increasing use of electronics had put the manufacture of indigenous military aircraft and airliners far out of reach of all except the United States and European consortiums. The country that gave the world bush flying sought instead to adapt its bush planes to appeal to the new breed of cost-conscious airline owners, the commuter market.

Toronto's Malton Airport in the 1950s. Canadian airports immediately after World War II were chaotic, overcrowded and dilapidated, forcing the Department of Transport to begin a program of air terminal construction.
AIR CANADA ARCHIVES

CHAPTER TWELVE

Learning to Fly Again

Between 1946 and 1956, annual passenger volume at Montreal's Dorval Airport rose from 246,359 to 1,092,000, and at Malton Airport, Toronto, from 180,307 to 900,000. Overlooked amid the glamour and noise of the jet age was the federal government's investment in airports and in electronic navigation systems.

THE AIRPORT PLAN

Canada had profited greatly from the 148 airports built or improved during the Second World War for the British Commonwealth Air Training Plan, the Northwest Staging Route and the Trans-Atlantic Ferry. In 1945, C. D. Howe, as minister of transport, announced a new policy aimed at adapting these to civil use: "Surplus airports were to be leased at a

The advances in air travel made during the Second World War democratized flying, bringing it within reach of middle-class Canadians like these honeymooners boarding a TCA North Star. AIR CANADA ARCHIVES

nominal sum to interested municipalities . . . on certain conditions which included an undertaking to operate a public airport."[1] This offer included the buildings on airport grounds, runway extensions, all radio equipment and all lighting. The federal government was also willing to provide financial assistance and annual subsidies for maintenance and improvements. There were several cities that were not enticed by these incentives, however, and the Department of Transport was forced to continue operating the airports at Lethbridge, London, Windsor, Toronto, Winnipeg and Moncton.

With the increased capacity of the North Stars and the Constellations, the passenger traffic that funnelled through Canadian airports doubled every five years, making the dilapidated, temporary terminal buildings left over from the DC-3 era dirty and over-crowded. In the United States, cities as wealthy as New York and Chicago threw up vast new airport complexes like La Guardia and O'Hare. Airports required longer runways, more ticket counters and more transit lounges to accommodate the new airliners and the masses of people they carried. In Canada, the Department of Transport embarked on a postwar program to build modern air terminal buildings at Gander, Montreal, Toronto, Winnipeg, Edmonton, Halifax and Ottawa.

The renovations at Ottawa's Uplands Airport, completed in early 1959, created a state-of-the-art glass and steel confection that cost the taxpayer $15 million. It was scheduled to be opened by Prime Minister Diefenbaker. But days before the inauguration of the new terminal was to take place, a USAF jet fighter (a model, ironically, that the Americans were trying to sell the RCAF as the Arrow's replacement) swooped low over the airport to demonstrate its speed and power. It broke the sound barrier—and every piece of glass in the new terminal, even tearing off the roof flashings and insulation. Ten months and $300,000 in repairs later, the prime minister officially opened the rebuilt Uplands Airport.

With improvements in airport terminals came developments in navigation systems that made mass air travel possible. The Instrument Landing System (ILS) had first been developed by the military during the war to bring its bombers safely home. The system consisted of a radio beam that defined the approach path in the horizontal plane (the localizer) and a separate beam that defined the path of the vertical plane (the glide slope). Other components of the system were three runway marker beacons that indicated for the pilot the distance from the runway as he lost altitude. By 1946, the ILS had been refined for civil use and, although supplanted today by the Microwave Landing System (MLS), it was the primary approach aid of the jet era. The first ILS in Canada was installed at Dorval Airport in 1948, and also that year at airports in Toronto, Winnipeg, Vancouver, Saskatoon, Calgary and Lethbridge. In

1961, Dorval became the first Canadian airport to have a hydrant refuelling system, which eliminated unsafe fuel trucks, and in 1966 the first to have air bridges, which ended forever the uncomfortable scurry across the tarmac and hike up the stairs to the aircraft door.

In 1970, the major airlines of the world carried 150 million people, three times more than they had in 1960. Nine years later, wide-bodied airliners like the Boeing 747 and early deregulation allowed the same airlines to carry 317 million passengers. The frequency of aircraft movements in and out of airports, the ability of pilots to land and take off in poor weather, and an airline safety record that the public took for granted (until the next crash) were the direct result of the sophisticated electronic systems that came into use in North America in the 1970s. The continuous improvements to airports and airways in Canada were a billion-dollar investment implemented just in time for the arrival of the first jets.

GETTING USED TO JETS

As the fate of the Avro Jetliner had demonstrated, American and Canadian airline operators initially had doubts about the use of jet engines to power commercial aircraft. Fighter pilots such as Chuck Yeager and Omer Levesque had just got the hang of

A CPA Bristol Britannia at Winnipeg Airport. The airline bought six of the sturdy, handsome airliners for its transcontinental service, leasing two more later. Displacing DC-6Bs in 1958, these were in turn displaced by DC-8s in 1961. CANADIAN AIRLINES ARCHIVES

jets, and to think of putting a little old lady in one was ridiculous. While suited to fighter sorties, the early jet engines were too thirsty and unreliable for commercial use, and the airlines were reluctant to gamble on innovation. Besides, jet engines frightened the public. In the late 1940s, they were one step below the realm of rockets and science fiction. Everyone had vague notions about what "breaking the sound barrier" meant, and as one passenger pointed out to a journalist, at least with piston engines you could check to see if the propellers were still turning.

The Americans were ahead of the British in jet aircraft design, but they had concentrated on the military aspect alone. Introduced in 1951, Strategic Air Command's B-47 was a swept-wing bomber with six jet engines that had the endurance to penetrate Soviet airspace, drop its bombs and return home. The attraction of such technology should have influenced both Boeing and Douglas to adapt it for civilian use, but both were backlogged with orders for the Korean War.

With its experience in building the B-47 Stratojet, Boeing got ahead of Douglas by launching the 707 in 1954, and it would not be until 1958 that the first DC-8 was rolled out. In 1961, both Air Canada and CPA bought DC-8 40s, which had Conway turbofans that made for quieter, more economical flights. CANADIAN AIRLINES ARCHIVES

While their American counterparts were building jet bombers, the British brought out the first jet airliner, the de Havilland Comet 1. Assured of a market for it with BOAC, the government airline, de Havilland flew the Comet prototype on July 27, 1949, in time for the Farnborough Air Show. In 1952, BOAC began scheduled jet flights from London to Africa and the Far East using the Comet. Pan American's Juan Trippe had no alternative but to order Comets for the prestigious Atlantic route until American-made jet airliners were built. The success of the first series of Comets led de Havilland to build the Comet 1A, which had an increased fuel and passenger capacity, and it was this version that Grant McConachie, the Royal Canadian Air Force and Air France ordered. McConachie, who had seen the de Havilland Comet 1 fly at the Farnborough Air Show, promptly drove to the company's plant at Hatfield and bought two for his Pacific routes. The Canadian Pacific Comets would not have the range to fly from Vancouver to Honolulu, so they were to be based in

Sydney. North Stars would take passengers to Honolulu, where they would be picked up by Comets and flown to Australia.

The first CPA Comet, the *Empress of Hawaii*, left Heathrow Airport for Sydney on March 1, 1953, flown by two experienced CPA pilots. All went well until March 3, at Karachi Airport, Pakistan, when at 3:00 A.M. the heavily laden aircraft lurched sluggishly down the runway and refused to become airborne. The pilots tried desperately to raise the Comet's nose before they ran out of runway and, with an extra few seconds, they might have succeeded. Instead, one of the wheels hit a drainage ditch, and the Comet plunged into an empty canal, shattering against its far wall. With so much fuel on board, the explosion was seen for many miles around. The British board of inquiry concluded that the cause of the accident was the pilots' inexperience with the aircraft's engines. Fortunately, as it was a proving flight, there were no passengers on board.

McConachie had lost some friends in the crash. Undaunted, he did his inflatable globe and string show for the CPA's board of directors and got their approval to buy three more Comets for the Pacific route. Then two BOAC Comets disappeared over the Mediterranean Sea, and the British grounded all the jet airliners.

One of the downed aircraft was brought to the

surface by the Royal Navy and painstakingly reassembled at Farnborough. Metal fatigue brought on by pressurization was found to be the cause, and de Havilland put its design through exhaustive tests over the next five years. Both CPA and BOAC bought Bristol Britannia turboprops instead, and in 1956 McConachie allowed his order for more Comets to lapse. It would not be until 1958, when de Havilland brought out its Comet IV, that BOAC began flying the Atlantic with jets once more. But by then it was too late for the Comet. Although expanded to carry a hundred passengers, the aircraft was too small to be profitable. The Americans had the larger Boeing 707 and DC-8 jets, both of which could carry 180 passengers. The Comet was reincarnated as the Nimrod maritime patrol aircraft for the Royal Air Force.

When Canadian Pacific's bread-and-butter DEW Line contracts ended in the late 1950s, the company sold its C-46s to Pacific Western Airlines and Quebecair. The airline had also sold off its North Stars by 1955 and was using DC-6Bs on its Vancouver–Keflavik–Amsterdam route, and a year later on flights to Lima, Buenos Aires and Santiago. The first Canadian "Over the Pole" flight was pioneered by the bush-flying legend Bob Randall. On June 3, 1955, CPA's DC-6B "CF-CUR" took off from Vancouver for Sondestrom, Greenland, and Amsterdam.

In 1957, CPA supplemented the DC-6Bs with six turboprop Bristol Britannias, which, at $2.9 million each, cut deeply into the CPR's dividends that year. The Britannias, nicknamed "the Brutes" by their crews, were magnificent, their turboprops so quiet that BOAC advertised theirs as "the Whispering Giants." The aircraft were more comfortable and faster than the DC-6Bs but—as anyone who has ever had the misfortune to own a Triumph sportscar knows—British electrical systems were the worst ever devised. By the time all the electrical malfunctions had been worked out, jets were in use and the Britannias could not compete. Passengers who had been afraid to fly in an aircraft that did not have propellers by 1962 wouldn't fly in one that did. Both CPA and BOAC sold the last of their Britannias in 1966.

Passenger comfort on this CP Air flight in 1971 is a far cry from the box lunches and cotton wool earplugs of the 1930s. CANADIAN AIRLINES ARCHIVES

The market for secondhand aircraft is always difficult to forecast and must have been more so for turboprops with jets on the horizon. But by a strange quirk of fate, some of the CPA Britannias were sold to the venerable British shipping line, Cunard. By 1967, for the first time in the history of the world, ocean-going ships were no longer the main vehicles of mass transportation; they had been relegated to the role of floating resorts for vacationers. Shipping lines were beginning to face up to the inevitable future, and along with the French and Italian lines, Cunard began to diversify into the leisure market with cruise ships. Cunard's chairman Sir Basil Smallpiece made the decision to build new ships like the *QE 2* with vacationers in mind and sell off his company's old ones, such as the *Queen Mary* and the *Queen Elizabeth*, which could not be converted.[2] As the private automobile had killed off the train, so the new airliners had sunk the passenger ship.

Coinciding with the shorter working hours and general prosperity of the decade, the introduction of jet airliners made hundreds of piston-engined aircraft available to the travel industry at bargain prices. This allowed savvy entrepreneurs like the British Freddie Laker and the Canadian Max Ward to begin their own charter airlines with little capital. Another airline that made good use of the second-hand Britannias was El Al Israeli Airlines. With their 4,000-mile range, the turboprop airliners did not need to refuel in Canada after crossing the Atlantic, allowing for memorable newspaper ads that declared, "No Goose! No Gander!"

BOEING TO THE FORE

During and after the war, Boeing marketed its chunky four-engined Stratoliner and Stratocruiser airliners, and although the passengers loved the latter's double deck and winding staircase, both aircraft were commercial failures, convincing the company to leave the civil field and concentrate on building jet bombers. When Boeing did reenter the commercial market in 1953, it was with the KC-135 jet tanker. To stay aloft for any length of time, Strategic Air Command's B-47 bombers depended on constant in-flight refuelling, and the United States Air Force maintained a large fleet of aerial tankers around the world, giving the airport at Goose Bay, made redundant by the use of turboprops, a new lease on life. Connecting two aircraft by a boom for refuelling was a difficult enough process at low altitudes, but it was a serious struggle for piston-engined tankers to keep up with jet bombers during the operation. The air force cried out for tankers with jet power. Given complete government financing and assured of a market with the military, Boeing began to produce KC-135s, an aircraft that could also be modified to carry passengers.[3]

His development costs paid for, Boeing's president, William Allen, then went to Juan Trippe. The czar of Pan American was still mourning the loss of his Comets, and he ordered twenty of the civilian conversions of the jet tanker. With Pan American in his pocket, Allen immediately renamed his tanker the 707 Dash 80, increased the aircraft's diameter to allow six-abreast seating and even got the wife of founder Bill Boeing to christen the first one when it

rolled out on May 14, 1954. It would take Douglas years to catch up with its DC-8 jet. With the 707, Boeing launched the jet age and changed the face of air travel.[4] Every major airline in the world has probably flown a 707. In 1972, when U.S. President Richard Nixon landed in the People's Republic of China aboard *Air Force One*, a Boeing 707, it was the greatest advertising coup that any aircraft manufacturer could pull off.[5] The Chinese ordered ten 707s that year and became steady customers from then on. In 1996, of the 354 jetliners flying in China, 216 were Boeing.[6] In the 1980s, finally too old and noisy for the commercial market, 707s found a new lease on life as E-3 Airborne Warning and Control Systems (AWACS) flying communications centres. By the time production of 707s stopped in May of 1991, Boeing had made 1,010 of the jets, almost double Douglas' sales of 550 DC-8s.

Donald Douglas's first DC-8 flew on May 30, 1958. The airlines liked the plane because it could cross the Atlantic nonstop from east to west, while the early 707s still had to land at Shannon Airport. Air Canada and Canadian Pacific Air Lines were two of the few airlines that didn't buy Boeing 707s, both opting for DC-8s.[7] These had the same airframe as the DC-8s used by Alitalia, Delta Airlines and United Airlines, but both CPA and Air Canada had the aircrafts' Pratt & Whitney engines replaced with Rolls-Royce Conway Turbofans.

Jet engines looked dramatic starting up, but all that roar and hot blast escaped into the air. In the 1950s, there were still engineers at Rolls-Royce in Britain who had trained with Frank Whittle, and the company, better known for its expensive cars, built a series of engines for the first RAF jet fighters. They developed a fan jet that captured some of the exhaust and used it to deliver more thrust with (welcome news to those who lived near airports) less noise. With the typical British sense of humour, the Rolls-Royce engineers named this revolutionary engine after a slow-moving local river, the Conway. With the Conways and later Pratt & Whitney fan jets, DC-8s were able to increase their range to over 4,000 miles, which allowed for the first nonstop

"But, I tell you, there <u>is</u> no powder room.
What do you think this is, TCA?"

*Next time she <u>will</u> choose TCA and enjoy the comfort of the DC-8 jet,
Vanguard or Viscount. Fast, luxurious and economical, too.*

Montreal to New York $44
Economy Return Fare

**TRANS-CANADA AIR LINES
AIR CANADA**

TCA/Air Canada advertisement. AIR CANADA ARCHIVES

An artist's impression of the future DHC-8 Series 400. A further stretch of the successful Dash family, in this aircraft the fuselage has been extended to fly 70 to 78 passengers, servicing "hub and spoke" regional markets. The company plans to sell it in 1999. BOMBARDIER/DE HAVILLAND ARCHIVES

flights across the Pacific. Then, as he had stretched the DC-2 into the DC-7, in 1966 Donald Douglas followed the original DC-8 with a "stretched" version. Both Air Canada and Canadian Pacific Air Lines purchased stretched DC-8s, which had accommodation for 259 passengers and, with the later Series 50, a range of 7,000 miles.

CPA FLIES CANADA

Even before the arrival of the jet age, CPA was ready to take on Trans-Canada Air Lines for the internal market. The fall of the Liberals in 1957 and C. D. Howe's retirement gave Grant McConachie the opportunity he needed to break the TCA monopoly. Diefenbaker's minister of transport was George

Hees, known to dislike the Trans-Canada Air Lines monopoly and reputed to have called the government airline "a spoiled child."[8] CPA applied to the Air Transport Board (ATB) for permission to fly three transcontinental routes between Vancouver and Montreal, stopping at either Calgary, Edmonton, Saskatoon, Winnipeg or Toronto. But after years of appearing before parliamentary committees, Gordon McGregor had the facts and figures ready to defend his airline's monopoly, something that McConachie's boyish charm could not rival. After a hearing that lasted three weeks, the board denied CPA a licence to fly those routes.

Political pressure did force the ATB to grant McConachie one daily flight, however: Vancouver–Winnipeg–Toronto–Montreal. It was hardly what he wanted, but it was a start. The cozy relationship between Trans-Canada Air Lines and the federal government had been breached. In anticipation of the traffic volume, McConachie ordered five DC-8s. By 1962 they were flying on CPA's international routes.

The first flight, nonstop Vancouver–Amsterdam on April 15, took nine hours. The DC-6B had taken twenty hours for the same journey.

When the Liberals returned to Ottawa in 1963, so did McConachie. This time he dealt with Jack Pickersgill, Prime Minister Lester Pearson's minister of transport. Pickersgill brought in the National Transportation Act in 1967, the year of the country's centennial. Canada had been created out of (or because of) protectionism and massive subsidies to its transport systems, first to the railroads and then to aviation. On the country's one-hundredth birthday, the act recognized for the first time a system of free competition among rail, road and air carriers. Canadian Pacific Air Lines was allowed to double its share of transcontinental traffic, and regional airlines such as Transair, Nordair and Quebecair were allocated the markets they were to serve. Preferential treatment of the Canadian National and Canadian Pacific Railways at the expense of airports was ended, with each mode of transport from now on to be compensated for the facilities and services they provided the public. The Air Transport Board was abolished, and the Canadian Transport Commission was created in its place.

Pickersgill opened the door further for Canadian Pacific Air Lines by allowing it a wider share of the international market. There would henceforth be "two flag carriers" with clearly defined areas of the world to fly in. Air Canada was given Britain, the Caribbean and Central Europe, and Canadian Pacific Air Lines, South America, the Far East, Australia and Amsterdam. Both CPA and Air Canada wanted exclusive rights to the lucrative market in the United States, but negotiations with Washington dragged on for so many years that routes would be awarded piecemeal to both companies.

The logical solution would have been for the duelling airlines to merge and present a united front to Ottawa. McGregor proposed this in 1960, pointing out that the duplication of services hurt the consumer as much as it did the companies' operating revenues. But McConachie argued that the only

countries with a single airline were in the Third World. Australia had three, France had three, the United States had eighteen, Britain had eleven. Canada could well support two, and more. McConachie hadn't flown fish and cajoled his way to the executive suite of Canadian Pacific Air Lines only to have McGregor buy him out.

By 1965, CPA had had three years of profits, and its shareholders and the railway's board of directors were pleased. When a reporter asked its president about the TCA merger, he is reported to have said, "Sure, how much do they want for TCA?"[9]

On June 29, 1965, in Los Angeles to negotiate the lease on another DC-6B, Grant McConachie suffered a fatal heart attack. The CPA DC-6B that brought his body home to Vancouver the next day had three passengers: McConachie's twenty-six-year-old son Don, John C. Gilmer, CPA vice-president and heir apparent, and Barney Phillips Jr., son of the gold prospector who had bankrolled a fleet of bush planes for McConachie.

McConachie had parlayed a bankrupt bush outfit into a profitable international airline, with a network that ranged from Amsterdam to Sydney, Vancouver to Santiago. He had successfully challenged the Trans-Canada Air Lines monopoly. For all his faults—and there were many—Grant McConachie had the allure of a swashbuckler and the optimism of a Mississippi riverboat gambler. His death brought to an end the day of maverick airline builders such as Juan Trippe, Eddie Rickenbaker and Howard Hughes. Just as computers now intruded into the cockpit, lawyers and accountants had taken over the airline boardrooms.

A NEW AGE DAWNS

This change in the industry was evident in Prime Minister Pierre Elliott Trudeau's appointment of Yves Pratte as the new chairman of Air Canada upon Gordon McGregor's retirement in 1968. Born the son of a Quebec City judge, Pratte had graduated summa cum laude from Laval University in law. He began his career as a junior partner with the Quebec firm of St. Laurent, Taschereau, Noel and Pratte.

Returning to Laval University's faculty of law, by 1962 he had risen through the academic ranks to become its dean. Quebec Premier Jean Lesage recruited Pratte as special advisor to his government, and he remained in that role with Premier Daniel Johnson. English Canada first heard of Pratte in 1966, when Prime Minister Lester Pearson appointed him as one of the three-member Royal Commission on National Security. When Trudeau, who contrary to popular belief had never met Pratte, made him CEO and chairman of the board of Air Canada, he knew that the Quebec lawyer had no airline experience at all, and this might well have been why he was appointed.[10]

At a time of rampant nationalism and FLQ turmoil in Montreal, the Trudeau government was very aware that the government airline was overstaffed, inefficiently run, and managed, so it seemed, by an English Canadian old boys' network. The fact that aviation fuel didn't run in Pratte's veins and that his heart didn't beater faster at the sound of the Conway was seen as a grievous fault among long-serving Air Canada employees. Their new CEO, on the other hand, thought that the airline had ossified, an inevitable fate of Crown corporations. Pratte commissioned an American management consulting firm, the McKinsey Company, to make recommendations as to how the airline could be reorganized to run more efficiently. Many employees felt that after a lifetime of loyalty to the airline, they were being cast aside for political expediency. As departments were fragmented and managers fired, morale at the airline's Place Ville Marie headquarters nose-dived, affecting customer service, which in turn affected profits. Then, on April 20, 1969, in opposition to Trudeau's wage and price freeze, machinists at Air Canada went on strike for more pay, grounding the fleet for thirty days.

Two events symbolized the changing of the guard at Air Canada. One was the appointment of Louise Ann Courtemanche to the post of executive assistant to the senior vice-president of sales, making her the first female executive in the airline. The other was Vice-President Herb Seagrim's retirement on March

31, 1970. Seagrim had joined TCA in 1937 and flown the first airmail from Winnipeg to Regina. More than three hundred well-wishers gathered for his farewell banquet, and when retired president Gordon McGregor took his turn at the microphone to tell of Seagrim's contribution to the airline, it must have seemed like the twilight of the gods. Seagrim soon began a second career, running his own boat charter company in Florida.

Pratte fired the first shots in the reorganization campaign on April 30, 1970, putting an end to the way Gordon McGregor had run Air Canada. "The fact that today we are embarking on major organizational changes in Air Canada in no way suggests a vote of non-confidence in past achievements," he wrote in the company newsletter. "It is simply a case of modifying our organizational mechanism so that we can bring to the new environment and the fresh challenges of the 70s the same skills and dedication that have proven so successful in the past. Our major challenge will be to more effectively market our product in an environment that is increasingly competitive and demanding."[11]

Effective May 1, Yves J. Menard, recruited from the advertising firm of Johnson & Johnson, was appointed vice-president of marketing. W. Gordon Wood, who had joined TCA in 1939, was appointed vice-president of government and industry affairs. Lindy Rood, the CGTAS pioneer, was made vice-president of flight operations. Jim McLean, who had joined the maintenance department in Winnipeg in 1941, was named vice-president of customer service, and Dave Tennant, who had been hired as a draughtsman by the airline in 1938, became vice-president of personnel. Pierre J. Jeanniot, on loan to the University of Quebec to set up their data processing system, was appointed to the position of vice-president of the computer systems; Bill Norberg, who had made his name with the CGTAS, was vice-president of maintenance; and Clayton H. Glenn, who had tested the Canadair North Star, the Viscount and the Vanguard, was now vice-president of operations planning.

Menard was the only appointment from "outside," but long-serving employees saw him as a symbol of all that was happening to the airline and, in effect, to the armed forces and the country in general. Their complaints ranged from enforced bilingualism to the cavalier firing of 350 of the airline's managers, from the Trudeau's government's political appointments to wage freezes. Scandals that uncovered villas in Barbados made good media copy, and it must have seemed to Pratte that resignations and early retirements among his staff took place daily. The Trudeau government, now embarrassed by its appointee, began to distance itself from him.

With the oil crisis, a spate of hijackings and the start of a recession, the early 1970s were a bad time for airlines everywhere. Air Canada in 1970 should have made C. D. Howe and Herb Symington proud. It carried more passengers, air freight and mail than at any time in its history. It had grown to 17,447 employees and had thirty-eight DC-8s, thirty-six DC-9s, twelve Vanguards and thirty-one Viscounts. It had Reservec II computers and Boeing 747s on order, and it trained air crew for other airlines such as Air Jamaica. It flew forty-one times a week between Canada and the United Kingdom and had expanded its international network to Prague. But the company also recorded a net loss of $1,072,000 that year, compared with a net profit of $1,548,000 in 1969. Prior to that, its last deficit year had been 1962, when the DC-8s were acquired, and since then the airline had enjoyed seven fat years with record profits. In 1968, Gordon McGregor's last year as president, it recorded its highest net income: $8 million.

The old Chinese curse of living in interesting times doomed Pratte. To make matters worse, Air Canada took delivery of three Boeing 747 "jumbo" jets in early 1971 at $25 million each. The financial reserves that Gordon McGregor had built up were melting away with alarming speed. A Crown corporation in deficit was bad enough, but a Crown corporation with morale problems deep enough to affect the way passengers were being treated was unforgivable.[12] The Trudeau government enacted a very Canadian solution. A Royal Commission was appointed to look into the malaise of the national airline, with hearings that dragged on through the summer of 1974. The commission's findings stopped short of suggesting it, but Transport Minister Otto Lang called for Pratte's resignation on November 28, 1975.

UP THROUGH THE RANKS

This time the new president was a company man who had worked his way up through the ranks to the position of vice-president of public affairs. Claude I. Taylor's credentials were eminently suitable. He was from a New Brunswick farming community, where his family were neighbours of RCAF Air Marshal Hugh Campbell and where, as a boy during the Second World War, his summer job had been carrying water to construction crews building the British Commonwealth Air Training Plan airfields. He had cycled twenty miles to Moncton Airport to watch the TCA Lodestars take off. Taylor had joined TCA as a reservations clerk in 1949, then earned a degree at night from McGill University when he was transferred to Montreal.[13] He was warm, outgoing and accessible.

The government had chosen well. In the years since McGregor had retired, employee morale at Air Canada had sunk to an all-time low, and Taylor faced the task of rebuilding it. His mission was to turn the airline into a leaner, meaner competitive machine—and that meant getting it out from under the Canadian National Railway and the federal government.

With its large freight door and ability to operate from 1,000-foot airstrips, the de Havilland Otter was made with Canadian bush pilots in mind. But it achieved worldwide fame when the U.S. Army Engineers bought 223 of the planes to carry fuel to Alaskan and Vietnamese landing strips for its helicopters. BOMBARDIER/DE HAVILLAND ARCHIVES

CHAPTER THIRTEEN

Bamboo Bombers and the Bottom Line

A long with hundreds of other demobbed pilots, Maxwell Ward knew what he was going to do. He had grown up around Edmonton's Blatchford Field, the cradle of bush aviation in the 1930s, and when the war began there was no question of not joining the RCAF. By 1945, he had accumulated 2,800 hours of flying time, was familiar with Tiger Moths and Ansons, and had saved most of his instructor's salary. His father-in-law and a

family friend put in $2,000 each, and with $6,000 in hand, in July 1946 Ward caught the TCA Lodestar flight for Toronto. He was going to buy an aircraft and become a bush pilot.

The postwar years marked the beginning of the modern air transport industry in northern Canada. Large-scale natural resource developments such as the ALCAN Kitimat project and the impact of Cold War defence construction brought basic changes in the region. And once more, as in 1918, there were thousands of war-surplus aircraft and desperate young pilots available. Some, like Max Ward, would live to see their dreams realized; others, like Ernie Boffa, would retire, no richer than they began, to their memories and scrapbooks.

A WING AND A PRAYER

In July 1945, Russ Baker and Karl Springer from Fort St. James leased a Beech 17 biplane and began Central British Columbia Airways. Frank Ross, a Montreal general contractor, bought a Norseman V, and in May 1947 began Boreal Airways from St. Felicien, Quebec. Milt Ashton and Roy Brown were former World War I pilots whose first company, Wings Ltd. of Manitoba, had been bought out in 1941 by Canadian Pacific. When aircraft, fuel and passengers became available again after the war, the pair bought British Commonwealth Air Training Plan surplus Ansons and RCAF Norsemen and reentered the bush-flying business with their new company, Central Northern Airways. Le Syndicate d'Aviation de Rimouski began in 1946 as a charter flight company on the Gaspé Peninsula, taking over the Canadian Pacific routes linking Matane, Mont Joli, Rimouski and Sept-Îles. In British Columbia, Jim Spilsbury began Queen Charlotte Airlines in May 1946, servicing the British Columbia coast with old Vickers Stranraer flying boats.

Older than any of these airlines was Maritime Central Airways (MCA), formed at Charlottetown, P.E.I., on September 30, 1941, by Carl Burke and Josiah Anderson. Anderson would be killed later flying for Ferry Command, and Burke awarded the Order of the British Empire in 1943 for rescuing four crew members of a crashed Anson from an ice floe in the Gulf of St. Lawrence. After the war, the airline resumed operations, and by 1948 MCA had the distinction of being the only bush airline to have an international air route, flying as it did from Sydney, Nova Scotia, to the French colony of St. Pierre.

The litany of undercapitalized, "wing and a prayer" outfits begun in postwar Canada also included Bradley Air Services, Associated Airways, Kamloops Air Service, Skeena Air Transport, Matane

Air Services, Superior Airways, A. Fecteau Transport Aerien and Mont Laurier Aviation, among others. They flew a variety of aircraft, picking up trade at drill camps, small mines, navigation stations and tourist lodges, and through government contracts. Their freight? One veteran remembers that it was anything the aircraft could take off with—Department of Transport inspectors were few and far between in the bush. Fuel drums, boats, burlap bags of stinking fish, families of trappers with their dogs, utility poles, diamond drills, flour sacks, sugar bags. More exotic cargoes were prisoners being escorted by the local Mountie, and sometimes even body bags containing murdered prospectors for autopsies.[1]

Even when flying without a load, bush pilots usually took what they called their "trading goods" on any trip into the isolated interior. These were newspapers, the latest Eaton's catalogues, fresh milk, razor blades, fresh vegetables and fruit—and any sort of alcohol. One pilot remembered that the isolation was especially hard on women in these settlements and took with him cosmetics, stockings and chocolates.[2]

On one occasion, young Max Ward flew three musk oxen (which hadn't been toilet-trained!) out of the Barrens using his new de Havilland Otter. Throughout his career, Ward upgraded his aircraft as suburban families might their cars, using the old ones as down payments for the new. It was his acquisition of an ex-TCA Bristol Freighter that moved Wardair out of the bush market. He had guessed that there was a market for airlifting, and with the Bristol carried a dismantled Beaver to England for de Havilland Canada, serviced DEW line stations in the Arctic, transported cars and trucks from Hay River, Alberta, to Yellowknife, NWT, and much later, with forty seats added, took passengers as well. Business was so good that, in 1961, Ward moved his operation from Yellowknife to an office in Edmonton and renamed his company Wardair Canada Ltd. He leased a CPA DC-6B from Grant McConachie and began flying tourists on charter flights to Europe. By 1966, Ward had made enough revenue to take delivery of a brand-new 727 from Boeing (appropri-

ately registered as "CF-FUN") and begin competing with CP Air and Air Canada for the vacation market.

Few other bush pilots had the wherewithal to buy a factory-fresh aircraft. The war had left thousands of trainers and light transports rotting at Crown Assets Disposal depots, and for a hundred dollars these could be carted away, rebuilt, fitted with either skis or floats—depending on the terrain and the time of year—and painted with a company logo. Before de Havilland entered the market with its specially designed Beaver, the term "bush aircraft" meant whatever was available. Every aircraft had its strengths and its peculiarities. Some faults were annoying, others fatal. The Bellanca, for example, had poorly designed fuel tanks; there were no baffles to prevent the gas from sloshing about, and if a pilot banked too sharply, the gas supply to the carburetor was cut off and the engine died. The Noorduyen Norseman, known as "the Thunderchicken," was well liked but needed a skilled pilot to handle it. After the war, Canadian Pacific Air Lines bought seven from Crown Assets Disposal, along with three Cansos.

Beech 18s were called "Wichita Wobblers" for their handling characteristics. Their tubular metal

The young Max Ward with his de Havilland Canada Fox Moth in 1947. Like many demobbed pilots, Ward used his entire savings to start a company, Polaris Charter Co. Ltd., parlaying that by 1985 into Wardair, the third Canadian international airline. BOMBARDIER/DE HAVILLAND ARCHIVES

frames made them heavy to fly and given to stalling when coming in to land. Bush pilot Welland "Weldy" Phipps, who began Atlas Aviation Ltd. in Resolute Bay, thought that they were the worst aircraft he had ever flown in his life. When parked overnight, the Beech's flex controls would freeze solid. Worse still, they would sometimes do this in mid-air. For every hour he flew a Beech, Phipps calculated he spent about fourteen hours on the ground working on one.[3]

The most docile of all the war-surplus bush aircraft were the lovable Avro Ansons. Max Ward reckoned they were proof that the military had a sense of humour. Ansons, he quipped, were old wooden gliders that happened to have a couple of engines installed.[4] The docile Ansons had been named after Baron Anson, the British seadog who trounced the French fleet off Cape Finisterre. The twin-engined canvas and plywood "Annies" were easy-going and

forgiving if flown correctly. In a stall, however, they had a tendency to flip over, with fatal results for all on board. Bush operators nicknamed them "Bamboo Bombers." They were cheap to buy and freezing to fly, and because of this were relegated to use as fish haulers. Inevitably, soaked in grease and fish scales, they rotted away within two or three winters. The greatest user of Ansons was Pacific Western Airlines (PWA), a descendant of Russ Baker's Central British Columbia Airways. PWA operated eleven Annies in 1955, selling them off only when it made the transition from a bush outfit to a regional airline a decade later.

There are more de Havilland Canada Beavers in the air now than there were ten years ago, although the company stopped making them in 1967. The Beaver and its cousins the Otter and the Twin Otter revolutionized bush flying forever. British Columbians might be most familiar with them today as the reconditioned commuter aircraft flown by Harbour Air or West Coast Air. But when introduced in 1947, the Beaver was the Swiss Army knife of aircraft—it could do anything. No longer did pilots have to trust their lives to fragile Tiger Moths or ancient Fokkers. Designed by aviators such as Punch Dickins and marketed by air ace Russ Bannock, Beavers and Otters soon earned the reputation of being able

to get out of any scrape or into any settlement, whether in the high Arctic or dense Ontario bush. Such is the market for these classics half a century later that Beavers rebuilt by Viking Air in Victoria today sell for $400,000, ten times what they originally cost.

THE DEW

Most bush outfits would have disappeared once youthful enthusiasm and demobbed savings ran out had it not been for a memorable Cold War project: the construction of the early warning radar defence. Between 1951 and 1958, three electronic tracking systems were strung across North America to warn of attack by Soviet aircraft. The Pine Tree Line was within the inhabited areas of Canada, the Mid-Canada Line ran along the 55th parallel, and the Distant Early Warning Line was constructed north of the Arctic Circle. The building of these three lines in record time would not have been possible without helicopters and bush aircraft. Several Canadian bush airlines took part in the airlifting of men and construction materials, purchasing larger DC-3s and DC-4s with their earnings.

The DEW Line's main contractors were Eastern Provincial Airways in the east and Pacific Western Airlines in the west. Lesser contracts were awarded

Between 1955 and 1956, Canadian Pacific Air Lines operated eight Curtiss C-46 freighters from Fort Nelson, B.C., on a contract to supply radar stations along the Distant Early Warning Line. CANADIAN AIRLINES ARCHIVES

to Ashton and Brown's outfit (now called Transair) and to Carl Burke's Maritime Central Airways. Canadian Pacific Air Lines, with its bush-pilot alumni and expertise, was awarded one of the largest supply contracts. While McConachie's Comets were grabbing the headlines, CPA purchased eight used C-46 aircraft for the project. The Curtiss C-46 had twice the cabin volume of the Douglas DC-3s that the other contractors used. This was because in 1940 Curtiss had planned to pressurize the upper half of the fuselage for passengers. But before that could happen, the U.S. military "drafted" the Curtiss C-46s as freighters, using them to fly supplies to Chiang Kai-shek's armies from India over "the Hump"—the Himalayas—to China.

Every DEW Line radar site came with a 6,000-foot gravel strip attached to it, and the CPA fleet of C-46s, based at Fort Nelson, flew supplies to each one on a rotating basis. CPA retiree Don O'Grady, a chief mechanic on the line, remembered it well: "We would haul a load of construction material out of Fort Nelson, B.C. to a designated site on the Arctic coast, stopping enroute northbound at Norman Wells, NWT to take on fuel. Once this load was delivered to the site, the plan then was to return to Norman Wells to take on a load of diesel fuel (contained in 45 Imp. Gal. drums), return once again to the site on the Arctic Coast and then back to Fort Nelson via Norman Wells once more to refuel."

The airline had bought the C-46s from Flying Tiger Airlines and a Cuban airline. "Most were previously operated in tropical climates, and winterization such as we required, was unheard of. Even to this day, how I remember those cold Arctic March winds and blowing snow blasting on the runway of Norman Wells." But O'Grady also never forgot "the vast splendour, the awesome scenery and yet, even in its very grotesque patterns, the cold naked beauty of our country's Arctic wasteland."[5]

BIG CHANGES FOR CPA

Two years after Grant McConachie's death, his ambitions for CPA were fulfilled: Minister of Transport J. W. Pickersgill allowed CPA 25 per cent of the capacity on transcontinental routes, and when the last of the DC-6Bs were sold, it became an all-jet airline. But the most glaring difference was its new livery and company logo. In 1968, the Canadian Pacific corporation had shed its old-fashioned railway image and exploded into the dayglo Swinging Sixties. The company was now called CP Air, and its new logo featured a triangle within a circle, suggesting an arrow of motion across the globe. But it was the distinctive bright orange that caught the public's eye, especially when used on the first CP Air Boeing 747, delivered on November 16, 1973. The name change and the new look were part of a corporate strategic plan to move away from the "Pacific" theme, now that the airline flew to Rome, Athens and Tel Aviv and had even organized a series of charter flights to Entebbe, Uganda, to pick up Asian immigrants fleeing the country.

The oil crisis and the recession of the 1970s cut into CP Air's revenues, as did competition from Pacific Western Airlines. McConachie's successor, Jack Gilmore, retired in 1976 and was replaced by another long-serving employee, Ian Gray. It was Gray's good fortune to inherit an airline that had finally broken into Air Canada's protected territory just as wide-body jets like the 747 and the DC-10 were coming on line. In 1978 the airline made its best operating profit ever, $43 million. With restrictions lifted on transcontinental travel, CP Air (like Air Canada) began buying up regional airlines. But route expansion is an expensive process, and this fact, coupled with the cost of the new aircraft fleet and rent at "hub and spoke" airports like Toronto, started to hurt the company. In 1981, annual costs exceeded revenue, and the airline lost $23 million. In the following year, it lost $39 million. The directors of the parent Canadian Pacific company began to lose patience with propping CP Air up annually.

In troubling times, an airline has several options. It can sell off aircraft and routes, replace its president

The Boeing 737 was first flown on April 19, 1967, to compete with the Douglas DC-9. CP Air took delivery of its first 737 in 1968, and it became the first of the company's aircraft to be painted in the new orange livery. CANADIAN AIRLINES ARCHIVES

or shed employees. In the United States, Pan American, in its eleventh hour of bankruptcy, chose first to sell off its Pacific routes to United Air Lines, its South American ones to Eastern Air Lines and its European ones to Lufthansa. When this was not enough, its Intercontinental hotel chain and finally the Manhattan landmark PANAM building were jettisoned. Juan Trippe did not live to see the dismantling of his company; the last of the airline-builders had died in 1980. Pan American was paying the price for decades of being "America's chosen instrument." Trippe had been proud that the world identified his airline with his country, like they did Coca-Cola and Hollywood, but this was eventually a liability, as Pan American became a symbol of American imperialism and a target for terrorists. As late as 1988, the airline might have staved off insolvency had not Flight 103 exploded over the Scottish town of Lockerbie, killing all on board and many below. The bad publicity and the billion-dollar insurance claims that followed wounded the airline mortally. On December 4, 1991, sixty years after it began, Pan American Airlines suspended operations.

Profits were a fading memory for CP Air, too, when president Ian Gray retired in 1982 and Daniel Colussy was hired in his place. A former president of Pan American, Colussy recognized what ailed the Canadian airline. Pan American had faced a similar problem: no domestic networks to feed its international ones. Worse, the Canadian airline's hub was isolated at the very edge of the Pacific coast in then-sleepy Vancouver.

To build a domestic network, Colussy embarked on a shopping spree to pick up small regional airlines, preferably those that were in trouble and could be bought cheaply. In 1984, Eastern Provincial Airways and Air Maritime were absorbed, giving CP Air a network in the east. Then, to Air Canada's dismay, Toronto's airport was targeted as CP Air's new headquarters.

Charter airlines such as Wardair and Nationair had steadily siphoned off the tourist market since the 1970s, so Colussy went after the "frequent fliers"— the business executives. In Europe, British Airways and KLM, having to compete with their national railways, had catered to business travellers for many years. But CP Air was the first in Canada to initiate a business section in their aircraft cabins, calling it "Attache" Class and designing it with wider seats and more room for briefcases. A low-density-seating shuttle service called "the Company Jet" was put into effect on the Montreal-Toronto corridor. On long-haul flights to Hong Kong and Tokyo, twelve fully reclining sleeperettes were installed for executives who had to begin a day's work as soon as they landed. Passengers who flew repeatedly with the airline were given points for each mile in an initiative later called the "frequent flier" program.

Executives loved it. This was Adam Smith with wings. For the first time in Canada there was an airline that embraced the capitalist philosophy of private enterprise and catered to the needs of executive passengers. Customers flocked to CP Air, and the airline showed a $9-million profit in 1984. This surplus was used to buy commuter airlines such as Nordair and Quebecair, whose extensive local networks firmly established CP Air as a domestic carrier.

Having launched CP Air on its new life in two frenzied years, Colussy returned to the United States to begin his own airline, and in 1985 Donald Carty was given his job. Canadians had reservations about entrusting their national airlines to Americans, and Carty was the best compromise CP Air's board of directors could come up with. He was an executive vice-president with the AMR Corporation of Dallas–Fort Worth, the parent company of American Airlines—and he was Canadian.

Under Carty, the airline shifted focus yet again. In 1986, the Asia-Pacific Rim was growing in importance, and the airline's focus shifted back to Vancouver. But its corporate logo, "CP Air," confused potential customers in Hong Kong, where the initials

"CPA" meant their own Cathay Pacific Airlines. Everywhere else, the name was too ambiguous for foreigners to associate with Canada. So Carty announced that the airline was reverting to its original name, Canadian Pacific Air Lines. Once more the livery was changed, this time to conservative red, white and blue, with stripes that signified speed on five continents. The four CP Air Boeing 747s were sold to Pakistan International Airlines, and the airline standardized its fleet on the DC-10s.

THE BOEING 747

Just as the DC-3 and the Boeing 707 had done in their day, the introduction of the "jumbo jet" revolutionized the industry. In the spring of 1971, just before the airline took delivery of its first Boeing 747, the Air Canada public relations people issued a press release describing the new aircraft:

CP Air 747 "Empress of Canada" publicizing Vancouver's Expo 86. Before rising fuel prices put an end to the service, the airline's 747s had an upstairs bar fitted out in a railway station motif, reflecting the company origins. CANADIAN AIRLINES ARCHIVES

The 747—Big by Any Standards

A pilot sits at the same level in the cockpit of a 747 as he would if he sat on the top of the tail of a DC-9.

The diameter of the aircraft's engine intake is 8 feet 5 inches, the same diameter as the DC-3 fuselage.

The Wright brother's first flight at Kitty Hawk could have been performed within the 150 foot Economy Section of the cabin. A man of average height can walk upright inside the aircraft's main fuel tanks. The fuel capacity (47,000 U.S. gallons) is sufficient to run the average family car for about 80 years. The tractor required to tow the 747 weighs more than a fully loaded Vanguard.

Four JN-4 Curtiss "Canucks" could be lined up on each of the 747's wings.

One section of the windshield weighs 152 pounds.

There are 16 cabin attendants, which is equivalent to a full load including passengers and crew of TCA's Lockheed 18.

The Air Canada 747s are configured to seat 32 passengers in First Class, with 333 in Economy—for a total of 365 people.[6]

The phenomenom of the Boeing 747 owes much to Pan American and Juan Trippe. As Trippe had influenced the design of the Clipper flying boats in the 1930s, so he would the jumbo jets forty years later. This time, it was Boeing's rival Lockheed that flew the world's first giant jet aircraft: the Galaxy. In the late 1960s, in response to Secretary of Defense Robert McNamara's foreign policy imperative that the United States be able to airlift armoured units anywhere in the world, Lockheed built its massive C-5A Galaxy.[7] The Soviet Union was building similar freighters, such as the Anatov AN-124.

It was too big and too slow to be a passenger airliner, but the Galaxy did set Boeing thinking about its own "jumbo" prototype, and Pan American, its main customer, was consulted. In 1965, the race between the Americans and the Europeans to build

piano. At one point, there was even talk of installing a small swimming pool![8] Delivery to the airlines began on January 22, 1970, with the first aircraft going to—naturally—Pan American.

THE ROUTE TO PRIVATIZATION

The heat was on over at Air Canada. The airline had started paying dividends, and Otto Lang, the minister of transport who had selected Claude Taylor as Air Canada's president, wanted to see the Crown corporation continue to be profitable. As long as Air Canada was part of the Canadian National Railway, its financing had to be approved by the Treasury. Worse, both the Liberals and the Conservatives, by being able to appoint members to the Air Canada board, used the airline as a source of patronage plums.[9]

In 1977, Lang guided the Air Canada Act through Parliament, cutting the airline's ties to the Canadian National Railway and allowing it to operate on a commercial basis. Both Lang and Taylor wanted to finish the process of privatizing the airline completely, but the government refused to give up its power over what the press called its "jewel in the Crown." There were still senior bureaucrats who saw the flag carrier primarily as a public utility.

When Joe Clark was elected prime minister (briefly) in 1979, Don Mazankowski was appointed minister of transport. Previous holders of the job had been archtypical mandarins. Pickersgill had been educated at Oxford and held positions in the diplomatic service. Lang was a Rhodes Scholar who had been dean of law at the University of Saskatchewan. "Maz" was different. The Member of Parliament from Vegreville, Alberta, caught the transportation bug as a car dealer and while working as a truck dispatcher in Chicago. Elected in 1968, Mazankowski

the first supersonic transport (SST) was on. The British Aircraft Corporation looked likely to win with its Concorde 01. Trippe had made it clear that he would buy whichever one came on the market first. Boeing, Lockheed and Douglas all had their own giant airliners called "wide-bodies" on the drawing board, but the contemporary thinking held that no one would choose to fly in a subsonic monster once the Concorde and American SSTs became available. Boeing initially designed its 747 as a flying freighter, configuring its interior diameter to carry containers two abreast. As with the C-5A Galaxy, the aircraft's nose would open up to admit the containers. The crew would sit out of the way in a hump above the fuselage.

But suddenly the 747 underwent a metamorphosis into a passenger aircraft. The loading door at the front disappeared, and a small cabin with a spiral staircase was put in behind the crew. This could only have been Trippe's idea. His double-deck Stratocruisers were famous for their circular staircases and lounges, and Trippe had never forgotten their popularity with passengers. The cabin behind the 747 cockpit was redesigned to house a bar with grand had served on parliamentary transport committees under both Diefenbaker and Robert Stanfield. In Claude Taylor, he found a soulmate—not only for baseball (they were frequently seen together in the corporate box at Montreal Expo games) but also for the privatization of Air Canada. But when Clark and his Conservatives lost the election in February 1980, Maz was unceremoniously dumped onto the Opposition benches. In 1978 the National Deregulation Act came into effect in the United States. President Jimmy Carter encouraged the Civil Aeronautics Board to ease restrictions on routes and airfares. The airlines, feeling the pinch of the oil crisis and the expense of buying ever-larger jets, took the opportunity afforded by deregulation to trim their routes to small towns and to elbow their way into "hub" cities such as Atlanta and Dallas–Fort Worth.

New adventurers also appeared on the scene. People's Express, Air Florida, New York Air and Southwest Airlines undercut the traditional carriers with "no frills" flying. Marginally profitable airlines such as Hughes Airwest and National Airlines were absorbed into larger ones. But as the dust settled, the established airlines began to match these new low prices, and the upstarts disappeared, taking with them commercial institutions such as Pan American, Braniff and Eastern Airlines.

Canadians watched the carnage below the border apprehensively. Claude Taylor and Prime Minister Trudeau's new Liberal minister of transport, Lloyd Axworthy, made a pilgrimage to Washington, and it soon became apparent to both that neither civil servants nor the public had any idea what deregulation would mean. Could Canadian airlines, so long protected, survive the free-for-all marketplace of competition? Labour unions prophesied massive layoffs of their members (correctly, as it turned out). The media played up the public's fears about airline safety. Provincial and municipal governments worried that their air connections would be cut, and the public hoped for cheaper airfares.

Axworthy wanted an end to regulations on all routes, but the entrenched airline interests within the Canadian Transport Commission (CTC) opposed

this. In May 1984, the transport minister publicly threatened to overrule the CTC if it refused to comply with his proposed new Canadian air policy. But before that policy could take effect, Prime Minister John Turner called an election. On January 14, 1985, the Conservative leader Brian Mulroney, playing to the hustings, vowed memorably, "Air Canada is not for sale. Canada needs a national airline. There is a possibility that shares in Air Canada will be sold to the public, but the Government would retain a majority interest."[10] In September Mulroney came to power, as did Claude Taylor's old friend Don Mazankowski.[11]

In 1995, after holding down several other portfolios, Mazankowski presented a White Paper on deregulation entitled "Freedom to Move," which took Axworthy's "New Canadian Air Policy" many steps forward. It was strongly opposed by the Canadian Union of Public Employees (CUPE), who had watched as market forces in the United States bankrupted some airlines and forced others to trim staffs, throwing their brothers and sisters out of work. In August 1986, the prime minister moved Maz to douse a fire somewhere else and made John Crosbie transport minister. But riding on the coattails of Free Trade, the government's commercial aviation continued apace.

In 1984, the Liberals had passed a bill requiring that any acquisition or divesture of a Crown corporation had to be approved by Parliament. By 1987, Crown corporations such as Petro Canada were being sold off, and Taylor couldn't help but notice that his travelling companions on Air Canada flights seemed, more and more, to be stockbrokers who pressed him for the Air Canada account. In Britain, Prime Minister Margaret Thatcher had successfully privatized British Airways, and Air Canada hired the British investment house of S.G. Warburg to advise it on the possible pitfalls of privatization. The firm pointed out that, in its deficit years, Air Canada had been granted loans on favourable terms, backed as it was by the government. If the same government were now to orphan it, so would the bankers. Bay Street financial analysts let it be known that selling

Tails of Maple Leaf at a Canadian airport in the 1980s hid the turmoil within Air Canada as it struggled to privatize, downsize and climb out of debt. AIR CANADA ARCHIVES

off up to 60 per cent of Air Canada might be acceptable to the banks. But Taylor, so close to his dream, refused to consider partial privatization: it was all or nothing.

Then, on October 19, the Great Stock Market Crash of 1987 occurred, taking with it recently privatized firms such as British Petroleum. The Air Canada president became so concerned that the topic of Air Canada's privatization would now disappear from Ottawa agendas that he was willing to accept even a partial measure. The airline desperately needed an infusion of hard cash, up to $3 billion, to purchase the fuel-efficient Airbuses that would enable it to compete in the marketplace. In April 1988, Bill C-129, which proposed the privatization of Air Canada, was introduced in the House. With Mazankowski now serving as deputy prime minister, Taylor knew that it had a chance of getting through.

THE FINAL DEBATE

The process by which Ottawa's grip on Air Canada was broken can be viewed as either the stuff of legend or a glimpse into the dark side of Canadian politics. John Turner, as leader of the Opposition, reminded the House of Brian Mulroney's election promise never to sell "our national birthright." He derisively referred to Air Canada as "Air Maz," linking it with Air America, the clandestine CIA outfit that carried out Washington's orders. Mazankowski replied that Canadians and, in particular, the Air Canada employees he had met in his travels welcomed the sale. Other MPs raised the perennial fear that cash-rich American corporations would buy a controlling interest in Canada's national airline and run it from New York, San Francisco or Dallas. But the deputy prime minister pointed out that no more than 25 per cent of the shares in Air Canada could be owned by non-residents of Canada, and that no more than 10 per cent could ever be owned or controlled by one individual. The

company's headquarters would remain in Montreal, guaranteeing that the Official Languages Act would apply to Air Canada. The Conservatives were successful, and the Air Canada Public Participation Act became law on September 10.

THE AIR CANADA CHALLENGE

Claude Taylor knew that the biggest challenge he faced now was the reinvention of the government airline. Rightly or wrongly, the public felt that their tax dollars had gone to create a monster with the efficiency and cold-heartedness of that other much-maligned institution, Canada Post. The airline's reorganization began with cost-saving measures that ranged from selling off the old DC-8s and Boeing 727s to wage freezes and the "downsizing" of management positions, making the airline leaner and more attractive to prospective share purchasers. In September 1988, 43 per cent of the shares went on sale, at $8 apiece, and all were bought up by Canadians. The airline grossed $246 million. Air Canada employees had been encouraged to "buy a piece of the employer," and of the 23,000 people on staff, 17,000 did so. When the remaining 57 per cent of shares were sold in July 1989, the airline's stock price had risen to $12, and by August it was $14.82.

But whatever cash and morale had been injected into the airline, their effects were minimized by the Gulf War in 1991, the doubling in price of jet fuel and the longest recession in Western history. Between 1991 and 1993, the world's airlines lost $15.8 billion U.S.—more than they had *made* since 1945. In 1992, at its lowest point, the Canadian airline industry posted a loss of more than $1 billion. Put in

With the purchase of 35 Airbus 319s, this one bearing the "Raptors" logo, Air Canada became the largest operator of the cost-effective Airbus airliners in North America, a major factor in the company's turnaround to profitability beginning in 1993. AIR CANADA ARCHIVES

that context, the financial losses incurred by Air Canada (and Canadian Pacific Air Lines), just as they were "rationalizing" their operations, are wholly understandable. Air Canada's deficit was $74 million in 1990, diving to $218 million the next year and a crippling $454 million in 1992. The airline was losing almost $2 million a day just by existing. Employees who had bought into the airline's rejuvenation saw their shares selling at $2.20.

As Howe had at the airline's birth, Air Canada's board of directors looked outside Canada for a successor to Claude Taylor, who had been CEO and president for sixteen years and was now sixty-seven years old. What was needed was a fresh perspective. The directors hired Hollis Harris, the former president of Delta Airlines. Harris began work at the Air Canada offices in Dorval in February 1992. The airline, as did much of the commercial aviation industry, stood at the crossroads. A year after Harris arrived, Air Canada proposed a two-year 5 per cent wage reduction for all employees—whose wages had been frozen since 1990—with Harris taking a 10 per cent

cut himself. At the annual general meeting in April 1993, he announced that employment would be reduced by 2,200 at the year's end.

The company's loss for the first quarter of 1993 was $293 million. But while few may have thought it then, the blood-letting at Air Canada was over. Harris bought part of the money-losing Continental Airlines. He also upgraded Air Canada's fleet with the purchase of 24 Canadair Regional Jets. In August 1993, he offered to buy Canadian Airlines' international routes for $1 billion. His offer was refused, but it was proof that the airline had successfully reinvented itself. As Delta had done, Air Canada built a web of global alliances, anchored by Lufthansa in Europe and United Airlines in the United States. With the signing of the "Open Skies" agreement in 1995, Harris began laying siege to the airline "hub" fortresses below the border, opening thirty new routes into the United States and code sharing with United and Continental Airlines.

Complementing the Canadair RJs were 35 Airbus A319s to replace the aged DC-9s, bought over 1996–97. With them, Air Canada would become the largest operator of Airbuses in North America, adding to its thirty-four A320s and three A340s with orders for more. Paul Brotto, the company's vice president of finance, credited the purchase of a young, cost-effective fleet (bought on deep discounts and cheap loans) with the start of the airline's turnaround.[12]

(Air Canada had first become interested in Airbuses in the mid-1980s as a replacement for their aged Boeing 727s. With its "fly-by-wire" technology (where six cathode ray tubes, like television screens, displayed the flight controls in the cockpit) and cheaper maintenance, the Airbus was chosen over the McDonnell-Douglas MD-88 and the Boeing 737 even though it was more expensive. The board of directors at Air Canada approved the purchase on March 30, 1988. At $1.8 billion for thirty-four airliners, it was the biggest aircraft purchase in Canadian aviation history.

(Boeing had complained for years that Airbus Industries, the A320's manufacturer, engaged in unethical practices to sell their aircraft. Air Canada was a Crown corporation, and the RCMP did investigate allegations that the European agents for the German, French and British consortium had paid secret commissions or "kickbacks" to members of the Conservative government to influence the purchase. Investigations were curtailed in 1989.

(In 1994, the rumours of kickbacks surfaced once more. The media smelled blood and closed in. The commission for the aircraft purchases was supposed to have been funnelled through International Aircraft Leasing, a Liechtenstein-based company owned by Karlheinz Schreiber, a Swiss-German businessman. Rumours alleged that Schreiber had had business dealings in the sale with former Newfoundland premier Frank Moores, lobbyist in Ottawa at the time Air Canada was evaluating the purchase. Moores and Schreiber denied any wrongdoing, but the media began calling for an examination of bank accounts in Zurich to reveal if payments had been made.

(In November 1995, the *Financial Post* reported both that the RCMP had written to Swiss authorities asking for their help in the restarted investigation and that former Prime Minister Brian Mulroney was mentioned in the letter along with Moores and Schreiber. Mulroney also denied any wrongdoing and launched a $50-million libel suit against the

South African Kevin Benson became CEO of Canadian Airlines on June 28, 1996, taking on the unenviable task of proving that the airline could successfully restructure. CANADIAN AIRLINES CORPORATE RELATIONS

RCMP and the justice department. In January 1997, just as the case was about to go to court, Minister of Justice Allan Rock and Mulroney settled out of court. The RCMP signed a document stating they had no evidence a former prime minister of Canada was involved in the "affair" and they regretted any damage the Mulroney family might have suffered because of their error. Mulroney agreed to drop the suit but wanted the federal government to foot the bill for his defence team, which conservatively amounted to $1 million. Moores and Schreiber were also issued apologies but were told they were responsible for their own legal expenses. RCMP commissioner Philip Murray was censured for his force's handling of the case, and Allan Rock also came under fire.)[13]

In May 1996, when Hollis Harris turned over Air Canada's reins to a protégé and fellow Georgian, Lamar Durrett, he could do so with justifiable pride. That year the airline had an operating profit of $275 million, the best in Air Canada's history. During Harris's term, Air Canada had also taken aim at the Pacific market and started to serve Seoul, Hong

An Air Canada 747 in its 1994 livery. The company's corporate makeover was seen as a way to make the final break with the public's perception of the airline as a Crown corporation. AIR CANADA ARCHIVES

Kong and Osaka, challenging Canadian Airlines on its own turf in the high-growth region.

But hiring Americans to whip a national institution into shape had its price. Harris felt that a corporate makeover of Air Canada, costing $22 million, was necessary to finally end the customer's perception of it being a Crown corporation. Canadians were still reeling from the news that the Royal Canadian Mounted Police had agreed to allow the Disney Corporation to market its trademark logo, and the country went into collective shock in January 1994 when it was revealed that the U.S. design company of Diefenbach Elkins, hired to change Air Canada's image, had recommended dropping the airline's familiar Maple Leaf from the logo. The embarrassing revelation forced the airline to instruct Diefenbach Elkins to retain the Maple Leaf. Air Canada learned that it was not wise to tamper with cultural icons, and in January 1996, when the airline changed the uniforms of its 16,000 employees, the new colours were given names such as "blue spruce," "evergreen," "polar moss" and "Canada red."

In May 1997, Air Canada posted a first quarter profit of $81 million, having sold off its shares in Continental Airlines. More significantly, for the first time in its sixty-year history, international markets to the Far East accounted for more than half the passenger revenue.

THE RISE OF PWA

If Air Canada had revamped itself in 1988, then Canadian Airlines was unrecognizable. In 1986, it had been bought by Pacific Western Airlines, and big changes were underway. Russ Baker, the founder of Pacific Western Airlines, had died in 1958, and Karl Springer sold his share of the airline to Bruce Samis, an investment dealer in Vancouver. Samis brought in Donald Watson as president. Like Max Ward, Watson was a savvy entrepreneur. He replaced PWA's bush aircraft with ex-CPA DC-6Bs and touted for long-range charter flights to Asia, the Cayman Islands and England. He bought a C-130 Hercules for supplying oil drilling companies and Lockheed Electras for Northern contracts, and when the CTC prevented PWA from carrying passengers on the lucrative Vancouver–Toronto route, the company took to flying to Buffalo, New York, and Seattle, Washington, busing passengers to their final destinations in Toronto and Vancouver. Profits doubled every year.

On August 1, 1974, Premier Peter Lougheed of Alberta paid $37 million to buy up all of the shares in PWA—before, he said, interests outside his province (like British Columbia's New Democratic

When Air Canada redesigned its employee uniforms in January 1996, it was careful to retain some Canadian identity with colours like "blue spruce," "polar moss" and "Canada red." AIR CANADA ARCHIVES

Below: Wardair stewardesses in the airline's heyday. CANADIAN AIRLINES ARCHIVES

government) could do so. PWA headquarters was transferred from Vancouver to Calgary, and Watson resigned. Under new president Rhys Eyton, PWA continued its upward streak. In 1977, it bought the Manitoba regional airline Transair and, in 1983, British Columbia's Time Air. It showed record profits from cross-Canada charters and contracts with Dome Petroleum and Panarctic, and when the Alberta government privatized PWA in 1983, the company's stock sold quickly. The following year, PWA sold sixteen of its Boeing 737s to the Irish aircraft leasing firm of Guiness Peat for $350 million, then leased them back at a profit. The Calgary airline was ready to expand out of the West and take advantage of deregulation. In 1986, with Eyton as CEO, PWA made $39 million in profits and acquired Calm Air of Manitoba. The word spread among financial analysts in Toronto that PWA now had enough money to take over either Air Canada or CP Air.

Eyton did contact Claude Taylor. A marriage of the two companies would infuse capital into the government airline and provide PWA with an international network. All Taylor had to do in return was to hand over a third of Air Canada's stock once the company was privatized. Taylor refused.

Then, in an announcement that amazed the country, on December 2, 1986, PWA paid $300 million for the mighty Canadian Pacific Air Lines, assuming CPA's debt of $600 million as well. By March 27, 1987, all PWA aircraft had been repainted

in Canadian Airlines International Ltd. (CAIL) colours, and two years later both airlines were fully integrated, with company headquarters in Calgary. When CAIL made $30.3 million in profits in 1988, Eyton started to cast an eye at Max Ward's airline, Wardair, which was fast running out of cash.

WARDAIR FLIES HIGH

Through dint of constant lobbying in Ottawa and the continual upgrading of his fleet, Ward had achieved what most bush pilots could only dream of.

Like Claude Taylor and Rhys Eyton, he was president of one of Canada's three international airlines. His blue-and-white 747s were named after those bush pilots he had worshipped as a boy—Wop May, Punch Dickins, Cy Becker. His company's in-flight service was so good that the international vacation magazine *Holiday Which?* proclaimed Wardair Canada Ltd. the best airline of the year in both 1986 and 1987. And his goal of capturing cost-conscious businesspeople had required Ward to compete head-on with Air Canada on the scheduled routes. By 1984, Wardair Canada Ltd. was flying scheduled flights to Puerto Rico, a year later to Britain and by 1986 across Canada. Ward ordered twelve of the latest A-310 Airbuses for a total of $650 million and added options to twenty-four Fokkers 100s to equip them for short-haul flights. He also got the European designer Nina Ricci to turn out uniforms for his stewardesses. It was a long way from hauling musk oxen in a cramped Otter.

But Ward learned to his cost (as Frank Lorenzo of Eastern Airlines in the United States had also) that shiny new aircraft do not an airline make. If china and crystal were all that were needed to run an airline, Wardair Canada Ltd. would still be flying. Air Canada and Canadian Air Lines International still had the most prominent counter space at terminals, the best landing slots at airports and the most convenient gates on the tarmac. Wardair passengers had to walk a good distance to their aircraft, and sometimes were forced to board them without the use of airbridges. Worse, the established airlines were able to keep the loyalty of the travel agent network—and their customers. As Britain's Freddie Laker too found out, the big boys played rough.

PUTTING BUMS ON SEATS

To understand why the 1980s would eventually be so disastrous for Canadian commercial carriers, it is necessary to look at the relationship between aircraft purchases and profits. Airliners are easily the costliest assets owned by airlines. In 1986, although amortized, aircraft purchases accounted for 81 per cent of the operating properties appearing on the balance sheets of Air Canada, Canadian Airlines International and Wardair. The cost of the workhorse Boeing 737 was then around $20 million, an Airbus about $40 million, a DC-10 $65 million and a Boeing 747 $100 million.[14] To put this in perspective: the construction costs of a high-rise building in downtown Toronto in 1987 were $1.1 million per floor, making the purchase of a single new Boeing 747 comparable to buying an eighteen-storey office building. Thus, for their fleets alone, the big airlines had to buy the equivalent of the downtown core of a medium-sized city every few years.

The renewal of aircraft fleets has occurred in very specific cycles in North America since the Second World War. Deliveries of new jet aircraft to Canadian carriers peaked during 1967–70, 1973–76 and 1979–83.[15] The next buying spree was to begin in 1988, when Canadian Airlines placed a $1.6 billion order for Airbuses and Boeings to be delivered in 1994, and Air Canada an order totalling $3.8 billion. Both Eyton and Taylor hoped that, by the time the planes were delivered, their companies would have sufficient passenger volume to ensure that the new aircraft began to earn their keep immediately.

In its purest form, an airline is only a means of selling seats at the lowest possible price. Freddie Laker used to say that, when it came down to it, the business was simply "putting bums on seats."[16] In Canada, the average proportion of seats sold per flight fell from a high of 70 per cent in 1987 to 64.5 per cent in 1991. (By 1995, it had risen only slightly to 65 per cent.) In retrospect, both Air Canada and Canadian Airlines began their tailspin into near-bankruptcy when the delivery of the aircraft they had ordered coincided with the recession.

Another factor was the overcapacity of aircraft. Traditionally, airlines paid for their new purchases by selling their old aircraft. This time, there was no market for them. There were acres of jet airliners—called "white tails"—in storage in the Mojave desert in Arizona, including three new Air Canada 747s that Claude Taylor couldn't use. Air Canada and Canadian had deep pockets, but Max Ward was too close to the margin for the banks to ignore. In the fall of 1988 they started calling in his loans of $300 million, and Ward looked about for money fast. He phoned PWA's CEO. The accountant in Eyton was well aware of Wardair's vulnerability, but he could not resist the opportunity to stage the biggest coup of his career. Unfortunately, it was only a matter of time before Wardair was put on the auction block and stripped piecemeal. In hindsight, Eyton should have let this demise take place at no risk to his company's own bank account. Instead, on January, 18, 1989, he bought Max Ward's dreams—and those of the airlines' 5,200 employees—for $250 million. With the addition of the Wardair fleet, Eyton's ambition (and that of his predecessor Grant McConachie) had been achieved: Canadian Airlines was finally as large as Air Canada.

Max Ward was given a seat on the CAIL board, and Eyton appointed thirty-two-year-old Kevin Jenkins as his proconsul at Wardair. But swallowing up Ward's dream gave PWA severe indigestion. Not only did Eyton shoulder a huge debt load, but he also took on a collection of aircraft that he couldn't use. There were well-meant promises to keep Wardair's logo on the aircraft and its people employed, but inevitably economics dictated that Wardair Canada Ltd. vanish from Canadian airports. It did so on January 1, 1990.

INTO THE RED

The early 1990s were the most disastrous in aviation history. The Gulf War, unpaid-for aircraft, rising fuel prices, deregulation, a depreciating Japanese yen, a recession that wouldn't let up—there is no single cause for both of Canada's airlines going into the red.

Whatever the reasons, CAIL, like Air Canada, was floundering. In 1989 the company lost $56 million; losses jumped to $161.7 million in 1991, $543.3 million in 1992. CAIL let 1,900 staff go, of which 1,017 were former Wardair employees. Eyton and Jenkins started to look around for partners. They looked south. In Calgary's sister city, Dallas, American Airlines president Bob Crandall had lifted his company from a mediocre position in the rankings to

premier place within a decade, largely by adopting a two-tiered approach to profitability. Crandall battered the company's unions into accepting low wages (as a main employer at a "hub" airport, he was able to get away with this), and, using DC-9s, concentrated on high-density short-haul routes. By 1989, American was the richest airline in the United States, with assets of over $2 billion, and it was looking for expansion.

On March 12, 1992, PWA, the parent company of Canadian Airlines, and AMR, the parent company of American Airlines, signed a letter of intent. In return for a one-third equity interest in Canadian Airlines, a 25 per cent voting interest (the highest allowed under law), and Canadian's signing of a "strategic alliance" of route and code-sharing (especially to the Far East), American would apply a financial tourniquet of $246 million to Canadian's wounds.

The deal hinged on Canadian Airlines being able to withdraw from the Gemini computer reservations system that it had shared with Air Canada since 1987. American Airlines, without Far Eastern routes, wanted access to Canadian's network through its Vancouver hub. To accomplish this, Canadian would have to become part of AMR's Sabre computer system.

When it seemed that this condition might kill the negotiations, Jenkins, in cowboy fashion, circled the wagons and then rode alone into hostile territory. On October 27, 1992, he attended an Air Canada board meeting to discuss a merger of the two airlines. There were those in the room, like Claude Taylor, who remember when Gordon McGregor proposed a similar merger to Grant McConachie. Air Canada told Jenkins they would be pleased to take over Canadian's Pacific Rim routes in return for a partial cash bail-out. The feeling among the assembled directors seemed to be: why bother offering concessions to an airline that was going to fold by year's end? After the meeting, Jenkins was told that a merger would only be possible if Ottawa agreed to put in more than $1 billion to help Air Canada out.

Both companies understood that the days of federal subsidies were over, and Jenkins returned home empty-handed. On November 19, Minister of

Transport Jean Corbeil tabled in the House of Commons the report of the Royal Commission on National Passenger Transportation. The commission's work had taken three years and cost $23 million, and it was the Mulroney government's final word on privatization. Their report recommended that market forces be allowed to decide what shape the Canadian aviation scene would take. Government subsidies were to be phased out, and there would be no more financial rescues for struggling carriers. In effect, the government was bowing out of commercial aviation.

A LAST-MINUTE BAILOUT

In early 1994, Canadian Airlines began suspending payments to its creditors and persuaded its employees to take wage cuts of between 5 and 17 per cent. In return, employees received $200 million in share entitlements at $13 a share. The airline's flight attendants, engineers and pilots belong to no less than six unions, ranging in size from the giant International Association of Machinists (IAW), the Canadian Union of Public Employees (CUPE) and the Canadian Auto Workers (CAW) to the tiny twenty-two-member Canadian Airline Simulator Technicians (CATS). Union leaders accepted the wage cuts for their members with definite reservations. American Airlines was holding out until Canadian could integrate into American's Sabre system, still making this a key prerequisite for the $246 million that the Dallas airline was going to invest.

Transport minister Doug Young and western minister Lloyd Axworthy came to the rescue, persuading Air Canada to allow Canadian Airlines to divorce itself from the shared Gemini system. In return, Air Canada would be allowed to fly to the lucrative Far East, traditionally Canadian's preserve. The AMR deal was finally consummated, and Rhys Eyton resigned on April 15, 1994, with Kevin Jenkins becoming CEO. But the airline's shares, trading on the Toronto Stock Exchange at $1.35, slumped to fifty cents, and all analysts considered the company a bad risk.

Through 1994, Ottawa, Alberta and British Columbia pumped $120 million in loan guarantees

into the airline—but to no avail, it seemed. Parent company AMR also began experiencing financial problems, stemming from a flight attendants' strike in November 1993 in which President Clinton had legislated staff back to work. Cutting 5,000 of its own employees and withdrawing from sixty-one markets, American Airlines had no money or sympathy for Canadian.

Instead of concentrating on rich foreign routes, CAIL management continued competing with Air Canada for the domestic market, putting its older Boeing 737s up against Air Canada's fuel-efficient 767s and Canadair jets. In July 1995, Jenkins predicted that Canadian would lose $35.4 million by the end of the year. By December, the airline press office had revised the figure to $185 million. Analysts attributed this revised figure to the work of Kevin Benson, who had been appointed that fall as chief financial officer. Jenkins resigned, and on June 28, 1996, Benson replaced him as CEO. A chartered accountant who had moved to Canada from South Africa in 1977, Benson had risen to become CEO of Trizec, one of the country's largest real estate companies. He loved racing cars, had flown aircraft in South Africa and accepted the position of chief financial officer with the remark that aviation "had more sex appeal than real estate."[17] He lured away key American Airlines staff such as Barbara Amster, who was made senior marketing and sales vice-president; George Mueller, senior vice-president of customer service; and Doug Carty, chief financial officer (and younger brother of former Canadian president Don Carty, who was now running American Airlines).

On November 1, 1996, Canadian Airlines announced a further 10 per cent pay cut to save $70 million annually, as well as the elimination of 250 jobs, a $70-million "downsizing" of administrative services and $60 million in aircraft efficiency improvements. Its shares were now closing as low as $1.05 (they had been $250 when Eyton bought Wardair in 1989), even as Air Canada's were trading as high as $6. On November 15, the company's entire board of directors resigned after receiving legal advice that they would be held personally liable if the airline went bankrupt. Benson warned that unless another rescue package was put together, the company would run out of money by January 1997.

This time he knew that neither AMR nor the six employee unions would be so understanding. CAW leader Buzz Hargrove's memorable quote summed up the unions' attitude: "Been there, done that, and now look where we are today."[18] Predictably, CAW and CUPE rejected the additional 8 per cent wage cut that Benson wanted from their members. As the airline still owed $30 million on loans it had obtained from Ottawa, Alberta and British Columbia in 1992, Benson understood that CAIL could not expect any further government help either.

A decade earlier, government money, whether provincial or federal, would have shored up a troubled industry and a local employer. With a federal election in the offing, there was little appetite for that in December 1996. Yet there was the conviction in the West that if Benson could restructure CAIL's finances and prove that it could fly on its own, Ottawa still had a moral responsibility to help. Apart from providing competition for Air Canada, the airline employed 16,400 people in Alberta and British Columbia, where it was also viewed as a symbol of the West's independence. If the related travel, food and petroleum industries were taken into account, more than 70,400 people would be unemployed if Canadian Airlines was allowed to die. The Liberals hoped to double their seats in the two westernmost provinces in the next election, and Ottawa knew that there would be a lot of anger if they refused Canadian's pleas, particularly since, in October, Prime Minister Jean Chrétien had given Quebec-based aerospace companies Bombardier $65 million and promised Pratt & Whitney $147 million. Chrétien kept a low profile throughout the whole drama, leading a previously scheduled trade mission to Japan. He allowed his minister of transport, David Anderson (who was from British Columbia), to take an active part, although any aid package would have to come from industry minister Michael Manley.

The details of the life-saving plan and the restructuring of the airline were played out before the nation in late 1996. Six unions, three provincial governments, two companies and Ottawa finally hammered out a deal. On November 30, CAIL suspended payments to seventy lenders and aircraft lessors; this gave it a "cash bridge" to allow its "Operational Restructuring Plan" to be fully implemented. The airline obtained the approval of all labour groups to accept salary and wage reductions for four years, commencing January 1, 1997. By reducing annual employee earnings over $25,000 by 10 per cent, Canadian Airlines estimated that it would save over $32 million. Moreover, expiry dates for all collective agreements were extended to December 31, 2000. In return, Canadian Airlines implemented a profit-sharing plan for employees.[19]

To its credit, Ottawa refused to return to regulating commercial aviation or to investing more money. Instead, it and the British Columbia government mitigated the impact of the wage reduction by contributing $38 million a year in the form of fuel tax rebates. The Alberta government permanently reduced fuel excise taxes. Benson, who had said that Canadian Airlines had only two years to become profitable, targeted a minimum of $70 million a year in overhead savings, outsourced engine maintenance and catering, cancelled money-losing flights to Frankfurt and Paris, and oriented the airline's cash-flow recovery to Tokyo, Beijing, Hong Kong, Taipei, Manila and Bangkok. Traffic on those routes was predicted to surge by 7 per cent annually, providing the potential for recovery.

The decade of the 1990s has not been a happy one for Canadian Airlines. Since it swallowed Wardair, it has found itself begging governments, creditors and employees for concessions with depressing regularity. Its mistake, according to analysts, was trying to compete domestically with wealthier Air Canada rather than doing what it did best—long-haul flying to the Far East, Australia and South America. After all, that is what Grant McConachie wanted for his airline in the first place.

CHAPTER FOURTEEN

Chariots of the Gods

If the last years of the twentieth century were tempestuous ones for airlines in Canada, the aircraft manufacturing industry knew no limits. In 1996, the Canadian aerospace industry was the sixth largest in the world, selling $12.5 billion worth of aircraft-related products. Bombardier had captured the business jet market, Messier-Dowty led with its landing gear systems and Pratt & Whitney Canada with its gas turbines, and CAE Electronics made 80 per cent of the world's flight simulators. By the turn of the century, Canada is scheduled to move into fourth place, behind the United States, France and Britain. Not since the Second World War has Canadian aviation achieved such status. Along with the traditional exports of lumber and grain, aircraft manufacturing has become a major foreign currency earner. In 1996, Bombardier alone employed 41,000 people worldwide—20,000 in Canada—producing $4.5 billion worth of goods, 75 per cent of which were exported.

But not only in executive jets is Canadian aviation a world leader. Less familiar is the statistic that today Canada accounts for the production of 57 per cent of the world's turbine helicopters.

THE FIRST HELICOPTERS

The first helicopter came to Canada in May 1945, appropriately enough on a mercy mission. Its inventor, Igor Sikorsky, was known for his flying boats, Canadian Airways having acquired one in 1932. Although he successfully flew a helicopter in 1939, it would not be until the end of the war that the United States military deployed Sikorsky's R-4, the first production helicopter. Some of the R-4s were assigned to the U.S. Coast Guard, who taught Canadians to fly them. The first practical use of a helicopter in Canada took place on May 19, 1945, when a Canso from RCAF 162 Squadron crash-landed in Labrador. Because the snow was too deep for a conventional rescue aircraft to land and get the crew, a U.S. military R-4 was transported in a cargo aircraft from New York to Goose Bay. The pilot flew it to the crash site and, because it could only take one passenger, airlifted the crew out of the Canso wreckage one at a time.

The early helicopters were too flimsy and unstable for commercial use, especially in the bush. They also had too short a range, as well as poor lifting capability, and they were three times the price of a more traditional aircraft. Only the RCAF could afford them, and in 1947 they bought Sikorsky s-5s, which remained in service for three decades. The first commercial helicopter was the Bell 47 "bubble" model used for medical evacuation in Korea and familiar to viewers of the long-running television series M*A*S*H. It was the Bell 47 that Canadian helicopter pioneer Carl Agar used in the mountainous terrain of British Columbia in the 1950s for construction projects and crop spraying.

BELL HELICOPTER TEXTRON

In 1958, Bell Helicopter of Fort Worth, Texas, was acquired by Textron Inc. of New Jersey, which also bought Cessna Aircraft and Lycoming Aero Engines.

The company's Bell HU-1 Iroquois medevac helicopter was reinvented as a gunship during the Vietnam War, with which it will forever be associated, and better known as the "Huey." In 1983, Bell Helicopter Textron at Fort Worth, Texas, decided to build the Jet Ranger in Canada, and three years later shifted production of all its models to a plant at Mirabel, north of Montreal. In this sprawling factory, helicopter shells made of composite material (including Kevlar) move down three different assembly lines: one for the 212 and the 412, one for the 206 and 407, and one for the 430. Parallel construction means that major components such as the tail booms are made up at the same time as the main aircraft structure and the engine/transmission assemblies are being put together. When production first began in 1986, it took 125 days to assemble a 206; ten years later, this had been shortened to 60 days. The original work force of 100 employees had mushroomed to 1,800 by 1996, with many trained at the local community college at St. Jerome. Some of the biggest users of the Bells are the Royal Canadian Mounted Police (with nine helicopters),[1] Vancouver Island Helicopters, Fletcher Challenge Canada and Universal Helicopters Newfoundland. Renewed energy exploration, led by deep-water flying to oil rigs further out at sea, promises that helicopter sales will only proliferate for years to come.

One Bell design demonstrated at Mirabel in 1995 would have been familiar to Canadair employees who remembered their own CL-84 tilt-wing transport from the 1960s. Bell had been experimenting with tilt-wing designs since 1943, and its XV-15 made its first full transition in 1979; it took twelve seconds to convert from vertical to horizontal flight. As a helicopter, the XV-15 could fly forward at 100 knots, backwards at 30 and sideways at 35. In partnership with Boeing, Bell has developed the V-22 Osprey, which will be operational with the United States Marines in 1999.

The infamous helicopter controversy during the 1993 federal election that helped bring down the administration of Prime Minister Kim Campbell also publicized the use of these aircraft in the

Canadian Armed Forces. Canada had agreed to buy fifty British-Italian EH-101 Cormorants, which were considered the Cadillacs of the helicopter world. Because they also came with a comparable price tag, the victorious Liberals cancelled the purchase, leaving the Canadian Coast Guard and the Navy to suffer their ancient Sea King and Labrador helicopters for another five years. The pain of the disgruntled British and Italian allies was nothing compared with that of Canadian taxpayers. Cancelling the EH-101s meant that the government had to pay the prime contractor, Unisys GSG Canada Inc. of Montreal, $166 million in compensation, which was to be shared among the other subcontractors.

The engines for the EH-101s were to have been made by General Electric Canada Inc., who had agreed that, if it got the contract, it would install a $20-million helicopter engine workshop at Abbotsford, B.C. B.C. had seen Ontario, Manitoba and Quebec benefit from the "pork barrelling" of defence contracts, and it was ready to elbow its way in. Subsequent cancellation of the EH-101s left British Columbia with nothing. This situation may have inspired the Vancouver aerospace software company MacDonald Dettwiler and Associates to put forward an audacious alternative: buying sturdy Russian helicopters called Kamovs, the Ladas of the industry, to fly off Canadian warships.

Instead, the federal government decided to shelve

Bell Helicopter Textron at Mirabel, Quebec, celebrated its 10th anniversary in 1996, producing models like the 206B Jet Ranger III. Except for sales to the Canadian government, all Mirabel-made helicopters are sold to the parent company at Fort Worth, Texas, for resale. BELL HELICOPTER TEXTRON

its helicopter shopping list, at least until after the next election. But in anticipation of the helicopter contract to come, three of the world's helicopter manufacturers set up Canadian partnerships. "Team Cormorant" comprised Westland Helicopters of the U.K., Augusta of Italy, Bristol Aerospace, CAE Electronics and Bombardier. "Team Cougar" consisted of Eurocopter Canada, Spar Aerospace, SNC-Lavalin and IMP Group International. Sikorsky's "Team Maplehawk" signed up CAE Aviation, Canadian Marconi, Litton Systems and General Electric Canada.

Fortunately, the land component of the Canadian Forces had already ordered Bell's CH-146 Griffons, made at Mirabel. Helicopter support is the mission of 10 Tactical Group, which replaced four older types of helicopters with the one hundred Griffons it bought. Within months of their purchase, several of the aircraft had already proven their worth. Eight Griffons supported fire-fighting operations in Roberval, northern Quebec, in June 1996, and fourteen took part in the rescue of Saguenay residents

from flood in July: in one day nine CAF Griffons evacuated 1,055 people from the town of La Baie, with their cats, dogs and birds. The 430 Squadron Griffons from Valcartier had the distinction of being the first to be used overseas when they replaced the CAF Hueys in Haiti in early 1997, providing Bell with the best advertisement it could have for its helicopters before several United Nations forces.

At Bell Helicopter Textron's tenth anniversary in Canada, Bob MacDonald, the first Canadian to become president, could safely say: "We've come a long way in a relatively short period of time. We took two years to roll out the first model. That cycle is now down to eight months. The best marketing tool we have is the factory floor. When you walk through the facility, you'll see a young workforce."[2] The company's biggest competitors, he said, were all the older Bell models still flying.

BOMBARDIER STARTS UP

One day in September 1992, de Havilland employees at Downsview noticed a new logo painted onto a company hangar. It was a stylized sprocket, with the word "Bombardier" splashed across it. The story spread through the growing crowd that it had been designed by company founder J. Bombardier himself to sell his home-built snowmobiles.

In the early 1940s, Joseph-Armand Bombardier had seen the need for a tracked vehicle to transport schoolchildren through the snow-bound Quebec countryside. No one cleared the roads then, and often whole communities were isolated in the winter. In the best tradition of all inventors, he started building a tracked vehicle with steerable skis in the front in his tiny garage at Valcourt, Quebec, registering the company as L'Auto-Neige Bombardier in 1942. There was a market for Bombardier's all-terrain ski and track snowmobiles with the military and forestry companies, but it would not be until 1959 that he designed a lighter machine for recreational use. He named it the "Ski-Dog," but through a printer's error, it became known as the "Ski-Doo." The sport of snowmobiling proliferated in the 1960s, making the Valcourt company a Canadian success story. When he died in 1964, Armand Bombardier was the word's leading manufacturer of snowmobiles.

The aging of the baby boomer generation and the 1973 oil crisis curbed the sport of recreational snowmobiling and forced governments to look at investing in mass transit. Now in the hands of Bombardier's son-in-law Laurent Beaudoin, the company began to diversify into mass transit rail systems. In 1975, with a $6.8-million financial incentive from the government of Quebec, Bombardier acquired an ailing Montreal locomotive factory to build cars for Montreal's Métro. The ski-doo works remained at Valcourt, but in 1978 Beaudoin moved the company headquarters to Montreal. Once more the Canadian government stepped in with financing to help Bombardier, securing a $1-billion contract to supply New York with subway trains. By 1985, the Quebec company employed 8,000 workers and had an annual revenue of $515 million. Under Beaudoin and his closest advisor, Yvan Allaire, the company motto might well have been flexibility and diversification.

THE GOVERNMENT STEPS IN

The turbulence experienced in the aerospace industries in the 1970s was brought on by the wasteful duplication of previous decades, which had resulted in white elephants (like the Concorde) or too many wide-body jets (like the DC-10) to be absorbed into the airlines. The low demand for civil aircraft just as the military contracts for the Cold War and Vietnam were drawing to an end caused assembly lines at aircraft factories from San Diego to Seattle to grind to a halt. So many employees at Boeing were made redundant that legend has it someone put up a sign at the Everett factory proclaiming, "Will the last person leaving Seattle please turn the lights off."

This aeronautical misery had widespread repercussions. De Havilland Canada, long isolated from its British parent, Hawker Siddeley, had even before the recession become what one day would be called a dysfunctional company. With the development of the DHC STOL Twin Otter, Hawker Siddeley had begun to view its Canadian branch as a serious rival in the world market, and started to wind it down. By 1970, the years of benign neglect and amateurish "making do" had taken an obvious toll, leaving in their wake rundown premises with a leaking roof,

thirty-year-old machinery and a worker rank and file that seemed constantly on strike.

The company's early successes with its versatile Caribou and Buffalo STOL freighters were followed by the hugely popular Twin Otter, of which eight hundred would eventually be made. But indications were that all three aircraft would be outstripped by de Havilland's ingenious Dash 7, known in the aviation world as "the quiet STOL airliner." The federal government feared that if Hawker Siddeley closed its subsidiary, the Canadian aviation industry would never recover. On June 26, 1974, the Trudeau government assumed control of de Havilland Canada, on the proviso that suitable investors must ultimately be found.

The federal rescue was not lost on the members of Parliament for Montreal, who had unemployed former Canadair workers in their ridings. The only project still going—sporadically—at Cartierville was the building of CL-215 water bombers. This aircraft was an unsophisticated, twin-engined amphibian equipped to scoop up water as it skimmed the surface of large lakes or rivers and then drop the contents on forest fires. There had been sales of the water bombers to the Quebec provincial government, France, Spain (which bought eight of them, exchanging the water bombers for an equivalent value in Spanish wine), Greece, Venezuela, China and Thailand. (The latter country still uses them as coastal patrol aircraft.)

But by the 1970s, the company that had built the North Star, the Sabre and the Yukon had shrunk to a skeleton. With the end of the federal contracts, there were no projects, and no hope of any. In 1968, Canadair employed 9,250 workers. By 1974 this had shrunk to 2,000, and core engineering staff were starting to drift away. Buildings at the Cartierville site were closed down, and the chance of picking up more than subcontracting work for American manufacturers seemed remote. Canadair's American parent, General Dynamics, itself strapped for money, began looking in 1975 to unload the company onto the Canadian government. On January 5, 1976, Ottawa bought the Cartierville company.

A dramatic shot of a CL-215 in service with the Spanish Air Force dropping fire retardant near Valencia. The foam is a liquid soap concentrate that is more effective than ordinary water. CLIFF SYMONS/BOMBARDIER/DE HAVILLAND ARCHIVES

Government-owned or -subsidized aviation firms have a reputation for building aircraft as "make-work" projects rather than to suit the market. To keep Northrop in business, for example, the United States gave so many of its F-5 fighters away under military assistance programs that there were more F-5s than any other aircraft in the inventories of Third World air forces.[3] The U.S. Secretary of Defense, Robert McNamara, even persuaded Canadian Minister of Defence Paul Hellyer in 1965 to have Canadair manufacture the F-5. Even though the recently unified Canadian Armed Forces protested, saying that the aircraft was too light and had insufficient range for Canadian needs, the program went ahead, and Canadair built a Canadian version called the CF-5. Forty-four of the CF-5s they produced were put into storage because by then they were already surplus to requirements. But the program had kept Canadair in business and even provided export orders to the Netherlands and Venezuela—for which Northrop sued the Canadian government, claiming the foreign sales were a contravention of their licensing agreement.

The Europeans have an even longer history of building aircraft as either make-work projects or items of national prestige, turning out everything from the Comet to the Concorde, which, while marvels of aeronautical engineering, were failures on the aviation market. The first aircraft to break with this tradition was the Aerospatiale A-300 Airbus, and its success was one that the Canadian government hoped to emulate. After the 1968 student riots in Paris, the French government feared that the insurrection would spread to industrial workers, so they merged the largely idle French aviation manufacturers and their work forces to build an airliner. Learning from the Concorde, designers ensured that the new aircraft would be utilitarian, have twin fuel-efficient engines and a 240-seat

capacity, and do exactly what its name implied: act as an "air bus."

In a radical departure, Paris arranged for the cost and manufacturing of the Airbus to be shared by British Aerospace, Deutsche Airbus, CASA of Spain and Fokker of the Netherlands, all of whom would be thus forced to become customers for the aircraft, or to share the blame if it did not sell. Bernard Lathiere, president of the consortium, is alleged to have summed up the philosophy behind the Airbus in true Gallic fashion when he said: "I loved Concorde as a mistress and Airbus as a son. At forty-four, I decided it was time to give up my mistress and concentrate on my son's upbringing." With such parents and prospects, the future of the wide-bodied twin jets was assured, and Boeing followed suit with similar twin-engined jets such as the 757 and the 767. It was the fuel-efficient Airbuses A-300s that Air Canada, Wardair and Canadian Airlines looked to purchase to turn their finances around, and they later purchased the Airbus A340-300s and A319s as well. When Wardair was merged with CAIL, the Canadian Armed Forces took over five of the surplus Airbuses. Outfitted as prime ministerial and troop transports, the Airbuses were painted a dove-grey colour and renamed Polarises.

THE CHALLENGER

Only European consortiums and American giants such as Boeing and McDonnell-Douglas had the wherewithal to manufacture large airliners; as the Avro Arrow had shown, the military market was too rich for a minor player like Canada. The search for an aircraft that would generate positive returns on its investment prompted Canadair's directors to embark on a radical venture. They looked south for inspiration. A decision was made to enter the executive jet field by buying from the aeronautical inventor William Powell Lear the rights to manufacture his LearStar 600. It was a bold move, fraught with risk, as there were already long-established competitors in the small jet sector such as Hawker Siddeley, Daussault and Lockheed—whose JetStar was used by Prime Minister Trudeau as a short-haul VIP aircraft.

The cockpit of the Canadair Challenger 604 in 1996. Its avionics system features six 7 1/4-inch-square CRT display monitors, which are multi-functional and include dual primary flight displays and the Engine Indication and Crew Alerting System (EICAS). BOMBARDIER/DE HAVILLAND ARCHIVES

The province of Quebec was on the eve of a provincial election that the Parti Québécois looked likely to win, prompting the federal government to guarantee $62.5 million in loans to keep Canadair afloat. On October 29, 1976, on the strength of twenty-eight orders and the loan, Minister of Industry, Trade and Commerce Jean Chrétien and Canadair president Fred Kearns held a news conference to announce the start of the executive jet program. The Parti Québécois won anyway.

Canadair dropped the LearStar name in favour of the name Challenger CL-600 in March 1977. By September of that year, the assembly of the three Challenger prototypes was in full swing, and the airborne courier Federal Express made a firm order for twenty-five of them. On the auspicious day of May 25, 1978, in a scene reminiscent of the inauguration of the North Star, the first Challenger was rolled out at Cartierville. If ever the fortunes of a company depended on the viability of a single aircraft, this was it. The first flight took place on November 8, after which the aircraft was ferried to a Mojave desert airfield for its certification. In addition to the initial commercial orders, two CL-600s were bought by the Canadian Armed Forces 412 Squadron at CFB Uplands to transport VIPs, and the German aerospace company Dornier and Swiss Air Ambulances placed orders for one each.

Bristol's CF-5 modernization program not only replaced the aircraft's critical components to extend its life but also installed advanced avionics in the thirty-year-old fighter.
BRISTOL AEROSPACE ARCHIVES

But as with every new aircraft, there were delays because of design modifications, and by the end of 1981, instead of the 113 forecast, only 33 aircraft had been delivered. Canadair was soon $370 million in debt, and the aircraft price had more than doubled, from $4.3 million to $9.5 million. The major problems with the Challenger were that the aircraft did not have the range to fly the Atlantic non-stop—an essential service for chairmen of large companies— and that its Avro Lyncoming turbofan engines were difficult to service. Canadair offered to install extra fuel tanks for its customers without charge. In all, 83 Challenger 600s were built. The next model, the Challenger 601, was rolled out on August 17, 1982. Significantly, its tail fairing was replaced with a tail-cone fuel tank, giving the aircraft a longer range of 3,955 miles, and it was powered by General Electric

CF34-1A turbofan engines. But by now, serious financial difficulties were threatening Canadair. In September 1982, 1,300 production workers were laid off for eight weeks, and 400 others were let go. Instead of five, production slowed to two Challengers monthly.

On November 23, 1982, the federal government transferred its shares in Canadair to the Canada Development Investment Corporation (CDIC), giving that corporation the responsibility for managing the government's investment. Poor sales were not helped when CBC television's investigative program *The Fifth*

Estate ran a series of three shows in April 1983 that was critical of the Challenger. Some customers even cancelled orders.

In May, Fred Kearns retired, and that summer the company was reorganized. Several of the management staff were fired and thousands of employees were laid off, some permanently. Canadair's finances were made public, revealing the loss of $1.4 billion. But Ottawa did some fancy accounting, bringing into being a new entity—Canadair Inc.—that was debt-free. The debts of the old Canadair were transferred to a paper company. This manoeuvre proved to be the turning point for Canadair. Freed of its debt burden, in 1984 the new company recorded a profit of $6 million. Transport Canada bought twelve 601s, the West German government ordered seven for the Luftwaffe, and the People's Republic of China took three. Profits for 1985 were $27.6 million, and with 148 firm orders, Canadair was on solid footing: so much so that, early in 1986, the federal government decided to sell it off.

THE CF-18 CONTRACT

While the government was considering possible buyers for Canadair, the CF-18 fighter contract gained national attention. The McDonnell-Douglas F-18 was the CAF's long-awaited replacement for its CF-104 Starfighter, which had been in front-line service since 1962. The contract to maintain and upgrade the CF-18s would be worth $2 billion and many hundreds of jobs.

Bristol Aerospace, the company founded by the MacDonald brothers on the banks of the Red River, was now owned by Rolls-Royce Industries Canada. Although it was Western Canada's biggest aerospace company and a major employer in Winnipeg, it had stagnated since, unlike Canadair or de Havilland Canada, it had relied on military orders during the Cold War. Bristol's managers saw the CF-18 contract as a means of reviving not only their fortunes but those of the city—and of the entire West. Along with Canadair, it submitted a bid to service the CF-18s. A team of independent experts studied both bids and concluded by favouring Bristol's, which was $65

million lower than Canadair's and technically superior. Bristol's management would later claim they were given assurances by the Department of National Defence that the contract was theirs.

The political choice, though, really came down to Montreal versus Winnipeg, Quebec versus Manitoba. If Bristol did not win, howls of protest could be expected from Manitoba Premier Howard Pawley and his New Democrats. The Conservative government in Ottawa could probably survive that, but how would it affect the chances of Saskatchewan's Tory leader Grant Devine, then running for election? The federal government's alleged favoritism for Quebec was an old rallying cry in the West. The decision was delayed through the summer. On October 20, Devine was elected, and the president of the Treasury Board, Robert de Cotret, confirmed on Hallowe'en night what the rest of Ottawa had already guessed: the CF-18 engineering support contract had been awarded to Canadair.

The choice of the Quebec firm was apparently made against the recommendation of the prime minister's own advisors, who warned that the Western backlash would return to haunt Brian Mulroney. The perception that the West had been betrayed yet again was used to fuel support for Preston Manning's Reform Party, which held its founding convention the following year. But by then Mulroney was busy with the constitutional wrangling at Meech Lake, in which he needed Quebec's support.

A NEW OWNER FOR CANADAIR

Among the parties interested in purchasing Canadair from the federal government were Fleet Industries of Fort Erie and the German firm of Dornier, who had liked their Challenger so much that they now wanted to buy the company. But Laurent Beaudoin saw an opportunity for Bombardier to diversify once more, this time into the aerospace industry. Canadair was purchased by Bombardier on December 23, 1986, for $121 million, a fraction of the company's real value; discounting the patents that Canadair owned, the price of the land at Cartierville alone was worth that amount.

Beaudoin and his team knew that while Canadian aviation manufacturing couldn't compete with Boeing or Aerospatiale, it could carve out a comfortable niche in the regional and business jet market. Robert E. Brown was made president of Canadair in 1990, and final assembly of the Challenger was moved to a state-of-the-art plant at Dorval Airport. The company also began design studies on the Canadair Regional Jet (CRJ) in August 1987. The CRJ could seat fifty passengers and had a range of between 1,127 miles and 1,531 miles, putting it in the small airliner class. When the aircraft was launched in 1994, Beaudoin's instincts proved correct. Until then, jets had made up barely 3 per cent of the regional airline fleets in North America because there were few economical alternatives to the turboprop airliners still being used. But as travel researchers discovered, if given a choice, passengers preferred the smoother, quieter ride of jets to the shuddering Convairs and Fokker F-27s still in use. Bombardier's competitors in the field were Fokker, Saab-Scania and, most aggressively, the Brazilian aircraft maker EMBRAER with its fifty-passenger commuter jet. At $14 million U.S., the EMBRAER jet was cheaper than the $18 million U.S. CRJ. But Bombardier had built up a solid reputation in North America, and the CRJ was faster, could fly further and had a wider fuselage, allowing passengers to sit four abreast rather than three. Lufthansa CityLine and Comair, the Cincinnati-based Delta Airlines feeder, were the CRJ's main users. Closer to home, Air Canada ordered twenty-four CRJs to fly its trans-border routes. The Open Skies treaty with the United States signed in February 1995 had increased the demand for an aircraft with the Regional Jet's capabilities, and Air Canada was able to open up several dozen new cross-border services, such as Toronto-Minneapolis and Ottawa-Chicago.

In the summer of 1986, Canadair had announced that it would make a turboprop version of the CL-215 water bomber. Although similar in appearance to its predecessor, the CL-415 was really a new aircraft, equipped as it was with Pratt & Whitney Canada PW123AF turboprop engines, an electronic flight instrument system and, best of all for firefighters, increased capacity water tanks that required only twelve seconds to scoop a load while skimming at high speed over water. The first production aircraft CL-415 was presented to Daniel Canepa, director general of the Securité Civile of France, on April 29, 1994. With an eye on the increase in the smuggling of people and contraband on the high seas, Bombardier also devised a system for launching and recovering boats from a CL-415, so that, in a coastal patrol role, the aircraft could land on the water and then launch a boat full of officers (customs, police or immigration) to board any suspect vessels.

The Seattle giant Boeing was also looking into the regional airline market. The company wanted to build a turboprop airliner for small airlines, so that when they upgraded to the Boeing 737, they would be locked into a Boeing family relationship. The jumbo-jet maker had worked with de Havilland on marketing the Dash 7, and liked the idea of owning a small (for Boeing) aircraft manufacturer that turned out legendary bush planes. It knew that the Downsview company had last made a profit in 1982, and it expected some complications when it bought de Havilland from the federal government in 1986. An antiquated factory and a militant labour force were part of the deal. Boeing poured $400 million into modernizing the plant's technology, taking it from the postwar era into the computer-controlled 1980s. Bits and pieces for aircraft that had been stored haphazardly in cardboard boxes were now inventoried and tracked by computer.[4] Parts for the Dash 7 that had been cut out and ground by a team of thirty-five people were now carved faultlessly by a computer and then monitored through to final assembly. In 1985, it took 130,000 person hours to put together a Dash 8. In 1992, it required less than half that.

But if Boeing thought that dragging de Havilland into the 1980s would earn them the gratitude of those on the assembly line, they were wrong. Sixteen months after the managers from Seattle (whom the Canadian workers claimed were arrogant and condescending) came to Downsview, unionized employees went on strike for the tenth time since 1954. The dispute lasted ten bitter weeks. Boeing management decided that the time had come to unload the expensive experiment on someone else.

In July 1990, the European consortium Avions de Transport Regional (ATR) announced that it was courting Boeing with the idea of buying de Havilland Canada. This must have frightened not only the suddenly subdued workers at Downsview but also politicians at Ottawa and Queen's Park. ATR made commuter aircraft and was a rival of DHC. The possibility that it might terminate the Dash series and lay off staff if it purchased DHC was very real. Worse, DHC would be forced to survive on subcontracting crumbs until the inevitable closure took place.

Bombardier's Laurent Beaudoin came to the rescue. After the Canadair purchase, Bombardier continued to expanded internationally, buying companies that were financially unsettled and acquiring the reputation in the aviation industry of an "ambulance chaser." In 1989, de Havilland's 6,000 workers turned out 141 aircraft. By 1991, this had dropped to 3,700 employees and 32 aircraft. Despite the computerization of the company, or perhaps because of it, morale at Downsview was low. The New Democratic premier of Ontario, Bob Rae, did not want to go down in history as the man who allowed another Avro Arrow exodus to take place. Neither did Michael Wilson, the federal minister of industry. As he had with his other acquisitions, Laurent Beaudoin waited in the wings for the incentives that he knew would come his way.

SOME FOREIGN ACQUISITIONS

Before the DHC deal was sealed, Bombardier practised some reverse colonialism by expanding to the other side of the Atlantic.

The Short brothers were Edwardian "aeronauts" who had made balloons in Britain in 1898. Their company got its start in aviation in 1916, when its float planes were the only aircraft used in the historic Battle of Jutland. Through the 1930s, at its Rochester factory, Shorts launched the C-Class Empire flying boats on the Medway, militarizing the model into Sunderland patrol aircraft just before the Second World War. In cooperation with the shipbuilders Harland & Wolff, Shorts moved to Belfast, Northern Ireland, where the British government bought up the company to provide local employment. Through the 1950s and '60s, Shorts' products ranged from the giant Belfast freighter to the agile Skyvans and Sherpas (which used Pratt & Whitney Canada engines) that competed on the STOL market with DHC's Twin Otters. It had built up a talented design and engineering department but, like de Havilland in Canada, Shorts had been mismanaged by its British parent and the government into near bankruptcy. When the British government let it be known that they would guarantee loans worth the equivalent of $1.3 billion to whoever took the lame duck off their hands, Bombardier became interested. Shorts would give the Canadians a foothold in Europe and access to small aircraft expertise. In October 1989, throwing in $60 million of its own money, the Montreal company bought the British firm.

Eight months later, Bombardier acquired the ailing Learjet Corp. of Wichita for $75 million, giving the Canadian company a dominant position in the business jet market in the United States. With the purchase came the Lear facility located in Tucson, Arizona, close enough to Latin and South America to give Bombardier a sales and service advantage. The hundred-acre plant at Tucson airport, formerly the location of Learjet production, is now mandated with the task of providing paint, avionics and interiors for Learjets and some of the Challengers. By 1995, Bombardier had a work force of 950, and it took advantage of the Tucson facility to complete its Global Express and Regional Jets on the site.

THE BOMBARDIER GLOBAL EXPRESS

Closer to home was the plum at Downsview, now ready for harvesting. The Montreal company wolfed down de Havilland Canada in March 1992, helped by sweeteners from Ottawa and Queens Park.

Michael Wilson gave the new owners $270 million in loans and subsidies, and Rae spent $49 million to buy Ontario taxpayers a 49 per cent stake in the company, adding $300 million in loans and subsidies later. At Queen's Park, the provincial opposition leader Mike Harris strenuously opposed the deal and vowed, if elected, to sell the province's stake in de Havilland as soon as possible.

A week after the takeover was announced, the Bombardier restructuring began. The Downsview workforce was cut by 700 employees. Aircraft output was reduced as well. In July, production was cut again, and 400 more jobs were eliminated. Cost-saving measures such as integrating the sales teams for the Challenger and the Dash 8 were put into effect. Challengers were flown to be finished at the company's "paint shop" in Tucson, and subcontracting work such as overhauling Canadair water bombers for the Spanish government (and later for the provincial fire service) was passed on to Downsview.

Some of de Havilland's old glory resurfaced when it announced the birth of the Dash 8-400 at the Paris Air Show in July 1995. De Havilland engineers had tried to convince Boeing to invest in a "stretched" version of the Dash 8, figuring that if a short-range airliner could be made to carry seventy passengers it could service the heaviest routes on hub and spoke terminals from regional airports. Boeing, trying to extricate itself from its Canadian venture, had refused. But when Bombardier became de Havilland's owner, it waited for the federal government to prime the pump with money. Through the $250-million-a-year Technology Partnerships Canada Fund, Ottawa put $57 million into de Havilland for the ongoing design of the Dash 8-400.

Beaudoin had defied all predictions with the Challenger and its cousins. But with his next aircraft, it seemed as if the ski-doo maker had finally overreached himself. The Bombardier Global Express is not just an airplane, it is a measure of wealth. Thirty metres long, 2.5 storeys high, it can carry executives from Tokyo to Miami, halfway across the world, at 580 miles per hour in 14 hours. It can

whisk movie moguls from Los Angeles to London in 9 hours, 38 minutes. It has enough wall-to-wall carpeting, hand-tooled leather furniture, polished boardroom tables, computers and fax machines to suit every Third World president or OPEC minister. If it were a commercial aircraft, it could seat fifty plebians in luxury. It also costs $34 million U.S., the price, wrote one journalist, of a medium-sized shopping mall. Selling ultra-long-range business jets in the recession-prone 1990s is difficult enough, but persuading a minimum of one hundred buyers to part with that amount of money even before the first Global Express flies in 1998 is the ultimate gamble.

The Global Express began life in February 1991 as the Next Model Executive Jet (NMEJ), planned to replace the Challenger. Discussions with potential clients and market analysis led the company to extend the aircraft's fuselage to the size of the Regional Jet and extend its range to 7,480 miles at Mach 0.80 to satisfy the requirement of flying from New York to Tokyo. When the final aircraft was rolled out at de Havilland, amid appropriate Cecil B. DeMille hoopla, in August 1996, Prime Minister Jean Chrétien was in ecstatic attendance. Not only did the prime minister attempt to associate himself firmly in the public's mind with the glamour of the jet-set jet (it was a lot more eye-catching than posing in front of an Abitibi paper mill), he was also well aware that Laurent Beaudoin is a prominent federalist who has openly criticized the government of Lucien Bouchard at provincial economic summits. With the Global Express, the prime minister could remind his audience that the federal government was a large contributor to a flagging Montreal economy.

By its speed and endurance, the Global Express distinguishes the really powerful from the merely rich. The private jet is no longer a luxury today. It is essential for those who fly often, but never commercially. Airport line-ups and delayed connections mean missed million-dollar deals. And resource companies fly today into obscure places that pilots of commercial 747s would not even be able to find, let alone land in. This is especially the case in emerging China, where not only Hong Kong entrepreneurs

The Bombardier Global Express is assembled at Montreal and Downsview, but the engines are made at BMW–Rolls-Royce in Germany, the wings and central fuselage at Mitsubishi in Japan, and the flight-control system at France's Sextant Avionique. GARTH DINGMAN/BOMBARDIER/DE HAVILLAND ARCHIVES

but military and government leaders rely on long-range private jets because of primitive airport and airline conditions in their country. In the early 1990s, the former Soviet Union and emerging Third World countries were able to use cellular and satellite technology to bypass their antiquated telephone and telex systems. Similarly, with the Global Express, pilots will now be able to overfly the crowded, inefficient big-city airports in those countries, delivering their charges directly from Wall Street to a Kazakstan oilfield. Security is another factor. If Fortune 500 executives, playboys and government ministers can travel nonstop to Beijing, Kinshasa or Riyadh without fear of hijacking or kidnapping, $34 million is a bargain.

THE BOMBARDIER GOLDEN TOUCH

In October 1996, Ottawa loaned Bombardier $85 million to help develop a stretched version of the Regional Jet, making the announcement the centrepiece of a $300-million batch of loans to the aerospace industry. Code-named the CRJ-X, the seventy-seater will cost $23 million. By February 1997, the company had signed up sixty-seven orders from eight airlines. Buyers range from Brit Air of France to Great China Airlines of Taiwan, which already operates twelve Dash 8s and has placed

orders for six more. The first flight is expected in 1999, with the program representing an investment of $476 million U.S. and providing 1,000 jobs in Canada and 750 at Shorts in Belfast.

Some of Bombardier's golden touch can be attributed to adopting Aerospatiale's strategy of passing around the risk. This is especially true of the Global Express. Agreements were signed with suppliers who bore some of the cost and would recoup their investment when and if the aircraft was sold. With instant electronic communications today, Mitsubishi Heavy Industries of Japan can make the wings and centre fuselage, BMW–Rolls-Royce GMBH of Germany the engine, Honeywell in the United States the avionics, and Sextant Avionique of France the flight controls. Of the $800 million spent to develop the Global Express, Bombardier had to put up only 50 per cent. "It's virtually a G-7 project," Prime Minister Chrétien boasted.[5]

Ironically, as cuts in armed forces around the

world have proliferated, Bombardier has capitalized on picking up the pieces. In 1987 Ottawa hoped it had placated Bristol Aerospace by designating the Winnipeg firm as the support centre for the air force's CF-5 fighter squadrons. Bristol was also awarded a $79-million contract in 1995 to upgrade thirty-six of the fighters for potential sales overseas. The Canadair CF-5s, part of the Hellyer legacy, were declared surplus in the 1994 White Paper on Defence, and the Canadian Commercial Corporation (the marketing agent for the federal government) hoped to export those not cannibalized for spare parts or donated to museums. Besides installing new electronics, heads-up displays and weapons targeting systems in the CF-5s, Bristol would also receive a 20 per cent commission from brokering the deals. Bristol scored a controversial coup in June 1996 when it unloaded thirteen of the refurbished CF-5s onto the tiny nation of Botswana for $50 million.

Understandably, the Department of Foreign Affairs (which plays down Canadian arms sales to emerging nations) was concerned that the CF-5s in Botswanan hands would "destabilize" the region— causing an arms race in southern Africa.[6] After some strategic sessions, it offered one possible explanation to non-governmental organizations concerned about the supersonic fighter sale—the Botswana Air Force could use the CF-5s as "anti-poaching" devices. Bristol president Keith Burrows announced that the remaining fighters would be offered for sale to countries such as the Philippines, Greece and Thailand.

Reflecting the worldwide slump in defence contracts and the recession, Bristol continued to shrink through the 1990s. In 1992 it had 1,950 employees and did $177 million in business. In 1996, it had 960 staff and $125 million in sales. The struggling aerospace company no longer fit into its British parent's long-term plans, and in 1997 Rolls-Royce decided to put it up for sale. Its aircraft overhaul and repair business certainly looked attractive to Bombardier, who was expected to bid for Bristol— as usual, only if the federal or provincial governments made its purchase worthwhile. But this time,

Toronto-based Magellan Aerospace Corporation beat Bombardier to the sale, acquiring Bristol on June 19, 1997. In a twist of fate, since Magellan also owns Orenda Corporation, which is participating in the CF-18 logistics support program with DND, Bristol Aerospace might get to service the fighters yet.

The downsized military establishment worldwide "can depend on Bombardier to do all the things that they don't absolutely have to do themselves," emphasizes David Huddleston, the former commander of Canadian Forces Air Command and now president of Bombardier Defence Services.[7] The company offers its Dash 8 as a maritime patrol aircraft, its Learjet for target towing or as an electronic warfare trainer, and its CL-327 UAV as a vertical take-off and landing surveillance system. The company's future plans include moving into the logistics support field as a progression of its NATO Flying Training in Canada (NFTC) program. After the Canadian Armed Forces turned over its primary pilot training at CFB Moose Jaw to Bombardier in 1991, the company put together a proposal to train pilots of NATO and "like-minded" countries as well. The view commonly held is that private industry can do many of the military's tasks more cheaply and more efficiently.[8]

The Canadian aviation industry has achieved good health because it weaned itself off defence contracts long before the Berlin Wall fell. In any case, in the final decade of the twentieth century, aircraft manufacturing has transcended national boundaries. There is no such thing as an all-American or a totally Canadian aircraft any more. Bombardier's worldwide subcontracting of its Global Express is the wave of the future in aircraft manufacturing. No one country can ever again afford to design, build and market an aircraft. Boeing, the biggest of them all, might still assemble the latest 777 in Seattle, but 20 per cent of the aircraft's components are made offshore in Japan, South Korea and China. Despite Aerospatiale's pride in European solidarity, 40 per cent of its Airbus is made in the United States, from the avionics to the brakes and the evacuation slides.

The heart of Canadian aviation might well be Dorval Airport, Montreal, which is located not two miles from Lakeside, site of the first Canadian Aerial Meet in 1910. Adjoining the main Air Canada base at Dorval is Bombardier's Plant 3, shown here on an Open House day in 1994. The runways at top were begun for ATFERO. CANADAIR ARCHIVES

CONCLUSION

Coming to an Airport near You . . .

At dawn yesterday, a Boeing 737 from the fictitious Cross Canada Airlines (CCA) took off from Toronto's Pearson Airport for Ottawa. After a half-hour stop there, it continued on to Rimouski, then to Charlottetown, then flew back to Ottawa.

Thirty years before, the airline's scheduling was done on huge sheets of paper by supervisors in white shirts with dark blue company ties who wielded magic markers and barked instructions over the phone to flight dispatchers. At that time the 737 would have returned to Toronto following its flight, then been cleaned and put away for the night. But no longer. The simple days of back-and-forth flights are long past. Under the eye of computer operators, the system now strives to keep as few CCA aircraft idle as possible. The Boeing 737 continued from Ottawa on to Oshawa, then to Yellowknife and then back to Toronto, followed by stops at Kenora, Sept-Îles, St. Jean and Montreal. At the airline's darkened, antiseptic systems operations room in Winnipeg, computer screens tracked the Boeing's odyssey minute by minute. The flights' routings were hardly random: they are the end product of the highly efficient use of machinery and personnel.

The mass of information punched in at ticket counters from Victoria to Gander—such as passengers' seating preferences, dietary considerations, the frequent fliers who are to be given preference, the connecting flights that passengers have to make, even the distance they will have to run from one gate to another—is fed into the CCA's central computer. Every minute that can be squeezed, every cent that can be saved, every glitch that could cause delays has been tied together. Then there is the flood of detail about the aircraft itself, transmitted by the electronic sensors on board. Parallel to both streams are the crew's work and rest periods; with different legally mandated schedules for pilots and flight attendants, the computers are forced to constantly recalculate times. (In 1996 Air Canada operated an average of 500 flights daily, with forty-two wide-body jets and ninety-eight narrow ones. No human mind could ever handle the countless variables that enter these equations.)

Twenty years before, as a back-up, CCA would have had an extra aircraft parked by the ramp, waiting to replace any plane with a defective engine. Today, with computers controlling the operational lives of both humans and machines, the system is as near perfect as it can be. An idle aircraft is, after all, a non-revenue producer. It is the proud boast of CCA that only 1.5 per cent of its aircraft are idle at any one time.

With computers, air travel has become a worldwide web of time and motion. When a CCA baggage handler misread a luggage label at Mexico City airport yesterday, he ultimately caused a forty-one-minute delay of the Winnipeg flight landing at Abbotsford today. In the 1980s, along with Air Canada and Canadian Airlines, CCA saw its revenues drown in pools of red ink. One of the major factors

in turning the airline around was computer technology, which enabled it to get near-perfect yield management for its aircraft and staff.

CCA has also profited from fast-paced feeding into the "hub and spoke" system. Through short-haul airliners like the CRJ and the Dash 8-400, it can inexpensively gather customers from various points into a hub and then offer them connecting flights at convenient times. If CCA does not fly to a certain destination, then one of the airlines that it has formed alliances with will, and the passenger and baggage are passed on through the same computer system.

What the computers cannot factor into their calculations is the unpredictable in air travel, things like oil crises or war. Yet the biggest threat established airlines face today are not rising fuel prices or terrorists but competition from cut-rate airlines.

According to Statistics Canada, the deregulation of the airline industry caused fares to soar in the 1990s. Created in part by rising government taxes on air travel and higher airport charges, the fare increases were passed on to the recession-weary traveller. Between 1987 and 1994 Canadians paid an increase of 66 per cent for their tickets on average, while the overall cost of living rose only 25 per cent. Consequently, there was an enormous demand for cheap fares.

Yet the economics of starting an airline are better now than they have been since 1945. Aircraft, labour and fuel are cheaper in 1996 than they were in the 1980s, when cut-price pioneers like People's Express first started out. The old bush pilot's dream of trading up his battered Norseman to a secondhand DC-6B still beats in the hearts of Canadian entrepreneurs. In 1996, Clive Beddoe began WestJet Airlines in Calgary with three 737s to serve British Columbia, Alberta and Saskatchewan. The bus company Greyhound Lines of Canada teamed up with Kelowna Flightcraft Air Charter Ltd. the same year to take to the skies with basic 727 equipment. And in London, Ontario, Thomas Syme leased a 737 to begin Vistajet, which operates a no-frills service between Ottawa, Toronto and Windsor. All three emulate Southwest Airlines of Texas, the original cut-rate airline, which offers its passengers no more than a seat and a packet of peanuts in return for rock-bottom prices.

But the Canadian aviation scene is littered with similar upstarts who were wiped out when Air Canada and Canadian Airlines matched their fares with better service: City Express (1991), Intair (1992), Nationair (1993), Air Astoria (1995). To guard against fly-by-night failures who leave unpaid bills and employees in their wake—and worse, who cut corners with shoddy equipment and poorly trained staff—the Canadian Transportation Agency (CTA) introduced tough new start-up requirements. Greyhound Air was grounded over Canadian ownership requirements. WestJet's launch was postponed for three weeks when the CTA decided that it had used the wrong maintenance manuals to service its fleet. And in May 1997, Vistajet failed to get a Transport Canada air operator's certificate because of its twenty-year-old Boeing 737. Yet while Greyhound reported a $9.8-million loss in its first year, WestJet claimed an undisclosed profit.

All three airlines hope that they will be able to profit from the boom in air travel in Canada, which is forecast to grow until at least 2014. World passenger traffic is predicted to rise by 5.1 per cent annually, with North America rising 3.8 per cent and the Asia-Pacific region 7.1 per cent. The Montreal-based International Civil Aviation Organization forecasts that, in 2003, the world's airlines will carry 1.8 billion passengers.

When flying first began at the turn of this century, an aircraft took off with the hope that it would remain in flight long enough to arrive at its intended destination. In the postwar period, a commercial airplane was launched in the hope that it would get to its destination on time and carry passengers in reasonable comfort. Today, airlines launch aircraft knowing where and when they will arrive; the focus is now on making money.

From the cabin cleaners to the board of directors, the people involved in Cross Canada Airlines know that the airline's future is not assured; the skies they operate in are unfriendly, and all the computers in the world cannot dull the pain of whatever hard decisions lie ahead. But as McCurdy, Richardson and McConachie well knew, financial uncertainty is a constant in Canadian commercial aviation. Those aerial pioneers understood that aviation is a passion, one that first bewitched us as a nation on a frozen lake at Baddeck long ago.

ENDNOTES

CHAPTER ONE

1. Jack Carpenter, *Pendulum: The Story of America's Three Aviation Pioneers: Wilbur Wright, Orville Wright and Glenn Curtiss, the Henry Ford of Aviation* (Carlisle, Massachusetts: Arsdalen, Bosch & Co., 1992), p. 22.
2. "Aerodrome" to Langley and Bell meant the whole aircraft, "aeroplane" only its wing.
3. Years later, when a magazine had Orville shouting "Eureka!" after the December 17 flight, he was furious enough to remonstrate with the editors that there was no single moment of discovery, but instead slow, painstaking scientific experimentation.
4. Carpenter, *Pendulum,* p. 91.

CHAPTER TWO

1. Throughout this chapter I have used information taken from the logbooks of the Curtiss Aviation School in the collection of the Public Archives of Canada (MG.28. III. 65 Vol. 1). I also owe aviation historian George Fuller my gratitude for his information on the subject.
2. S. F. Wise, *Canadian Airmen in the First World War: The Official History of the Royal Canadian Air Force* (Toronto: University of Toronto Press, 1980), pp. 607–608.

CHAPTER THREE

1. This quotation, and other information about Ernie Boffa, is taken from Florence Whyard's book *Ernie Boffa, Canadian Bush Pilot* (Whitehorse: Beringian Books, 1994).
2. Frank H. Ellis, *Canada's Flying Heritage* (Toronto: University of Toronto Press, 1954), p. 63.
3. Dennis Duffy and Carol Crane, eds. *The Magnificent Distances: Early Aviation in British Columbia* (Victoria: Provincial Archives of British Columbia, 1980), p. 49.
4. Locklear was so good that Universal Studios signed him up in 1919 to play an airmail pilot who thwarts a gang of aerial pirates in a six-reel feature called *The Great Air Robbery*. The following year, Fox Studios asked him to perform a tailspin for their movie *The Skywayman*. He did so, and died when he couldn't pull out in time. The director kept the camera rolling and advertised the movie as "Showing Locklear's Spectacular (and Fatal) Crash."
5. While this rhyme is known in American aviation circles, its origin is vague, probably pertaining to Samuel Langley's failure. The rhyme was picked up by vaudeville performers, who would always portray the would-be aviator as a funny but doomed figure.
6. The reason for the fiery crashes was that the exhaust pipe from the engine ran alongside the gas tank and, after a few hard landings, cracked enough for sparks to ignite the gas fumes.
7. The beginning of aircraft registration in Canada is a British legacy. "G" was assigned to all countries within the British Commonwealth and Empire, and "C" to Canada. Only in 1927, with the passing of the Washington Radio Telegraph Convention, were groups of five-letter call signs given to each country. Canada was allotted thirteen such groups, and on January 1, 1929, Ottawa chose "CF" as the first series to be used.
8. On May 26, 1919, Groome and his partner Edward Clarke flew from Regina to Moose Jaw, delivering the first newspaper by air. Because of this service, the Regina *Leader* could be bought on the streets of Moose Jaw before 7:00 A.M.

9. Randall's aviation career culminated as captain of a Canadian Pacific Air Lines DC-8 in 1968. His sons and grandson are pilots now for Canadian Airlines.

10. Ronald A. Keith, *Bush Pilot with a Briefcase: The Happy-Go-Lucky Story of Grant McConachie* (Toronto: PaperJacks Ltd., 1973), p. 39.

11. Lindbergh was completely unaware of what he had accomplished. When he landed at Le Bourget, he pulled a note out of his pocket and asked a bystander: "Do you know this Paris hotel? I understand it's quite reasonable." The American ambassador quickly took control, hustling Lindbergh off to the official residence, where the bed the Lone Eagle slept in became part of the tour of the ambassador's mansion.

12. Hollywood studio head William Fox had recently put sound into his *Movietone News*, enabling Lindbergh not only to be seen but also to talk to his admirers. When his speech was played in moviehouses in the United States and Canada, audiences would give Lindbergh a standing ovation. Few events did more to publicize aviation.

CHAPTER FOUR

1. W. L. Brintnell, *The Bulletin* (Winnipeg: Western Canada Airways), Vol. 4, 1930.

2. K. M. Molson, *Pioneering in Canadian Air Transport* (Winnipeg: James Richardson & Sons, 1974), p. 153.

CHAPTER FIVE

1. Allan Loughead discovered, when he went looking for capital to build his aircraft, that people misspelled or mispronounced his name as "Loghead" or, worse, "Loafhead." His accountant finally insisted that it be spelled phonetically, and in 1926 the Lockheed Aircraft Corporation opened for business.

2. Juan Terry Trippe graduated from Yale in 1923 and bought some old Navy trainers to fly his former classmates about in. All his life he took great pride in his Yale connections, decades later ensuring that his Pan Am building in Manhattan could be seen from the dining-room windows of the Yale Club.

3. The studio on Wilshire Boulevard Douglas used was where the Dauntless dive bomber, the aircraft that won the Battle of Midway for the United States, was designed. Douglas was proud of his Scottish heritage, and he played the bagpipes, quoted Robbie Burns to anyone who would listen and attended board meetings accompanied by his Scottish terrier, which Wall Street called the best-informed dog in the aviation business.

4. Philip Smith, *It Seems Like Only Yesterday: Air Canada, the First Fifty Years* (Toronto: McClelland & Stewart, 1986), p. 17.

5. One of those to escape the RCAF downsizing was Bob Bowker, who would go on to have a successful career in Trans-Canada Air Lines. Bowker was a batman at the air force station at Rockcliffe, painting the toilet at the officers' mess while the upheavals were taking place. When he emerged from the toilet, after a week of "slinging the lead," he was told that the government had been overzealous, and there were now so few pilots left that Bowker was ordered to report to Camp Borden for training as one. He went on to fly some of the first TCA trans-Atlantic flights. Source: Personal interview with the author.

6. Molson, *Pioneering in Canadian Air Transport*, p. 118.

7. Even the British purchased the Lockheed 10A, the first American aircraft they would own.

8. Robert Bothwell and William Kilbourn, *C. D. Howe* (Toronto: McClelland & Stewart, 1979), p. 106–107.

9. Transport Canada Newsletter, fiftieth anniversary issue, Summer 1997.

10. As a Battle of Britain pilot and war hero, McGregor never forgave Hellyer for the unification of the Canadian Armed forces.

CHAPTER SIX

1. Howard White, *The Accidental Airline* (Madeira Park, B.C.: Harbour Publishing, 1988), p. 8.

2. This and subsequent reminiscences about the early days of Trans-Canada Air Lines are from the company magazine, *Horizons*, the fortieth anniversary issue, No. 479, April 10, 1977.

3. So many of the crew and passengers who perished with the R-101 had come to St. Hubert with the R-100 that the government ordered all flags in Canada be flown at half mast.

4. Air Canada anniversary issue, *The L10A Sentimental Journey*, 1986.

5. Ibid.

CHAPTER SEVEN

1. Lindbergh had raised $15,000 in 1926 from nine St. Louis businessmen to build his monoplane.

2. The citizens of Harbour Grace had built the tiny airfield themselves, with their own funds and labour. It remains in use today.

3. This was not the end of the Albatross, however. De Havilland would use its advanced design for that "Wooden Wonder," the Mosquito bomber, which would be flown by BOAC, carrying VIPs between Britain and Sweden.

4. Besides their other obvious passenger comforts, the Boeings had the first flush toilets. Unfortunately, on the proving flight from San Francisco to Honolulu, both flushes jammed. It was later discovered that they were designed by Boeing to function efficiently on two-ply paper, while Pan American, sparing no expense, had installed three-ply.

5. Duffy and Crane, *Those Magnificent Distances*, p. 68.

6. Howe's son, serving in the Royal Navy, would also be torpedoed, but by the Japanese fleet off Ceylon. Until he was rescued, his father tried to cheer up the rest of the family by saying that the Howes were "unsinkable."

7. On October 25, 1967, a Lockheed Hudson bomber memorial was unveiled at Gander by former Imperial Airways pilot Don Bennett C.B., C.B.E., D.S.O., now Air Vice Marshal of the Royal Air Force, to commemorate an airlift that made Allied victory possible and mass trans-Atlantic travel inevitable.

8. One of the RCAF's Liberators would later be modified for King, who would use it to attend the first United Nations conference in San Francisco.

9. Vincent Massey, *What's Past Is Prologue: The Memoirs of the Right Honourable Vincent Massey, C. H.* (Toronto: The Macmillan Co., 1963), p. 206.

10. Ross Smyth, *Horizons*, May 3, 1977, pp. 2–3.

11. David Clark MacKenzie, *Canada and International Civil Aviation 1932–1948* (Toronto: University of Toronto Press, 1989), pp. 82–3.

12. The Lancastrians ended their days in various ways. One took part in the Berlin Airlift, another two fell apart in smuggling and gun-running, and rumour has it that a fourth was sold to the Pakistani Air Force, which promptly crashed it.

CHAPTER EIGHT

1. The company made a half-hearted attempt to get into the airline business in 1937 by buying five new Barkley-Grow aircraft.

2. Elsie MacGill became the first woman to be employed as technical advisor to the International Civil Aviation Organization and in 1967 was appointed by Prime Minister Lester B. Pearson to the Royal Commission on the Status of Women. She was elected to Canada's Aviation Hall of Fame in 1973.

3. Not until the building of the dams at Lake Manuane, Quebec, and the airlifting of some 3,000 tons of supplies to that remote area in 1940–41 did aluminium become available.

4. Howe had to pay in advance. Although gratified by the business, Jacobs waited for the Canadian government's cheque to clear its New York bank before beginning work. The possibility of the British losing to the Nazis was very real in 1941.

5. The *Ruhr Express* was assigned to RCAF 419 (Moose) Squadron, then at Middleton St. George in England, part of 6 Group.

6. Ivan Rendall, *Reaching for the Skies* (London: BBC Books), 1988, p. 269.

7. MacKenzie, *Canada & Civil Aviation*, p. 112.

8. Ibid.

9. Anthony Sampson, *Empires of the Sky* (London: Doubleday & Co., 1988), p. 70.

10. My favourite story concerning C. D. Howe and the British took place shortly after the war when Trans-Canada Air Lines was trying to extend its routes to the British colonies of Bermuda and the West Indies. Britain wanted to keep the routes to the popular vacation areas for BOAC alone, and at a meeting in London told Howe that "because of technical difficulties" TCA could not land in the West Indies. Howe accepted this calmly, and as he was leaving the room remarked: "By the way, beginning Monday, the only Canadian airport that BOAC will be able to land at is Quebec City." Everyone knew that the runways at Quebec City were too small for trans-Atlantic aircraft. When Howe got back to his hotel, there was a phone call from the British to say that the "technical difficulties" had been cleared up, and TCA could start flying into the Caribbean. Source: Susan Goldenberg, *Troubled Skies: Crisis, Competition and Control in Canada's Airline Industry* (Whitby: McGraw-Hill Ryerson Ltd., 1994), pp. 13–14.

CHAPTER NINE

1. Edward Jablonski, *A Pictorial History of the World War II Years* (New York: Doubleday & Co., 1977), p. 113.

2. Keith, *Bush Pilot with a Briefcase*, p. 249.

3. Ibid, p. 257.

4. Today the Canadian Airlines International Boeing 747s are named after countries, the DC-10s after provinces and cities, and the Boeing 737s after North American cities. Air Canada does not name its aircraft.

5. For a study of Hong Kong in this period, the author's work *Hong Kong Rising: The History of a Remarkable Place* (Ottawa: General Store Publishing House, 1995), is recommended.

6. Nothing proved the strength and versatility of the DC-4 better than the events over the German city of Berlin in the late summer of 1948, when streams of C-54s flew in 80 per cent of the city's food and fuel, landing every three minutes.

7. In Canada, the War Assets Corporation was responsible for disposing of war surplus aircraft. In 1946, Hamilton, Ontario, scrap merchant Cameron Logan bought nineteen Fairey Swordfish, seventy-two Hurricanes and scores of Ansons for $50 each. He resold the Hurricanes for $100 apiece, the remainder for scrap. In total, he made $1,191. Only one of the Swordfish survived, and it is at the Shearwater Museum in Nova Scotia.

8. It was in a Canadair Argonaut that Princess Elizabeth and the Duke of Edinburgh visited Kenya in 1952. When news came of her father King George VI's death, the same aircraft brought Queen Elizabeth home.

CHAPTER TEN

1. This quotation, and all others from McGregor in this chapter, are taken from Gordon R. McGregor, *The Adolescence of an Airline* (Montreal: Air Canada, 1970).

2. It had been intended that Symington would be succeeded by Howe himself, but the prime minister kept Howe on in the Cabinet to help incoming leader Louis St. Laurent.

3. Smith, *It Seems Like Only Yesterday*, p. 123.

4. Throughout his political career, whatever his portfolio, Howe kept Trans-Canada Air Lines under his personal control. He frequently dreamed of leaving politics to become its president. A telling incident occurred during the war, when Howe was the most powerful person in King's Cabinet. Friends recalled him walking down Ottawa's Wellington Street one day and pointing to a TCA Lockheed far overhead, saying, "Now what I would really like to be is head of that!" Source: Bothwell and Kilbourn, *C.D. Howe*, p. 113.

5. Smith, *It Seems Like Only Yesterday*, p. 127.

6. "Between Ourselves," Air Canada newsletter, April 10, 1977.

7. Ibid.

8. The new radio systems had made the radio operator's position redundant.

9. Mr. Glenn very kindly made his memoirs available to the author for this book.

10. Personal interview with the author, March 30, 1997.

11. Ross Smyth, "The Unforgettable Gordon McGregor: From War Hero to President," *Aviation Quarterly*, vol. 1, no. 4, Winter 1995/1996, pp. 8–14.

12. The only criticism passengers had about the Viscount was that, at a certain speed, the rotating propellers looked as if they had stopped. It was an optical illusion caused by the anti-collision light illuminating the propeller blades when they were in the same radial position.

13. When British Airways had the BAC 1-11 foisted on them instead of the Boeing 727s they really wanted, the British government gave the airline $75 million to cover the higher operating costs. As for Air France, when it wanted the Boeing 727s instead of the aged Caravelles, the French minister of finance threatened to fire its board of directors for their lack of patriotism. It would not be until 1978 that Air France was allowed to buy U.S.-made aircraft.

14. Lawrence Martin, *Chrétien: The Will to Win* (Toronto: Lester Publishing, 1995), pp. 151–2.

15. "Between Ourselves," Air Canada newsletter, September 1967, p. 2.

16. A. P. Wavell, *Other Men's Flowers* (London: Penguin Books, 1944), pp. 90–94.

CHAPTER ELEVEN

1. Roe died in 1959, the same year that the most technologically advanced aircraft to bear his name—the Avro Arrow—would also "die."

2. The RCAF were using British-made de Havilland Vampire jets at the time. The Vampire was the first jet aircraft to fly the Atlantic.

3. The unsubstantiated story is that Air Vice Marshal Wilfrid Curtis, who was old enough to remember the World War I Canuck—the first aircraft built in any quantity in Canada—gave the CF-100 its name.

4. James Floyd, "The Canadian Approach to All-Weather Interceptor Development," *Journal of the Royal Aeronautical Society*, vol. 62, no. 5-76, December 1958, p. 861.

5. Julius Lukasiewicz, Dept. of Mechanical and Aerospace Engineering, Carleton University, Ottawa, in a letter to the editor, *Ottawa Citizen*, March 3, 1997.

6. Denis Smith, *Rogue Tory: The Life and Legend of John G. Diefenbaker* (Toronto: MacFarlane, Walter and Ross, 1995), pp. 307–25.

7. PCG was on such good terms with his employees that even during the strike he commuted to work from his summer home in Muskoka in a company Beaver with his regular passenger William Brown, a neighbour and one of the strikers. Each morning, on arrival, Garratt went to his office and Brown to the picket line. Each evening they returned home to Muskoka in the Beaver.

8. W. Carlson and D. Newey, *Fifty Years of Technology* (Winnipeg: Bristol Aerospace Ltd., 1983), p. 101.

9. Iceland was not part of IATA, but it did have the vital USAF airbase on its territory. In exchange for its use, the United States gave Iceland airline landing rights at New York and, as

Luxembourg was not part of IATA either, it became the airline's mainland destination.

CHAPTER TWELVE

1. T. M. McGrath, *History of Canadian Airports* (Toronto: Lugus Publications, 1992), p. 48.

2. Despite his surname, Sir Basil Smallpiece was given to grand decisions. In his previous job, he had been the managing director of BOAC, where, to compete with Pan American and Boeing, he ordered forty-five expensive Vickers VC-10As. The order almost bankrupted the airline, and, when it was reduced to thirty, nearly put Vickers into receivership as well. Smallpiece was forced to resign, and BOAC was allowed to buy the cheaper Boeing 707s.

3. In 1973, when the USAF was looking to replace its tanker fleet of KC-135s, McDonnell Douglas designed the KC-10A for the air force, which enabled the company to offer the DC-10 airliner at a reduced cost and extend the line to the MD-11. Canadian Airlines International is one of the largest users of the DC-10.

4. The Canadian Armed Forces replaced the prime minister's VIP C-5 with a CC-137, a military version of the Boeing 707, and continued to use it as a strategic airlifter and aerial refueller well into the late 1990s.

5. Old China hands (such as the author) will never forget the first Pan American Boeing 747 to land in that part of the world. Recalling the flying-boat era, the aircraft was to have the words *China Clipper*, in both English and Mandarin, emblazoned across its nose. Unfortunately, this had been literally translated into *China Barber*, which only served to affirm the Chinese belief then that the West thought of them only as laundry-workers, waiters and barbers.

6. In 1979, when then Vice Premier Deng Xiaoping toured the Boeing plant at Seattle, company managers resurrected the memory of Wang Tsu, a Beijing-born engineer whom Bill Boeing had hired in 1918 to help him design an aircraft for the U.S. Navy.

7. Canadian Pacific Air Lines did lease one Boeing 707 from a Seattle airline in 1967, complete with crew, to cope with a busy season.

8. Goldenberg, *Troubled Skies*, p. 18.

9. Keith, *Bush Pilot with a Briefcase*, p. 307.

10. At least Pratte had impressive academic qualifications. Later political appointments to Air Canada were worse. When Brian Mulroney named Gayle Christie, a municipal Tory politician, to the airline's board, she told a reporter that her only relevant experience in the field of transportation was being able to drive a car.

11. "Between Ourselves," Air Canada newsletter, May 1970, p. 1.

12. Not every customer was unappreciative of Air Canada in those dark days. One passenger mailed in all the salt and pepper shakers that he had taken as souvenirs from the aircraft. His conscience had bothered him, and he was afraid that "there would be a shortage of shakers and that the next person to occupy my seat would do without." The airline sent him a set of Air Canada napkin rings and glasses in the

hope that he would fly with them again. Source: "Between Ourselves," Air Canada newsletter, July 1971, p. 3.

13. Claude I. Taylor, in a personal interview with the author, told a wonderful story about how he joined TCA. As a young man, his landlady played bridge with the mother of the local TCA agent. On her recommendation, one day he applied for a job with the airline . . . and got it.

CHAPTER THIRTEEN

1. Legend has it that while transporting the dead was considered part of frontier life, no one would take the victim of a drowning on board.

2. Veteran bush pilot Jean-Jacques Bastein, now a member of the Department of Foreign Affairs and International Trade in Ottawa, told the author that when he flew in the Quebec bush, the most eagerly anticipated part of his cargo at mining camps was not fresh vegetables or razor blades but the latest issue of *Playboy* magazine.

3. In 1949 Phipps flew the unlikeliest war-surplus bush aircraft of them all. Spartan Air Services had the contract for high-altitude photography in the North, and to aid in mapping the terrain for the DEW Line construction, Phipps flew a P-38 Lockheed Lightning fighter with cameras where its nose cannon would have been. He was awarded the McKee Trophy in 1961 for inventing the "Phipps Special," a lightweight balloon tire with superior shock absorbency that allowed bush pilots to land anywhere on the tundra. He died in Ottawa on October 29, 1996.

4. Max Ward, *The Max Ward Story* (Toronto: McClelland & Stewart, 1991), p. 27.

5. Personal interview with the author.

6. "Between Ourselves," Air Canada newsletter, January 1970, p. 1.

7. One of the hundreds of subcontractors for parts was Canadair.

8. D. M. Bain, *Canadian Pacific Air Lines: Its History and Aircraft* (Calgary: Kishorn Publications, 1987), p. 100.

9. Every member serving on the board gets an unlimited free pass on Air Canada for the duration of his or her appointment.

10. My major source for information on the privatization of Air Canada was Anne Shortell, "A Wing and a Prayer," *Financial Times of Canada*, August 15, 1988, pp. 12–14.

11. There have always been stories in Ottawa that Turner lost the election because his wife, Geills, threw a celebrated tantrum on board an Air Canada flight from Vancouver to Toronto. She refused to sit next to a mother and a crying baby on a crowded aircraft and, when the captain landed the aircraft in

Toronto, continued her yelling at the Air Canada counter.

12. Brenda Branswell, "Unfriendly Skies," *Maclean's*, November 18, 1996, pp. 34–35.

13. Bruce Campion-Smith, *Toronto Star*, December 11, 1995; A. Wilson-Smith, "Revenge! Ottawa Folds Its Cards and Apologizes," *Maclean's*, January 20, 1997, pp. 16–21.

14. All prices are in U.S. dollars. The payment was always made outside the United States to avoid taxes.

15. W. Jordan, *Comparative Analysis of Airline Performance in Canada and the United States* (Toronto: York University, 1987), pp. 122–25.

16. Freddie Laker was a source of memorable quotes, my favourite being: "Aeroplanes are just an aluminium tube that you can use to make money. You can't love them the way you can do a boat." When he lost his Laker Skytrain in 1982, he turned his back on Britain and retired to the Bahamas to live on his eighty-foot yacht.

17. Michael Posner, "Flight into Oblivion," *Report on Business Magazine*, November 1996, p. 68.

18. Buzz Hargrove on CTV television news, November 28, 1996.

19. All information on the restructuring plan was supplied by Canadian Airlines Corporate Communications/D. Hedley.

CHAPTER FOURTEEN

1. By comparison, in Los Angeles, the police department has sixteen of its own helicopters, the City has twelve, the department of water and power six, and the fire department another six. The city limits stretch over 466 miles, making surveillance by auto alone impossible. In 1995, LAPD helicopters responded to 42,487 calls, and on 14,981 occasions they were the first police on the scene.

2. Ken Pole, "The Canadian Influence," *Helicopter*, January 1997, p. 13.

3. Many F-5s were left behind in Vietnam after the U.S. withdrawal and were repainted in the colours of the Communist air force. Bristol Aviation of Winnipeg has been trying to get the contract to upgrade the Vietnamese F-5s.

4. Kenneth Kidd, "Cleared for Take Off," *Report on Business Magazine*, November 1992, p. 49.

5. John Ibbitson, *Ottawa Citizen*, August 26, 1996.

6. Israel, Kuwait and Turkey were also trying to sell their surplus jet fighters to Botswana.

7. *Jane's Defence Weekly*, April 16, 1997, p. 16–23.

8. With the retirement of its Boeing 707 tankers in 1997, the CAF is considering leasing its next generation of aerial refuellers from a private consortium based in Dublin, Ireland.

SOURCES

In writing this history of commercial aviation in Canada, I am keenly aware of the debt that I owe my predecessors. The original aviation historian of this country was undoubtedly F. H. Ellis, whose *Canada's Flying Heritage* served as a primer for my generation. It is also inevitable that the research and interpretations of Canadian aviation authors such as J. R. K. Main, K. M. Molson, J. A. Wilson, T. M. McGrath and G. A. Fuller have consciously (or unconsciously) found their way into *Flying Colours*. Commercial aviation in Canada is recent enough for the primary sources to include interviews with men and women who witnessed its birth, and I would be remiss in not acknowledging their generosity and enthusiasm in giving me access to their log-books, memories and photographs. This is especially true for bush pilots Bob Randall and Ernie Boffa; the founding members of both Canadian Pacific and Trans-Canada Air Lines; Jim Floyd; and Claude Taylor.

Aymar, Brandt, ed. *Men in the Air: The Best Flight Stories of All Time from Greek Mythology to the Space Age.* New York: Crown Publishers, 1990.

Bain, D. M. *Canadian Pacific Air Lines: Its History and Aircraft.* Calgary: Kishorn Publications, 1987.

Borden, Henry, ed. *Robert Laird Borden: His Memoirs.* London: Macmillan & Co., 1938.

Bothwell, Robert, and William Kilbourn. *C. D. Howe.* Toronto: McClelland & Stewart, 1979.

Campagna, Palmiro. *Storms of Controversy: The Secret Avro Arrow Files Revealed.* Toronto: Stoddart Publishing, 1992.

Canadair Limited. Montreal: Canadair, A.P. 292, September 1965.

Carlson, W., and D. Newey. *Fifty Years of Technology.* Winnipeg: Bristol Aerospace Ltd., 1983.

Carpenter, Jack. *Pendulum: The Story of America's Three Aviation Pioneers: Wilbur Wright, Orville Wright and Glenn Curtiss, the Henry Ford of Aviation.* Carlisle: Arsdalen, Bosch & Co., 1992.

Christie, Carl A. *Ocean Bridge: The History of R.A.F. Ferry Command.* Toronto: University of Toronto Press, 1995.

Duffy, Dennis, and Carol Crane, eds. *The Magnificent Distances: Early Aviation in British Columbia 1910–1940.* Victoria: Provincial Archives of British Columbia, 1980.

Ellis, Frank H. *Canada's Flying Heritage.* Toronto: University of Toronto Press, 1954.

Fuller, G. A., J. A. Griffin and K. M. Molson. *125 Years of Canadian Aeronautics: A Chronology 1840–1965.* Toronto: The Canadian Aviation Historical Society, 1967.

Goldenberg, Susan. *Troubled Skies: Crisis, Competition and Control in Canada's Airline Industry.* Whitby: McGraw-Hill Ryerson Ltd., 1994.

Gunston, Bill, ed. *Chronicle of Aviation.* Liberty, Mo.: JL International Publishing, 1992.

Hotson, Fred W. *The de Havilland Canada Story.* Toronto: CANAV Books, 1983.

Howard, Fred. *Wilbur and Orville: A Biography of the Wright Brothers.* New York: Alfred A. Knopf, 1987.

Hudson, Kenneth, and Julian Pettifer. *Diamonds in the Sky: A Social History of Air Travel*. London: The Bodley Head, 1979.

Jablonski, Edward. *A Pictorial History of the World War II Years*. New York: Doubleday & Co., 1977.

Keith, Ronald A. *Bush Pilot with a Briefcase: The Happy-Go-Lucky Story of Grant McConachie*. Markham: PaperJacks Ltd., 1973.

McGrath, T. M. *History of Canadian Airports*. Second edition. Toronto: Lugus Publications, 1992.

McGregor, Gordon R. *The Adolescence of an Airline*. Montreal: Air Canada, 1970.

McIntyre, Bob. *Canadair CF-5*. Ottawa: Sabre Publishing, 1985.

MacKenzie, David Clark. *Canada and International Civil Aviation 1932–1948*. Toronto: University of Toronto Press, 1989.

McLaren, Duncan D. *From Bush to Boardroom: A Personal View of Five Decades of Aviation History*. Winnipeg: Watson & Dwyer, 1992.

Main, J.R.K. *Voyageurs of the Air: A History of Civil Aviation in Canada, 1858–1967*. Ottawa: Queen's Printer, 1968.

Massey, Vincent. *What's Past Is Prologue: The Memoirs of the Right Honourable Vincent Massey*. Toronto: The Macmillan Company of Canada, 1963.

Milberry, Larry. *Aviation in Canada*. Toronto: McGraw-Hill Ryerson Ltd., 1979.

Milberry, Larry. *The Canadair North Star*. Toronto: CANAV Books, 1982.

Molson, K. M. *Pioneering in Canadian Air Transport*. Winnipeg: James Richardson & Sons, 1974.

Molson, K. M., and H. A. Taylor. *Canadian Aircraft since 1909*. Stittsville: Canada's Wings, 1982.

Page, R. D. *Fleet: The Flying Years*. Erin, Ontario: Boston Mills Press, 1990.

Penrose, Harald. *Wings across the World: An Illustrated History of British Airways*. London: Cassell Ltd., 1980.

Pickler, Ronald A. *The First Forty Years: A Record of Canadair Operations 1944–1984*. Montreal: Canadair Public Relations, 1985.

Pickler, Ronald A., and Larry Milberry. *Canadair: The First 50 Years*. Toronto: CANAV Books, 1995.

Public Archives of Canada (PAC). Files 3564-1011-1-5.

Rendall, Ivan. *Reaching for the Skies*. London: BBC Books, 1988.

Sampson, Anthony. *Empires of the Sky*. London: Doubleday & Co., 1988.

Skene, Wayne. *Turbulence: How Deregulation Destroyed Canada's Airlines*. Vancouver: Douglas & McIntyre, 1994.

Smith, Denis. *Rogue Tory: The Life and Legend of John G. Diefenbaker*. Toronto: MacFarlane, Walter & Ross, 1995.

Smith, Philip. *It Seems Like Only Yesterday: Air Canada, the First Fifty Years*. Toronto: McClelland & Stewart, 1986.

Solberg, Carl. *Conquest of the Skies: A History of Commercial Aviation in America*. Boston: Little, Brown & Company, 1979.

Spring, Joyce. *Daring Lady Flyers: Canadian Women in the Early Years of Aviation*. Lawrencetown Beach: Pottersfield Press, 1994.

Sullivan, Kenneth H., and Larry Milberry. *Power: The Pratt & Whitney Canada Story*. Toronto: CANAV Books, 1989.

Sutherland, Alice Gibson. *Canada's Aviation Pioneers: 50 Years of McKee Trophy Winners*. Toronto: McGraw-Hill Ryerson, 1979.

This is Canadair. Montreal: Canadair, 1956.

Wagner, R. *The North American Sabre*. London: MacDonald & Co., 1963.

Ward, Max. *The Max Ward Story: A Bush Pilot in the Bureaucratic Jungle*. Toronto: McClelland & Stewart, 1991.

White, Howard. *The Accidental Airline*. Madeira Park, B.C.: Harbour Publishing, 1988.

Whyard, Florence. *Ernie Boffa, Canadian Bush Pilot*. Whitehorse: Beringian Books, 1994.

Wilson, J.A. *Aviation in Canada: 1897–1948*. Ottawa: King's Printer, 1949.

Wise, S. F. *Canadian Airmen in the First World War: The Official History of the Royal Canadian Air Force*. Toronto: University of Toronto Press, 1980.

ACKNOWLEDGEMENTS

It is impossible to write a book such as this without the support and assistance of a number of individuals and institutions. I am much indebted to the following people: Claude I. Taylor, Brian Losito and Ross MacKenzie of Air Canada, Shannon Ohama and Andrew Geider of Canadian Airlines International, Catherine Chase and Garth Dingman of Bombardier Inc./Canadair, Colin Fisher of de Havilland, Ann Wrelesworth of James Richardson & Sons, Ltd., Vicki Hinchcliff-Stuart of Bell Helicopter Textron, Clayton Glenn, Herb Seagrim, Ross Smyth, Fraser Muir, Bob Robbins, Bob Randall, Ernie Boffa, Florence Whyard, George Fuller, the staff at the Canadian Forces Photographic Unit, the Saskatchewan Archives Board, the National Aviation Museum, the City of Toronto Photographic Archives and, as always, everyone in my own Lester B. Pearson Library.

INDEX